3 3013 00010 8096

WITHDRAWN

E
815
.S35

Schmidt, Karl
Henry Wallace

BRADNER LIBRARY
SCHOOLCRAFT COLLEGE
LIVONIA, MICHIGAN 48152

# HENRY A. WALLACE:

## Quixotic Crusade 1948

*Men and Movements Series*

# HENRY A. WALLACE:

## Quixotic Crusade 1948

☆

*Karl M. Schmidt*

SYRACUSE UNIVERSITY PRESS

1960

E
815
.S35

*Library of Congress Catalog Card:* 60-16440

COPYRIGHT © 1960, SYRACUSE UNIVERSITY PRESS

ALL RIGHTS RESERVED

MANUFACTURED IN THE UNITED STATES OF AMERICA

BY THE VAIL-BALLOU PRESS, INC., BINGHAMTON, NEW YORK

*For Jill and Glen*

# Preface

THE TWO-PARTY system has been a feature of the American political scene for all except a few brief periods in our history. Yet, during most of the last 130 years, the traditional two major parties have had in virtually every election at least one minor-party competitor. Despite this persistence, there has been a continuing pattern of failure. Never has an American third party been successful in displacing a major competitor. (Both the Whigs and the Republicans grew and came to power in two of those rare periods when a single major party was dominant.)

The presidential campaign of 1948 was not exceptional in that it witnessed new minor-party challenges to Democratic and Republican supremacy. One of these movements took shape as Henry A. Wallace's Progressive Party. The present study attempts to examine the background, the leaders, the organization, the campaign, and finally the disintegration of this third party. It attempts to present a history of the Wallace Progressive Party—a political history based to the greatest possible extent upon the firsthand accounts of those who participated in a movement sufficiently distinctive to merit the title of "crusade"—a quixotic crusade.

Why is it that minor parties have never been successful in this country? It appears that there must be substantial reasons for the repeated pattern of failure that has greeted their persistence. Professor William B. Hesseltine had indicated some of them in *The Rise and Fall of Third Parties:*

> . . . The obstacles that line the . . . way are indeed discouraging. In general they fall into two classes, the practical and the philosophical, and neither can be dismissed as unimportant. Both are imperatives—liberals must find a base upon which to make a valid appeal to the reason and conscience of the voters, and they must create a practical organization to carry out the program.
>
> The practical handicaps which a new party must overcome fall into two groups: financial and legal. . . . candor compels the admission that the barriers are formidable.

A postscript might be added that a successful third party also requires a fertile soil of crisis or a favorable climate of unrest in which to flourish. Surrounding conditions may not, of course, be created by the party; they may only be utilized. Nevertheless, their presence or absence may spell life or death to a minor party.

In examining these factors to ascertain the role they played in the life cycle of one third party, that of Henry A. Wallace, inquiry will first be made into the currents—streams both philosophical and political—contributing to the initial decision to embark upon such a venture. Since the party was essentially the creation and creature of one man, it seems necessary to examine briefly his personal philosophy, characteristics, and attributes that were to play so great a part in this undertaking. Attention must also be given to the "practical" obstacles mentioned by Professor Hesseltine: matters of party organization—the attempt to establish a new nation-wide group able to compete on the ward and precinct level with well-established party machines and the attempt to set up a structure sturdy enough to endure, regardless of the fate of the individuals connected with it. Part and parcel of these practical considerations are the dual legal-financial barriers referred to, including the statutory weapons so often used by parties in power to discourage or eliminate third-party competition by keeping insurgent groups off the ballot. Included also are fiscal obstacles—the need to secure funds to meet the tremendous expense of organizing and conducting a nation-wide campaign against well-entrenched machines possessing established donors as well as patronage favors to dispense.

In addition, there are numerous other obstacles that confront a third party—the traditional adherence of the American voter to the party of his forbears, the loss of popular policies to major-party "thunder-stealers," the feeling that pressure group activity may be more productive, defeatism resulting from rebuffs at the polls, and the opinion that more certain—if more restricted—benefits will accrue from working within the two-party framework. Virtually all of these considerations played a part in the yearlong 1948 campaign of the Wallace Progressive Party, its rejection at the polls, and its subsequent attempts to carry on into the following years.

Besides these customary barriers to minor-party success, the Wallace venture was subjected to certain additional and very special handicaps—handicaps attendant upon the nature of the Party's underlying doctrines and its attempts to introduce what might be described as tolerant politics into a period of intolerance. These special disadvantages must be inquired into—particularly as they were reflected in two aspects of the 1948 campaign: the Philadelphia Convention and the Communist-domination charges so persistently hurled at the party by a hostile press.

Ultimately, an evaluation must be made of the party's performance in carrying out the announced objectives of its founder—Henry A. Wallace—and of its impact on the American political scene. Acting upon his basic faith in and desire to assist the "common man," Wallace felt this third-party venture was a means—the only means—of carrying his "fight for peace" over the head of the President of the United States to the American people. For Wallace, the campaign battle reached far beyond America's shores; it was a battle for a war-free world in which the common men of all nations might live and prosper. If both major parties failed to give the American voter an opportunity to urge peaceful alternatives upon his government, then a new party must come into being—eventually to supplant one of them. "The people," said Wallace, "must have a choice."

But, beyond the immediate hopes and expectations of its founder and its followers, what was the party's impact? What were its ultimate effects on the American political scene, upon the conduct of American government? Here the additional perspective provided by the passage of time and the policies of succeeding administrations may prove helpful in arriving at a more balanced picture.

Much was written about the 1948 Progressive Party—at least in the columns of the press at the time—but little systematic attempt has been made to inquire with any measure of objectivity into the many facets of its history. Accordingly, it has been necessary to rely in great measure upon sources other than written for the present study.

The primary sources employed have included materials contained in the files of the Progressive Party (to the limited extent that party officials were willing to make them available), reports filed with the Clerk of the United States House of Representatives (for financial matters), and data gathered by the author and other persons during the course of the 1948 campaign—such as party press releases, letters of instruction to local affiliates, and other official communications.

However, more important than these documentary sources of information have been the personal interviews with officials of the Progressive Party and others connected with the Wallace campaign. On the basis of firsthand reports from the people actually involved in the organization of the party, and from others who observed from points of vantage, it has been possible to fill in many of the gaps that otherwise would have existed.

This interview method of research, it should be noted, possesses both advantages and disadvantages. Persons close to events in which they played an important role are sometimes reticent, sometimes intent on proving a special point or on justifying their own actions. Other individuals, muted by the social climate in which our investigations were conducted, proved unwilling to admit even an interest, let alone actual participation, in the Wallace party. On the other hand, secondhand reports, hearsay, and unsubstantiated allegations must be evaluated for their worth and credibility. Consequently, it has been necessary for the author to make judgments concerning the relative merit of many conflicting claims. In instances where there has seemed to be substantial support for contradictory positions, an attempt has been made to indicate both sides, as well as the author's own opinion.

Inasmuch as this study constitutes a political history, it seems wise to keep in mind the telling remark attributed to the late Charles A. Beard: "History may be objective, historians never are." The author does not claim exception to this rule. In fact, had a sympathetic interest in this third-party venture of Henry A. Wallace's not existed, it seems unlikely that this work would ever have been undertaken. But this very sympathy, coupled with the author's own participation (slight as it was, as chairman of a student group—Republicans for Wallace—at Colgate University, Hamilton, New York) in the campaign, may have served to qualify him for a better understanding of the problems faced and a clearer judgment of the solutions adopted by the third party.

Because the interviews, research, and preparation for this book covered an extended period of time, the author finds it difficult to acknowledge in a brief space the contributions of all those who have given assistance at one stage or another of the project.

Nevertheless, gratitude must be expressed to some whose contributions have been most substantial. Foremost of these has been Professor Malcolm C. Moos of the Johns Hopkins University, under whose guidance the work was planned, organized, and ultimately carried to completion. Indebtedness must also be expressed to those members of the Progressive Party who gave their wholehearted cooperation—particularly to the Honorable Henry A. Wallace, former Vice President of the United States, and to the Honorable Glen H. Taylor, former United States Senator from Idaho. Ladies and gentlemen of the press also provided many worthwhile suggestions. Thanks must be expressed to all of them who aided—particularly to Miss Helen Fuller of *New Republic* and to Mr. Barney Conal of *National Guardian,* who gave most generously of their time and personal recollections.

For the assistance rendered by these persons and the many others who must remain unmentioned, the author expresses his appreciation. For any errors of fact or interpretation which may remain, he accepts full responsibility.

Karl M. Schmidt

*Syracuse, New York*
*Summer, 1960*

# Contents

# HENRY A. WALLACE:

## Quixotic Crusade 1948

# CHAPTER 1

# New Currents Forming

New York casts 23 votes for Wallace, 69½ votes for Truman, ½ vote for Barkley.

Ohio casts 24½ votes for Wallace, 19½ votes for Truman.

Pennsylvania casts 46½ votes for Wallace, 23½ votes for Truman.

THE TIME—July, 1944. The place—Chicago. The occasion—the Democratic National Convention. This extract is a portion of the roll call of the states to select a running mate for Franklin D. Roosevelt in the fall campaign—a vice-presidential candidate destined by fate to become President of the United States. And with this vote there came to the surface the swirling currents that only four years later were to culminate in the organization of a third party—a new Progressive Party—the Wallace Progressive Party of 1948.

On this first ballot, the roll call noted above, Vice President Henry A. Wallace received 429½ votes and Senator Harry S. Truman 319½ votes, with the balance—some 428 votes—divided among fourteen favorite sons and local choices. Since 589 votes would have given him the requisite majority, Wallace had fallen short, by a margin of some 160 votes, of regaining the candidacy for Vice President at this strategic moment. On the second ballot, the band wagon of the bosses began to roll, sweeping Truman to the nomination, thence election, and ultimately the White House.

What lay behind the scene just described? What significant undercurrents contributed to it? First, there was a growing rift in the Democratic Party organization apparent in the split votes of the major state delegations. Second, there were sections of the nation in which streams of third-party sentiment and tradition existed and were rising. Then there were the wellsprings of an ideological discontent that was to emerge in the midst of the Truman administration and completely divide the Democratic camp. It is our task to survey these various streams that were to flow into the third-party channel and to measure their velocity—to explore the ultimate diversion of others originally expected to swell the Wallace tide, thus emerging with a clear chart of the new currents forming the 1948 Progressive Party.

At the outset, what were the contending forces within the Democratic Party?

In the 1940 Democratic Convention, President Franklin D. Roosevelt had virtually dictated the selection of Henry A. Wallace, then Secretary of Agriculture, as his fellow candidate, threatening to refuse the third-term nomination for himself if his wishes were not met. The reluctant delegates had to accept as Roosevelt's running mate a man who was anathema to many, a "renegade Republican" to others, and an unwanted candidate to practically all.

By 1944, however, the situation was nearly reversed. Despite the majority popular support indicated in the polls and the political strength exhibited on the convention floor, Wallace received what amounted to a kiss of death from Roosevelt. Instead of giving to Wallace the strong support of 1940, or the clear-cut endorsement that would have sufficed in 1944, the President saw fit to send a letter to Senator Samuel D. Jackson, permanent chairman of the Chicago National Convention, in which he announced that he "would vote for him [Wallace] personally if he were a delegate," but that he had "no desire to appear to dictate to the convention."

A few days later, with Wallace still in the thick of the fight for the nomination, despite this lukewarm endorsement, a second letter was sent by Roosevelt—this time to National Committee Chairman Robert Hannegan, who was also manager of the Truman forces—stating that either Truman or William O. Douglas would be an acceptable running mate. The original order of preference in the letter had been "Douglas or Truman," but the two names had been reversed prior to press release.[1] The Presidential communication proved decisive. Although the personal appearance of Wallace on the convention floor, together with his speech seconding Roosevelt's nomination, created demonstrations that almost turned the tide, the opposition strategy of postponing the vice-presidential balloting overnight prevailed.

It proved impossible to hold together for a second ballot the jerry-built Wallace convention machine. Commitments were too weak to keep the delegates in line. So confident had he been of the President's support up to the time of the convention letter, the Vice President had not deemed necessary an organization for returning him to office. Indeed, he had even neglected to secure a floor manager. Wallace has observed that as late as the Friday before the convention, the President, seated at his desk after a cabinet meeting, had put his arm around Wallace and pulled his head down to whisper, "Henry, I hope it's going to be the same old team." Only after arriving in Chicago did some of the Wallace supporters make a last desperate attempt to fill the gap, prevailing upon the aging Pennsylvanian Senator Joseph Guffey to lead the last-ditch battle. But the power of the big city bosses, the professional politicians, and the Southern Conservatives—working behind the scenes—proved too

---

[1] Wallace has ascribed the change to Hannegan, but Raymond Moley has claimed it was done at Roosevelt's request.

much. The house of cards collapsed. Led by Mayor Ed Kelly of Chicago, Ed Flynn and Paul Fitzpatrick of New York, and Frank Hague of Jersey City, with an assist from the National Committee Chairman Hannegan, the opposition forces which had seemed hopelessly divided at first finally agreed on Harry S. Truman as an available candidate who would, in the words of Ed Flynn, "offend no one" and be "acceptable" to almost all the contending groups.

This decision, however, was not made until the Political Action Committee of the Congress of Industrial Organizations, under Sidney Hillman, had effectively vetoed "Assistant President" James F. Byrnes—first choice of the Southern Conservatives. In this action Hillman had been supported by Flynn's protests that Byrnes—convert from Catholicism to Protestantism during his youth—would lose the votes of his former coreligionists in the crucial state of New York. Moreover, Byrnes possessed little appeal to the numerous Negro voters, whose support the Democrats hoped to retain. The liberal Douglas, with his name relegated to second place in Roosevelt's letter, was never seriously in contention, since he was most acceptable to those groups preferring Wallace.

The excuse advanced that Wallace was sacrificed for fear of costing F.D.R. votes in November is not supported by polls taken at the time. Far from a people's choice in 1940, he had nearly a majority of the rank-and-file Democrats supporting him by March of 1944, and by June this following had swelled to 65 per cent according to the Gallup surveys. At best, his abandonment may have led both southerners and city bosses to a stronger support of him than would otherwise have been forthcoming.

The results were succinctly expressed in an editorial in the *Manchester Guardian:*

The party bosses, . . . the machines, and the conservatives of the South could not stand Mr. Wallace who in the popular mind embodied the New Deal and racial equality. So they turned to the colorless Truman who has never upset anyone's prejudices.

Nor does it seem likely that the nomination of Wallace would have caused the Southern Conservatives to break completely with the administration or secede from the party. Unlike the situation four years later, the promise of victory and the magic of the Roosevelt name were insurance of at least nominal support.

For our purposes, however, the bitter floor fight over the Wallace nomination not only emphasized the basic division in the party but also made clear the specific cleavage of interests and ideologies—temporarily bridged by the personal appeal and magnetism, as well as the vote-getting ability, of the "Chief." On one side were the five principal groups of Wallace supporters: first, the old line New Dealers—Rex Tugwell, Ellis Arnall, Claude Pepper, Helen Gahagan Douglas, to mention a few; second, the CIO Political Action Committee group, as evidenced by the CIO's top leader, Sidney Hillman, and by Richard Frankensteen of the United Auto Workers, who singlehandedly had almost kept Michigan in line for Wallace; third, the Negro leaders who feared the Byrd-Byrnes drive and were at best lukewarm to Truman; fourth, a small group of professional politicians—particularly those with strong union constituencies, such as Senators Joseph Guffey of Pennsylvania and James Mead and Robert Wagner of New York; finally, the Communist fringe of the party—the fellow travelers and "daily workers," noisy though feeble, with their line of wartime "cooperation."

Against these Wallace supporters were arrayed three main groups: first, the big city machines and Conservative Northern Democrats, such as Flynn, Kelly, Hague, and Farley; second, the Southern Bourbons—remnants of a slow-dying southern conservatism—Byrd, Byrnes, Bankhead, and the

Virginia and South Carolina machines, among others; finally, the Anti-Wallace Liberals, more difficult to define but including those who desired to make haste more slowly. Counting in their ranks men like Justice William O. Douglas, Thomas Corcoran, Harold Ickes, Representative Estes Kefauver, and Senator Alben W. Barkley, as well as some of the Southern Liberals, this third group considered Wallace impractical and visionary.

Senator Truman's great virtue was that all groups could and would accept him, since Roosevelt would be *the* name on the ballot. Thus, the breach had been closed, at least on the surface, and the rather motley array of the Democratic Party closed ranks for the election battle with a common Republican enemy. As Arthur Krock so aptly put it in the *New York Times,* Henry A. Wallace had been "sacrificed to expediency."

Despite the convention rebuff, Wallace, with the opening of the fall campaign, began working actively for the Democratic ticket. Speculation began about the role he might play in a new Roosevelt administration. With the election issue still undecided, there came a rumor that he was to succeed the aging Cordell Hull as Secretary of State. In fact, this report gained such widespread circulation that the President saw fit to deny it publicly.

Following the election, word reached the press that, in return for his "sacrifice" at Chicago, the former Vice President had been offered his choice of Cabinet posts, with the sole exception of State, and that he had decided upon Commerce. Wallace himself has stated that, late in 1944, he had heard rumors of the impending retirement of Commerce Secretary Jesse Jones and that since he was not anxious to "push anyone out" of the Cabinet, he requested the Commerce post.

On January 22, 1945, President Roosevelt submitted the name of Henry A. Wallace to the Senate to succeed Jones in this position. After a bitter battle on Capitol Hill, in the course of which the post was stripped of many of its powers, including that of control over Reconstruction Finance Corporation funds, the appointment was finally confirmed. Wallace, after a four-year interval as Vice President of the United States, resumed his place at the head of an executive department.

As Secretary of Commerce, Wallace weathered the advent of Harry S. Truman to the Presidency in April of 1945 and, in contrast to his usual accompaniment of controversy, settled down into relative obscurity for nearly a year. However, during this period significant changes took place within the ornate walls of the Commerce Building. A strong friend of small business was now in power. Expansion of technical and other assistance for small firms from $300,000 to $4,500,000 per year was initiated.

In addition to performing his administrative duties, Wallace found time to oppose strenuously Republican attempts to undermine the reciprocal trade agreements in favor of higher protective tariffs. Citing the unemployment of the 1930's as an example of the ill effects caused in part at least by previous tariff policy, he argued that there could be no stability of employment without continued export-import agreements of the Cordell Hull pattern. While such views intensified the enmity of certain business groups, they seem to have left the general public apathetic.

Finally, to culminate the period of calm before the storm, Wallace's postwar doctrine of socio-economic planning emerged in book form as *60 Million Jobs*. But, with rapid reconversion and business boom making this figure reality in short order, the author was spared much of the customary attack on his "impossible dreaming."

This discussion summarizes the situation of the Democratic Party in late 1945. The rifts revealed at the Chicago Convention the previous year had indicated the deep and basic divisions within the party. But those had been healed over—at least on the surface. Liberal Left and Conservative Right had once more been reconciled. Viewed from Washington, any possibility of a third-party movement seemed remote indeed.

But what of the earlier background of Henry Wallace, this man of peace now standing on the verge of the most fateful decision in his whole career? What had been his governmental experience? What was his popular role?

Henry Agard Wallace had not been the first of his family to head the sprawling agencies of our largest peacetime instrument of government—the Department of Agriculture. His father, lifetime Republican Henry C. Wallace, had filled this same post during the 1920's in the Cabinet of Warren G. Harding. But along with so many other midwestern Republicans, the son had found long-standing political adherence challenged by the farm problems of the twenties and thirties and the failure of the GOP to move far enough or fast enough. He had become a Democrat, a public supporter of Franklin Roosevelt in the pages of the family journal, *Wallace's Farmer,* and had gone on to become one of Roosevelt's first Cabinet appointees.

Throughout his many years in public service—first as Secretary of Agriculture, then as Vice President—Wallace had found himself the target of unprecedented abuse and the object of unrestrained praise, with the former clearly predominating in the pages of the press. During the period of the New Deal and the Presidency of Franklin D. Roosevelt, Wallace had become much more than just another Cabinet politician. He had become a symbol for those Americans conscious that in the midst of the plenty, the means of production, and the know-how—in the midst of all these riches—one third of their nation was still ill-fed, ill-clothed, and ill-housed. Liberal groups, labor groups, and groups of the common people had rallied to the Wallace call "for a better world right now." Despite the unending press campaign of vituperation waged against him as a "visionary," a "radical," a "mystic," and an "idealist," Wallace had remained unswerving in his devotion to the common man. As he remarked cheerfully on one occasion, "The people who are fighting against me know that they are not fighting a starry-eyed liberal or mystic. If they really thought that, they wouldn't be worried."

Confident of the rightness of his position, Wallace had pressed the fight throughout his public career and had seen his popularity with the American public climb slowly but steadily to the high point recorded prior to the 1944 convention. With the death of Franklin D. Roosevelt in 1945, many of these persons came to feel that the true spiritual heir to the New Deal had been passed over. Pointing to the administration's handling of domestic and foreign affairs, those close to the scene concluded that Henry A. Wallace, rather than Harry S. Truman, represented the legitimate line of descent for the policies of the late President.

This description represents the man and the scene in Washington in late 1945. Although the crusader may have been mentally testing his armor, he was scarcely prepared for embarkation, nor was there yet any indication on that shore of the flood tide appropriate to the launching of a third-party venture.

What political attitudes were prevalent in other sections of the nation? What were some of the movements outside the Democratic Party that were to furnish tributary currents of varying size for the main stream of third-party sentiment in 1948? There were two regions of primary significance— the Middle West, traditional seat of third-party unrest, and New York, home of an existing balance-of-power third party. The year 1946 witnessed important developments in both areas.

There was the final dissolution of the Progressive Party in Wisconsin. Although founded as late as 1934, its roots went much deeper, even beyond 1912 and the Teddy Roosevelt movement. Through all these years it had been linked to the name of La Follette—first old "Fighting Bob," standard-bearer in the presidential race of 1924, and later his two sons, "Young Bob," who replaced his father as Senator, and Phillip, who became Governor of the state.

The party had built up a substantial following for itself and for its ideas of governmental reform, becoming, indeed, one of the state's two major parties. By 1944, however, it had fallen to third place at the polls, receiving only 5 per cent of the popular vote. And in 1946 it seemed that even the magic of the La Follette name would be insufficient to re-elect Young Bob to the Senate on its slate. Practical politics dictated a merger with one of the major parties.

Secretary of Commerce Wallace addressed a personal letter to the Senator, urging that the Progressives "with their great tradition of liberal action come home to the party of Roosevelt, rather than return to the party of Hoover." But, impelled by the desire to see La Follette re-elected, in state convention the party overcame the protests of a minority that wished to remain independent and decided to rejoin a reluctant GOP.

Labor groups within the party, however, had battled for acceptance of the Wallace invitation. Defeated, they withdrew from the Progressive-Republican coalition and entered their candidates in the Democratic primary. The defection proved fatal for La Follette in his Republican primary race, for the Conservative wing was busy engineering his replacement with a state circuit judge, Joseph R. McCarthy, distinguished chiefly by his youth (the youngest person ever elected to the state's circuit court), his political brashness, and his wartime service as a marine, rather than by his judicial competence or behavior (he had been censured by the state bar association for unethical practices). The loss of the labor votes—particularly in Milwaukee County—that had previously given Robert M. La Follette his margin of victory cost him the primary and his seat in the Senate.

For the first time in years, no member of the La Follette family held a high post in the Wisconsin government. But even more important, leaders who had crusaded for the Progressive banners, voters with a long tradition of independence, now felt that they had no place to go. Seemingly, there was fertile soil for a new third party in the state of Wisconsin, and the state convention had revealed substantial Wallace support—particularly among younger segments of the old Progressive Party.

At about the same time there came significant rumblings from the neighboring state of Minnesota, where, according to Malcolm Moos and E. W. Kenworthy, "Greenbackism and Populism and Bryanism are still slogans that awaken memories, and where 'Wall Street' and 'malefactors of great wealth' make the eyes see red and the blood pound in the veins."

In Minnesota, a Farmer-Labor Party had grown in the years following World War I from the merger of urban labor sentiment represented by the Socialist Party and rural unrest stemming from the Nonpartisan League. For two decades it had been highly important in state politics, but with the advent of a progressive Republican organization under Harold Stassen, it had gone into decline. A deathbed wedding with the Democratic Party had been arranged in 1942, but now this uneasy alliance showed signs of splitting. As in Wisconsin, there had been many persons—including former Governor Elmer Benson—who had never been completely reconciled to operating within the confines of a major party. And Benson's sympathy with the Wallace movement was clearly emerging.

Further indications of a right-left split in the Democratic Farmer-Labor alignment were present. In its traditional stronghold, the Iron Range, the DFL candidate for Congress was the pro-Wallace John Blatnik. Within the state organization, power seemed to rest with the malcontents. They promised sturdy roots for the grafting of a new nation-wide third party. Only one caution was in order—the Moos-Kenworthy warning that "despite the agrarian radicalism of Minnesota farmers, they want no truck with communism, and have an abiding fear and distrust of Russia."

Turning from agricultural to industrial America, the year 1946 marked significant developments in New York State. Evidence of growing support for a third-party movement can be traced to two parties there—the American Labor Party and the Communist Party—both centered in the New York City area.

The American Labor Party, a product of the 1930's, had already achieved a balance-of-power position for the entire state on the basis of its strength in the metropolitan New York City area. Despite the fact that it had already been rent by one anti-Communist fission—the departure of the Liberal Party group headed by David Dubinsky and the powerful International Ladies' Garment Workers Union—it had survived, and even thrived. Although this group had become the second party in only a small number of New York City districts, it possessed a solid regularly-voting core of some 350,000 to 400,000—a turnout large enough to spell the difference between victory and defeat for the Democratic candidates that the party tended to support.

The American Labor Party, after a running battle between left and right wings for many years, appeared to have stabilized itself in 1946 under the chairmanship of Representative Vito Marcantonio ("Marc"). A protégé of Fiorello H. La Guardia, Marcantonio had at various times been the congressional nominee of both major parties, as well as of the American Labor Party. He had also earned for himself the title of "Communist party-line follower" by such tactics as his rapid shift from anti- to pro-interventionist with the invasion of the Soviet Union in 1941. Nevertheless, it should be noted that Marc's leadership was based on a very solid foundation of precinct- and ward-level organization that had gained him the respect, if not the admiration, of Tammany and GOP workers in his district.

Having established his control over the state American Labor Party machine, Marcantonio left little doubt about his position on forcing a new third party, or the number of votes he expected to be able to deliver in New York. Following Wallace's dismissal from the Cabinet, he was to tell a Transport Workers Union Convention:

> This crisis . . . marks the beginning of the disintegration of the two American parties. I don't know which will go, but the historic condition is present for the creation of a new party resolving the question of peace and progress on the side of the people.
>
> 500,000 votes on Row C, the American Labor Party line, will be the forerunner of leadership given to the great movement for a new political party in America.[2]

In much the same vein, he repeated this call to a meeting of the American Youth for Democracy, saying, "We must build now for the establishment of a new political party in the United States. We must move now and not when it is too late." It should be noted, however, that not all of the American Labor Party membership was in accord with these sentiments. Jacob Potofsky of the Amalgamated Clothing

[2] *New York Times,* September 27, 1946.

Workers Union consistently opposed tying the party to a national Wallace third party and eventually walked out when the decision was made to do so.

Nor had the Communist Party yet determined its new course of action. During the war years, under the leadership of Earl Browder, the Communist Party line had been one of cooperation with the Democratic Party. It had attempted to employ infiltration tactics, the boring-from-within technique, as evidenced at the 1944 Convention.

Finding this tactic ineffective, the Communist Party, in late 1945, suddenly changed its line and replaced Browder as chairman with William Z. Foster. This emergency convention action to adopt the "popular front" approach successfully employed in Europe was reportedly in response to the international policy directives of Jacques Duclos from abroad.

Later evidence suggests that the Communists based their strategy upon the hope of developing a balance-of-power party, in which they would be able, by virtue of bloc cohesiveness, to exercise disproportionate power.

Many other ideas have been advanced concerning their reasons for supporting the Wallace party. It was suggested, particularly in labor circles, that they desired to split the Democrats to insure the election of a reactionary Republican President, thus making inevitable their predicted "capitalistic depression" and gaining them converts faster than any device of their own making. Another possibility was that the Communists desired to force the Democrats so far to the right that all Liberals would then flock to a new major party, in which the Communists, by being in on the ground floor, would have an important role. Quite possibly they realized that their endorsement of Wallace would be the kiss of death for him and that, by tagging him with the Red label, they might effectively eliminate the moderate reform element so feared by them in European countries.

However, in view of their own writings, and in view of

their limited American political experience, it seems more reasonable to credit them with attempting to follow the observed pattern of New York State rather than with formulating any supercrafty strategic concepts.

As Robert Minor wrote later in the *Daily Worker:*

> The central task of the Communist party . . . is to help forge the broadest people's anti-monopoly and peace coalition, in which the working class must play the leading role . . . . It is to curb the war-mongers and pro-fascists and *break once and for all the reactionary two-party system* of the monopolies.
> . . . a correct picture of the New Party [is] as the beginning of a break up of "The Two-Party System." . . . One of the most dangerous mistakes we made [was] when we accepted the anti-Marxist theoretical proposition made by Browder that the political struggles of the country could be fought out within the two-party system.[3]

Regardless of the reasoning behind the decision, the Communist Party continued to be one of the strongest advocates of third-party activity for the 1948 campaign. They may have wavered in choosing their candidate, but never in planning their strategy.

Having thus surveyed some of the significant developments outside the Democratic Party and outside the Truman administration, let us now return to the Washington scene where, for our account, the most dramatic single incident since 1944 was being prepared. The central character was again the same—Henry A. Wallace.

The year 1946 marked the development of two broad areas

[3] Robert Minor, "Lessons of Past Third Parties," *Daily Worker* (New York), August 2, 1948. Italics supplied.

of discontent with administration planning—discontent with
the administration's shift from the policies of Franklin D.
Roosevelt. First, there were signs of increased questioning
of the altered policy toward the Soviet Union. Second, there
was growing unrest with its changed handling of labor affairs
at home. At first, it was the foreign policy opponents who
favored continued action within the Democratic Party, while
the disaffected labor segment began to demand third-party
action.

Under newly appointed Secretary of State James F. Byrnes,
former "Assistant President" and vice-presidential hopeful
of 1944, there was a perceptible change in foreign outlook;
the previous Roosevelt attitude that the United States and
the U.S.S.R. could live together in peace despite their different political and economic systems was gradually replaced
by a firm policy toward Russia.

Many groups in the nation viewed the worsening relations between the former allies with misgiving, especially as
the United States initiated steps interpreted as by-passing
the United Nations. There were pacifists, religious leaders,
scientists, and old-time midwestern isolationists in this critical category, as well as the professional friends of Russia. All
were spurred on by the threatened devastation of a third
world war. Mankind, they agreed, possessed the means—
atomic, chemical, and bacteriological—of exterminating itself now in any new conflict. Consequently, any course of action by the administration tending to increase tension and
build up public acceptance of the inevitability of a future war
with Russia was to be deplored. These dissenters viewed the
Truman-Byrnes program as leading inevitably to hostilities.

On the other hand, the administration defended its course
as the only road to peace. The Russians, they said, could be
deterred from plans of world conquest only if the American
government took a firm stand to contain communism.

Thus, a broad cleavage began to develop over foreign

policy, with an ever increasing tendency on the part of some to interpret all criticism of American conduct of foreign affairs as communism or following the party line. Thus Mississippi Representative John Rankin was one of the first to trot out the Red label for Wallace, while a number of his fellow southern Congressmen conspicuously absented themselves from a Jackson Day dinner at which the Secretary of Commerce was to speak. These incidents followed a series of speeches and press releases early in 1946, in which Wallace decried the talk of war with the U.S.S.R. and urged a foreign policy that would build the United Nations as the stepping stone to an eventual world federation.

Notwithstanding his increasingly critical attitude toward the Truman-Byrnes conduct of American foreign policy, there were, at this time, no signs of his splitting completely with the Democratic administration. In fact, on May 25, 1946, in a speech to the American Labor Party in New York City, Wallace stated his opposition to any third-party move. As he phrased it, "Because of the election laws in any states, it [a third party] would give a reactionary victory by dividing the votes of the progressives."

The fact that such a rebuff was necessary indicates that some new current of sentiment favorable to the creation of just such an organization was already stirring on the extreme left. However, most foreign policy critics, including Senator Claude Pepper of Florida, agreed with Wallace that the most promising course was to work within the framework of the Democratic Party.

There had been a shift to the right in the domestic policies of the administration. Labor dissatisfaction was growing, stoked most of all by President Truman's threat to draft the striking railroad workers. The President's veto of the Case bill, which would have restricted labor's right to strike, had been interpreted by many as an attempt to stay on the fence—a last-ditch effort to avert a complete withdrawal of the labor segment of the Roosevelt coalition and the formation of a new third party. In addition, Truman was accused of responsibility for appointing to high office large numbers of men representing Wall Street, big business, and the military to replace the Roosevelt New Deal team.

Indications of the growing labor-liberal dissatisfaction were to be found in the statement of the National Citizens Political Action Committee, at this time allied with the CIO Political Action Committee. While placing its hopes for 1946 in the Democratic Party, the National Citizens Political Action Committee came out with a stinging statement that the party was in need of a rebirth. At about the same time David Dubinsky, speaking from both a labor (International Ladies' Garment Workers Union) and a third-party (liberal) viewpoint, called for a union of labor forces behind a new party. The boring-from-within technique of labor in major parties was inadequate, he said, since it would never create the necessary machinery for an organized labor party strong enough to run its own candidates for office on a national scale.

Thus by the summer of 1946 there were two main currents of unrest brewing under Harry S. Truman—one, which was critical of foreign policy, led by the Secretary of Commerce, who urged action within the Democratic Party; the second, critical of domestic policy, headed by labor leaders thinking in terms of a new and powerful labor party. Although scattered geographically, there was already a long-enduring undercurrent of third-party sentiment among groups as diverse ideologically as midwestern isolationists and Union Square Russophiles.

# CHAPTER 2

# *"The Fight for Peace"*

THE SMOLDERING unrest finally erupted with Henry A. Wallace's Madison Square Garden speech on September 12, 1946. This incident, more than any other single happening, served to crystallize third-party opinion, to widen the split between Conservatives and New Dealers within the Democratic Party, and to confuse the ranks of the Liberals themselves. What were the events that launched the Wallace "fight for peace"?

The Secretary of Commerce had personally presented to President Truman the text of a speech on foreign policy to be delivered at an anti-Republican, anti-Dewey rally to be held in New York City, actually reading the complete address to the President so that there could be no possible misunderstanding through misreading, or omission. After covering the speech, sentence by sentence, in the course of a private White House conference, the President suggested only one alteration—a strengthening of one section. Following this change, and in advance of the speech's delivery, according to James Reston:

> President Truman said in his press conference today that he approved the speech [to be] delivered in New York tonight by Secretary of Commerce Henry A. Wallace and that he considered it to be in line with the policies of Secretary of State James F. Byrnes.[1]

[1] *New York Times*, September 13, 1946.

Concerning the speech itself, next morning the *New York Times* reported that "Secretary Wallace . . . was hissed and heckled at several points in his speech when he talked of the need for Russian understanding of American aims." Wallace interpreted this unfavorable reception as being caused by the fact that the speech "followed a straight American line." In his estimation, it was "neither pro-British or anti-British, neither pro- nor anti-Russian." Although Wallace endorsed the stated administration objective of seeking peace through United Nations cooperation, he presented three main points of departure: (1) a warning against allowing American foreign policy to be dominated by the British; (2) a warning that "the tougher we get with Russia, the tougher they will get with us"; and (3) a tacit acceptance of a Russian sphere of influence in Eastern Europe, much as the Monroe Doctrine had implied an American sphere of influence in Latin America.

Since the speech attacked the firm policy of the Secretary of State toward Russia—a policy which Mr. Byrnes was even then outlining to a Paris meeting of the United Nations—and since the President had so definitely approved the speech in advance, there was immediate speculation about a possible shift in American foreign policy. Strong repercussions were felt in Paris, although in this country the speech was interpreted as being primarily political and designed to secure the campaign support of dissident leftwing elements in New York—elements of major importance in the coming state election.

From Paris, the American delegation protested immediately and strenuously. Senator Tom Connally of Texas put it this way, according to the *New York Times,* "If the United States is to speak with an influential voice, there must be no division behind the lines." Senator Vandenberg, the Michigan Republican, complained, "We can cooperate with [only] one Secretary of State at a time."

As a result of these protests, President Truman backtracked, stating that he meant to approve only Wallace's right to speak, not "the speech as constituting a statement of the foreign policy of this country." He then announced, following rumors of Wallace's forced resignation, that the Secretary of Commerce would remain in the Cabinet under an agreement that no further foreign policy speeches would be made until after the Paris meeting had adjourned.

But this solution was not sufficient to appease the Secretary of State. Byrnes, maintaining a public silence, delivered to the President in a private teletype conversation a Wallace-goes-or-I-do ultimatum. Denied at the time, the report of this communication was later confirmed by Byrnes himself in his book *Speaking Frankly*. It was Wallace's belief that Senator Vandenberg, more than anyone else, influenced Byrnes to take this stand. However, Bernard Baruch, the elder statesman who had recently participated in a public exchange with Wallace over their respective plans for control of atomic energy, also reputedly played a considerable part in putting on the pressure. The President's hand having been forced, he reversed his previous announcement and, in a telephone conversation, requested the resignation of his Secretary of Commerce. Wallace complied, promising at the same time to continue his "fight for peace, in which I am sure that I have your full and continued support." Thus the last of the original New Dealers left the Cabinet.

An overt realignment of political forces began to take place. With Wallace's departure, many of the radical and leftist elements in the Democratic Party—those antagonized by the President's foreign or domestic policies—intensified their battle against their titular head. The split that until now had been more or less concealed came fully to the front and was widened by publicity.

The Brotherhood of Railway Trainmen, headed by A. F. Whitney, still smarting from his earlier encounter with the President over the threatened draft of striking railroaders, issued an invitation to Wallace to address the union's forthcoming convention. At the same time Whitney condemned Truman for having "removed every progressive appointed by Franklin D. Roosevelt," and declared that "Secretary Wallace is now available to lead a movement for sound and progressive government." Since Whitney and the Trainmen had supported the La Follette Progressive candidacy in 1924, this seemed not just an idle threat but the promise of substantial labor support for a third-party venture.

National Citizens Political Action Committee spokesmen Frank Kingdon and C. B. "Beanie" Baldwin labeled President Truman's action in dismissing Wallace a blow to peace, charging the abandonment of F.D.R.'s foreign policy. Jack Kroll, director of the powerful CIO Political Action Committee, was quoted in the *New York Times* as saying, "Wallace now has the opportunity to bring the real facts on this crucial issue to the American people." Grant Oakes, president of the leftwing CIO United Farm Equipment and Metal Workers Union, alleging that Truman had chosen the path to war, declared that "he leaves the people no alternative but to organize a third party of their own in 1948."

In New York, the American Labor Party went on record as supporting Wallace's position, as did such diverse groups as the American Slav Congress, the Executive Committee of the Methodist Federation of Social Service, and the New Council of American Business, Inc. Vito Marcantonio, ALP spokesman, termed the Wallace dismissal the beginning of disintegration of the Democratic Party and called for a new party backed by labor.

The Communists, taking advantage of the furor created and realizing that their initial interpretation and dislike of the speech must have been erroneous, reversed themselves abruptly to praise the Wallace stand. Their *Daily Worker* had been highly critical the morning after its delivery. Their news columns played down the Wallace role in the rally with no mention of his comments until the ninth paragraph, while editorially they complained:

While expounding the peace ideals of the late President Roosevelt, Henry Wallace defended the policies which are undermining those ideals.

.  .  .  .  .

He advanced views, however, which covered up American imperialism's aggressive role.

.  .  .  .  .

. . . he implied the U.S. was innocent in this struggle between Britain and Soviet Russia.[2]

But with the growing furor that the speech was kicking up three days later, they tempered this statement in their early Sunday edition, saying:

Unfortunately, Mr. Wallace didn't do [the] job of showing up American foreign policy . . . although he did say a lot of good things in his speech at Madison Square Garden Thursday night.[3]

Then, with President Truman's disavowal of the speech and hints of Wallace's impending dismissal, this second opinion was altered, *in later editions for the same day,* to lukewarm praise:

Henry Wallace's speech, last Thursday night despite all its shortcomings, was a repetition of the deep worry which pervades our people over the present war trend of the administration.
. . . Despite inconsistencies, Wallace expressed the desires of the people.
. . . Wallace and Pepper should fight for their policies.[4]

Finally, by Tuesday, the Communists had adopted Mr. Wallace completely for their own, declaring:

[2] *Daily Worker,* September 13, 1946.
[3] Editorial, *Worker* (New York), September 15, 1946, 1st edition.
[4] Editorial, *Worker,* September 15, 1946, later edition; also reprinted in *Daily Worker,* September 16, 1946.

. . . As for ourselves we declare frankly that the main features of Mr. Wallace's represented a criticism which we have long been making in our own modest way. The things on which we disagree with Mr. Wallace, though important, are secondary to the main areas of agreement.[5]

While some Liberals, such as Senators Claude Pepper and Glen Taylor, supported the Wallace position, many others condemned the speech. The American Liberal Party assailed his acceptance of spheres of influence as inimical to world unity as well as to the United Nations and declared that he had "forfeited support of Liberals working for one world, not two."

Socialist leaders were equally critical, Norman Thomas calling Wallace the "heir to the policy of appeasement disastrously followed by Chamberlain . . . and by Roosevelt and Truman at Cairo, Teheran, Yalta, and Potsdam." However, they, too, agreed that the Wallace episode marked "the beginning of the crack-up of the Democratic party."

The Conservative wing of the Democratic Party was far from unhappy at Wallace's departure. Men like James Farley, erstwhile party strategist, and Jesse Jones, Wallace's predecessor in the Commerce post, supported Byrnes wholeheartedly. The *New York Times* was able to quote numerous prominent members of both House and Senate, virtually unanimous in their approval of the President's action.

A broad range of political thought expressed condemnation of Wallace; the United Mine Workers commented editorially on Wallace as an "impractical dreamer," while Harold J. Laski, writing for the *Nation,* assailed not the content of the speech but its timing. In his opinion, it should have been delivered some three months earlier, prior to the Paris talks, to have had any chance of being effective.

[5] Editorial, *Daily Worker,* September 17, 1946, later edition, p. 1; also reprinted Monday, September 16, 1946.

With respect to new party currents, it can be said that the Madison Square Garden speech stirred up a maelstrom of conflict: Those who accepted the Wallace views on foreign policy were not agreed on the relative advisability of creating a third party or of working within the Democratic Party. Those who were strongly committed to minor-party endeavor, such as the Socialists, the Liberals, and the American Labor Party, found themselves split over the foreign policy issue.

The first tangible political event to come out of this turmoil was the Conference of Progressives held at Chicago two weeks later—September 28 and 29, 1946. This meeting, called by the National Citizens Political Action Committee and the Independent Citizens Committee of the Arts, Sciences and Professions, proposed to "discuss common political strategy for independent progressive organizations." Specifically, it aimed at a showdown over the Wallace ouster and at the formation of a compact power bloc by those Democrats espousing the Roosevelt New Deal traditions, which, they claimed, the Truman administration was gradually deserting.

The conference set as its goal the task of getting out a 50,000,000 vote in the 1946 congressional elections so that liberalism might be reinforced in the coming Eightieth Congress. For the more distant future they set their sights on the selection of Liberal delegates to the 1948 Democratic National Convention. A broad segment of Liberal thought was represented at this Chicago assemblage. The speakers included Henry Morgenthau, Jr., Secretary of the Treasury under Roosevelt; former Interior Secretary Harold Ickes; Florida Democratic Senator Claude A. Pepper; Phillip Murray and Jack Kroll of the CIO; James Patton of the Farmers Union; Clark Foreman of the Southern Conference for Human Welfare; and Walter White of the National Association for the Advancement of Colored People.

Morgenthau attacked talk of forming a third party and thus falling into the "trap set by reactionary elements of the

Republican and Democratic parties," while Walter White
pointed out that it would take six years to get a third party
listed in all the states. Nonetheless, the vehemence of their
remarks in trying to quell the ardor for a third-party move
strongly suggests the existence of considerable sentiment
among the delegates for just such action.

Another alternative was suggested by former Secretary of
the Interior Ickes. Since it was highly improbable that their
group would be able to capture either major party, he urged
the self-proclaimed New Deal heirs to cross party lines and
elect Liberals wherever they were to be found.

Unable to reach agreement on the broader aspects of political strategy, the meeting did unite on some of the minor
details—building from the ground up, ringing doorbells, and
working on the precinct level. Moreover, the conference arrived at an acceptable platform—twelve domestic planks
based on the 1944 Democratic stand and seven foreign policy
ones based on the views of Henry A. Wallace, as outlined in
a letter to President Truman in July of 1946. This accomplished, the group adjourned, but not without Phillip Murray's attempt to read out of the movement "and out of progressive and liberal ranks those of Communist persuasions."

Meanwhile, the Democratic campaign was getting under
way. Representative John J. Sparkman announced that Wallace and Pepper had been dropped from the congressional
Speakers Committee as a result of their foreign policy views.
After a six-week quasi-retirement from the political scene,
however, Wallace was summoned by James Roosevelt, son of
the late President and chairman of the California Democratic
State Committee, to deliver a series of speeches in behalf of
Liberal West Coast candidates whose congressional seats were
in danger. Wallace followed this California trip with a brief
tour of the Middle West. He wound up the campaign speaking in New York, despite the disapproval of the city machine.

Here, while urging the election of Democratic candidates James Mead and Herbert Lehman in the 1946 New York State races, he joined Senator Pepper in issuing a call for a progressive candidate for President in 1948.

This last-minute visit seemed to many a clear-cut threat to the Democrats of leftwing withdrawal and organization of a third party, if necessary, for the 1948 campaign. But, while National Citizens Political Action Committee leaders Frank Kingdon and C. B. "Beanie" Baldwin declared that

> Unless the national administration changes its course, the progressives will sever their bonds of allegiance and form a new third party in the next two years,

Wallace declined to commit himself definitely, saying:

> I don't mean that the day after tomorrow we are going to form a third party, but I do say that new currents will be forming.[6]

Immediately following the Republican landslide in the 1946 elections, in which candidates supported by the CIO Political Action Committee won in only 73 of 318 races, the Continuations Committee of the Conference of Progressives met to discuss strategy in view of the disaster at the polls. The decision was reached to continue work within the frame of the major parties. Former Secretary of the Treasury Morgenthau told the press that a third party "had not been discussed."

Despite this disavowal, it was a matter of only a few weeks before the leftwing elements of the conference were again meeting—on December 30, 1946—this time to organize the Progressive Citizens of America. Even though the PCA stated that its immediate object was to make the Democratic Party

[6] *New York Times,* November 5, 1946.

"out and out progressive," others felt that this was the first serious step toward creating the independent nucleus of a third party. The new group adopted the Wallace foreign policy plank of "peace, prosperity and freedom in one world" and called for widespread domestic reforms.

Thus, by the close of 1946, new currents were running that were to lead eventually to a new party. The Madison Square Garden speech had provided the catalytic agent for translating discontent into political action. It now seemed possible that the divided forces of the Liberals might unite—on both policy and strategy—to carry out the Wallace "fight for peace."

Inasmuch as the Progressive Citizens of America had been formed with the Political Action Committee of the CIO as one of its main advocates, there was reason to believe that its political endeavors would receive considerable labor support. However, events soon took place that were to eliminate this possibility. First, a group of Liberals and New Dealers, including Mrs. Eleanor Roosevelt, banded together to reorganize the existing but feeble Union for Democratic Action into a stronger non-Communist left which would oppose the Progressive Citizens of America. They said that their new group, Americans for Democratic Action, would further Liberal aims through the medium of the Democratic Party. It would bar from membership the Communists and fellow travelers who, it claimed, dominated the PCA. Significantly, Walter Reuther, President of the CIO United Auto Workers, was among the founders of the Americans for Democratic Action.

A rift in the ranks of the CIO itself now seemed imminent with CIO President Phillip Murray listed as vice president of the Progressive Citizens of America, and the leader of one of his strongest unions enrolled in the Americans for Democratic

Action. It may well have been this threat of internecine strife in the CIO that led Murray to withdraw his name from the PCA and at the same time urge the CIO to disassociate itself officially from both PCA and ADA. In this manner, a split within the union was averted, but the Progressive movement was effectively deprived of the strong organized labor support without which any attempt to establish a third party was foredoomed to failure.

Meanwhile, the Progressive Citizens of America continued to support the Wallace foreign policy, sponsoring a series of speeches in which the former Secretary of Commerce assailed the Truman doctrine of aid to Greece and Turkey as inviting a fatal arms race between the United States and the U.S.S.R. and dividing the world into two armed camps. At the same time, Vito Marcantonio of the New York American Labor Party continued to call for the formation of a new third party. Whereas a year before certain members of the Democratic Party had walked out on him at the annual Jackson Day Democratic festivities, this time it was Wallace who absented himself.

In the midst of the American debate on foreign policy, the former Vice President now embarked on a tour of Western European democracies. In a series of speeches delivered in England, Sweden, and France during April, 1947, he was highly critical of administration policy, accusing it of undercutting the U.N., which he termed the world's "best, perhaps only, hope for peace."

These speeches, warmly received in some circles abroad, became the immediate target of attack at home. Representative John Rankin, chairman of the House Committee on un-American Activities, urged that the Logan Act of 1799 be invoked to prosecute the former Vice President for "dealing with foreign nations to defeat American measures." In this argument, Rankin received the warm support of many southern Congressmen. Similarly, the Veterans of Foreign Wars urged that Wallace's passport be revoked. On the other hand, the Americans for Democratic Action contented itself with opposing the Wallace views but not his right to state them.

With the increasing strength of his attacks upon the Truman administration, third-party rumors began to fly in earnest. Wallace, however, disclaimed any ambitions for himself, suggesting that Senator Claude Pepper of Florida, a firm supporter of the United Nations, would be the ideal choice to head such a movement. Senator Pepper immediately tossed the ball back to Wallace, stating that he would "remain in the Democratic party as long as it is truly liberal."

Upon his return from the controversial European tour, Wallace embarked, under sponsorship of the Progressive Citizens of America, on another American tour—continuing to urge economic aid to Europe (still some weeks prior to the enunciation of the Marshall plan [7]) and to oppose what he termed "war preparations." In his own words, the purpose of the tour was to "liberalize the Democratic party." Stating that he did not know whether he would back Truman in 1948, he continued to urge that the President meet with Premier Stalin to settle American-Russian differences.

By the first of June, this stumping tour of the country was beginning to have noticeable effects. Cabell Phillips remarked in the *New York Times:*

> As Henry Wallace stumps the country in advocacy of his program for altering the course of American foreign policy, he is leaving in his wake a recrudescence of that familiar form of political rebellion that seeks its ends through the formation of a third party.[8]

[7] Wallace's speech to the French Chamber of Deputies in which he proposed a fifty-billion-dollar world reconstruction program was delivered April 23, 1947. Under Secretary of State Acheson's speech at Cleveland, Mississippi—the forerunner of the Marshall plan—was delivered May 8, 1947.

[8] *New York Times,* June 1, 1947.

But at the same time there were serious obstacles in the way of a new party—the lack of any cohesive organizational control, the difficulty of securing a place on the state ballots, much greater than in the days of La Follette, and the belief that the "balance of power technique [would] yield more practical results in the next few years at least." Moreover, while the movement was acquiring perhaps a few supporters, it was making many enemies.

The persistence of the Wallace attacks on foreign policy continued to draw the fire of those who had opposed his Madison Square Garden speech. In New York David Dubinsky again attacked the Wallace position, while former Under Secretary of State A. A. Berle, Jr., urged Wallace to leave the "Appeasement Party," as he termed the Progressive Citizens of America. Socialists Norman Thomas and Louis Waldman continued their barrage, as did the old Democratic Party war horse Jim Farley.

A suggestion by Wallace that "liberal Republicans" might be willing to support a new alignment drew a sharp rebuff from Senator Wayne Morse (Oregon), who at this time still maintained that "the only hope for sane and sound progressive politics is through liberalizing the Republican party."

The only new accretion to the strength of the movement during the first months of 1947 came with announcement that Dr. Francis Townsend and his old-age pension group would support a third party because they had "lost faith in the sincerity of both of the old parties." Wallace continued to urge that organized labor, small businessmen, and farmers cooperate within the Democratic Party to end the "feudal leadership" of the Southern Democrats, while he parried all suggestions that a third party was in the making. His, he insisted, was a struggle to make possible the survival of the Democratic Party by persuading it to adopt a policy of peace and disarmament.

But at the same time his followers in the Far West were

posing a much greater threat to party harmony. A considerable segment of the California Liberal wing of the
Democratic Party, led by Robert W. Kenny, former Attorney
General and candidate for Governor, met at Fresno on July
19, 1947, to organize a move to elect Wallace-pledged delegates to the 1948 National Convention. If this move failed,
they said, they planned to launch a third party with the former
Vice President at its head.

And when the Southern Democratic bloc in Congress combined with the Republicans to pass the Taft-Hartley Bill in
June, it again seemed possible that large groups of organized
labor might bolt their Democratic traces. The General Executive Board of the International Ladies' Garment Workers
Union called for action leading to the ultimate organization
of a third party. Their doubts concerning the advisability of
such a move had seemingly been dispelled by the possibility
of President Truman's signing the measure, or of its becoming law over his veto. They urged that it was time for the
AFL to abandon its traditional nonpartisan role in favor of
positive action.

The seriousness of this latter threat, however, is rather to
be doubted in the light of their actions once the measure
passed over the Truman veto. As with the earlier Case anti-
strike bill, it seems possible that much of the force was
directed at pushing a decision upon a wavering President.
While it is difficult to determine the amount of influence that
such declarations had in bringing about the veto, there is
less doubt that the Truman message, couched in strong
terms, proved one of the greatest blows to the possibility of a
new and strong third-party alignment. It turned the labor
tide that had been receding from the Democrats and inter-
mittently threatening independent-party action. Despite the
fact that a large number of Democrats joined with the Republicans to override the President, his waning prestige with

labor and with Liberal groups was considerably restored by his action.

One immediate effect was that A. F. Whitney, who just a year previously had been threatening to raise a "million-dollar slush fund" to defeat Truman, now in July, 1947, advised his Brotherhood of Railway Trainmen that the Taft-Hartley veto "vindicated [Truman] in the eyes of Labor." He went further to state that a third party would be "suicidal" and "out of the question," as it would merely serve to help the Republicans. This declaration was a damaging blow, since for three years, ever since the 1944 Convention fight, Whitney's Trainmen had been firm supporters of Wallace, and their organized support, to say nothing of their financial assistance, would have been significant in any attempt to create a third party.

At the same time it was observed that while many Liberals thought that a "third party will ultimately be necessary," they added that "it must have a grass roots origin, not now considered possible," according to Clayton Knowles in the *New York Times*. Coupled with the backing off by labor leaders, there came a sudden waning of strength in California, with the announcement that James Roosevelt, who had earlier been highly critical of the Truman foreign policy, was now back in the Democratic fold.

When, in September, Wallace announced that it was his "intention to work within the Democratic party realm" and President Truman rebuked Gael Sullivan, acting national chairman of the Democrats, for singlehandedly reading Wallace and Pepper out of the party, it seemed that threats of a third party had nearly vanished.

Yet, at the same time that Wallace was expressing his intent of working within the Democratic Party, he was also keeping the door open for a change in plans "if the Democratic party is a war party . . . [and] continues to attack civil liberties." Furthermore, he went on to say, "If both parties stand for high prices and depression, then the people must have a new party of liberty and peace. The people must have a choice." And while most of the labor support for a third party was withering away, the International Longshoremen's and Warehousemen's Union, a leftwing CIO affiliate headed by Harry Bridges, came out in open support of a third party to be headed by Wallace. This was more than counterbalanced by the final decision of the CIO Political Action Committee, as announced by Jack Kroll on October 16, that this group would not lead in the formation of any new party organization.

Thus it can be seen that by the fall of 1947 most of the third-party agitation stemming from the domestic labor policies of the first Truman administration was beginning to subside. The sole main current still running strongly in favor of a third party was that impelled by groups in opposition to its foreign policy. During this period, with many of his supporters wavering and returning to the Democratic ranks, Wallace embarked upon a three-week visit to Palestine to survey at first hand the situation in the infant state of Israel. Nor was this trip devoid of political significance in view of the large numbers of Jewish voters who might thereby be attracted to the Wallace banners.

By the time he returned, the situation in California had become increasingly critical. The withdrawal of the Roosevelt support and the desire of many Liberals to work only within the Democratic Party left the newly formed Independent Progressive Party in the hands of Hugh Bryson, president of the Marine Cooks and Stewards (CIO), supported by some seventy CIO locals and a few AFL affiliates. The Independent Progressive Party had the support of the Townsend organization, but the Southern California chapters of the Progressive Citizens of America had adopted a wait-and-see attitude.

Owing to stringent California requirements on nominating petitions,[9] a total of 275,970 signatures would be required by March 18, 1948—only three months away—if the party were to have a place on the November ballot. While it was still hoped that Wallace-pledged delegates to the Democratic Convention could be elected, there was an immediate necessity to establish contingent machinery should that plan fail. And with the reluctance of Wallace to announce his candidacy, the task of obtaining the required signatures seemed hopeless. Word was received from the Coast that unless a positive commitment was forthcoming by January 1, the Wallace drive would have to be completely abandoned.

Spurred on by this deadline, the National Executive Committee of the Progressive Citizens of America announced on December 17 that it had decided to support Wallace for the Presidency and urged the immediate formation of third-party machinery to place the name of its candidates on the ballots of all the states. This decision was arrived at only at the cost of a complete break within the Progressive Citizens of America leadership. According to Wallace, during 1947 co-leader Frank Kingdon had "put more pressure on" him than anyone else to form a third party. But now Kingdon, his eye on the Democratic senatorial nomination in New Jersey, announced his resignation, stating that while he supported the Wallace foreign policy, and would have worked for the *Democratic* nomination for Wallace, he was opposed to the attempt to organize a third party.

Kingdon's resignation was followed by that of Bartley Crum as national vice-chairman. Of the original substantial leadership in the Progressive Citizens of America, only a shadow now remained. The potential third-party ranks were further diminished by the announcement that the Amalgamated

[9] According to California law, 10 per cent of the number of votes in the last gubernatorial election must be secured as signatures to any nominating petition prior to both the state primaries and the na tional conventions.

Clothing Workers was ready to withdraw from the American Labor Party if, as anticipated, that party should become the vehicle for a Wallace candidacy in New York State.

Wallace himself remained silent while all these maneuvers were taking place during mid-December, but his acceptance of sponsorship by the Progressive Citizens of America for an upstate New York speaking tour indicated probable receptivity to the formal bid now tendered him. Hence, his declaration of candidacy on December 29 came as no great surprise. As J. Howard McGrath, Democratic national chairman, put it, this announcement merely served to "clear the atmosphere."

In a radio address to the American people, Wallace explained the reasons for his decision:

> Peace and abundance mean so much to me that I have said . . . . "If the Democratic party continues to be a party of war and depression, I will see to it that the people have a chance to vote for peace and prosperity."
>
> When the old parties rot, the people have a right to be heard through a new party . . . . The people must again have an opportunity to speak out with their votes in 1948 . . . .
>
> A new party must stand for a positive peace program of abundance and security, not scarcity and war . . . .
>
> . . . I have fought and shall continue to fight programs which give guns to people when they want plows . . . . Those whom we buy politically with our food will soon desert us. They will pay us in the base coin of temporary gratitude and then turn to hate us because our policies are destroying their freedom.
>
> . . . We are acting in the same way as France and England after the last war and the end result will be the same —confusion, digression and war.
>
> It just doesn't need to happen. The cost of organizing for

peace, prosperity and progress is infinitely less than organizing for war . . . .

Thousands of people all over the United States have asked me to engage in this great fight. The people are on the march . . . .

By God's grace, the people's peace will usher in the century of the common man.[10]

It should be noted, however, that in the same speech Wallace left the door open to a possible reconciliation with Democratic leaders prior to the election, provided that they would drop their proposal for universal military training and get rid of what he called the "Wall Street–Military appointees" whom he saw as leading the administration toward a war with Soviet Russia.

With this final definite announcement, the new currents that had been swirling about for so many months now entered straighter, narrower, and more discernible channels. Of the five main groups that had composed Wallace's chief support at the 1944 Convention—the old line New Dealers, the CIO Political Action Committee, labor leaders, the Negro groups, the sprinkling of professional politicians, and the Communist fringe—only one group—the Communists—now remained intact and firmly behind the third-party candidacy. Wallace had declared his opposition to any and all forms of Red-baiting and his willingness to accept the support of any and every group working in the interests of peace, with the wistful hope that the Communist Party would avoid passing any resolutions of support for him. The Communists proceeded at once to offer him their firm support.

The old line New Dealers split over the Wallace move, with only a few—such as Rexford Tugwell and Elmer Benson—supporting the new-party decision. The balance—Harold

[10] Text of Wallace's Address, *New York Herald Tribune*, December 30, 1947.

Ickes, Leon Henderson, Wilson Wyatt, Chester Bowles, and Mrs. Eleanor Roosevelt—had returned through the Americans for Democratic Action into the Democratic fold. Their belief that only through an immediate victory in the 1948 election could the cause of liberalism be advanced was soon to be exhibited by their myopic espousal of the presidential nomination of General Dwight D. Eisenhower—a man whose political views were virtually unknown, and the known few conservative—since in early 1948 he seemed the only nominee with enough strength to carry a lagging Democratic Party to victory.

Labor, too, was now divided; only a few leftwing CIO national unions—the United Electrical Workers and the International Longshoremen's and Warehousemen's Union—were openly supporting Wallace, although it appeared that some locals as well as many of the rank and file might cling to his banner. The great power of the CIO, with its Political Action Committee, was gone from the camps of the third party. The Railway Brotherhoods were gone. In re-electing Walter Reuther as its head the United Auto Workers had evidenced that it too was in the camp of the Americans for Democratic Action rather than that of the Progressive Citizens of America.

The National Association for the Advancement of Colored People, through Secretary Walter White, seemed similarly in the ADA lineup, although here again there were indications that many individuals would continue to support Wallace. Finally, the professional politicians, quick to sense the trend, stayed away from the Wallace camp in large numbers. The task of organizing the new party would be left almost completely in the hands of the amateurs, except in New York where the American Labor Party was well established.

Of the groups outside the Democratic Party, only the American Labor Party and the Communist Party could be counted upon for complete support. The American Labor Party had been greatly weakened by the withdrawal of its greatest single constituent group—the Amalgamated Clothing Workers. Communist Party support was of dubious value at best. Indeed, Wallace estimated later that its 100,000 votes (or less) would probably cost him 3,000,000 non-Communist supporters. The Progressive Party had expired in Wisconsin, and the remaining independent threads sustained by the *Progressive* magazine would soon endorse the Socialist candidate, Norman Thomas. It should be noted that at this time, however, there was still some substantial hope of capturing the Democratic Farmer-Labor Party in Minnesota.

Elsewhere in the agricultural areas, farm support for the onetime Secretary of Agriculture was almost completely lacking. Even the National Farmers Union, through President James Patton, announced that it would take no stand on his candidacy, although they realized that "undoubtedly many farmers of the NFU [would] support Henry Wallace for President."

Of the press, only the Communist *Daily Worker* and "Jess" Gitt's York, Pennsylvania, *Gazette and Daily* promised support. Publisher Gitt was one of those who had earlier placed pressure on Wallace, saying, "If you don't run, some one else will." Such liberal publications as the *Nation* and *New Republic* took an exceedingly dim view of the proceedings. As the *Nation* editorialized:

> There is still a gulf between the two [major] parties taking them by and large, both in intention and in program . . . [and] by 1952 the fate of the American economy may well have been sealed and the question of war or peace decided. Never before has a serious progressive group in this country even thought of launching a third party without major support from the trade unions . . . the only result can be to confuse enough Progressives to assure a Republican vic-

tory without establishing a mass base for a future third
party movement.[11]

Small wonder, then, that political observers shrugged their
shoulders and shook their heads as Henry A. Wallace, former
Vice President of the United States, announced that he had
"assembled a Gideon's Army, small in number, powerful in
conviction, ready for action" and that he would "run as an
independent candidate for President of the United States in
1948." Small wonder that the whole scheme of the Wallace–
Progressive Citizens of America group was dubbed "quixotic
politics."

[11] *Nation*, 165 (December 27, 1947), 693.

CHAPTER 3

# The Wallace-Taylor Team

WITH A new party thus launched by Henry A. Wallace's decision to run for the Presidency so that the American people might "have a choice," the immediate problem became that of selecting his running mate. The Progressive forces found themselves severely limited in the ranks from which to choose—in the numbers of the politically prominent willing to stake their futures on the same principle—the all-important Wallace principle of opposing the bipartisan foreign policy endorsed by the Republican opposition as well as by the Truman administration.

Senator Claude Pepper of Florida, prominent New Dealer and firm supporter of the Roosevelt foreign policy throughout both prewar and World War II periods, had already indicated his decision not to bolt. Although a severe critic of the Truman doctrine of military aid to Greece and Turkey and the sponsor of an unsuccessful Senate amendment for routing economic aid to Europe through the United Nations, Senator Pepper had finally voted for passage of the administration's Marshall plan. He now promised to continue to press for policy modifications from within the ranks of the Democratic Party.

Professor Rexford Guy Tugwell, former Wallace aide in the Department of Agriculture and more recently Governor

41

of Puerto Rico, was a possible nominee. But although Professor Tugwell was later to serve on the party's Platform Committee, he apparently received little serious consideration as the Wallace running mate.

Then there was O. John Rogge, an avowed candidate for the nomination. A lawyer who had served as Assistant Attorney of the United States, Rogge was not well known outside the New York–Washington area. Moreover, like Wallace, he was a resident of New York State, thus posing the theoretical if unlikely constitutional problem of electors from a single state being unable to vote for two candidates from that state in a presidential election. Should the Progressives carry the Empire State, their electors would be unable to vote for their vice-presidential candidate.

From the very beginning, however, the leading contender for the second position was Democratic Senator Glen H. Taylor of Idaho. Elected without strong state organizational support, Taylor felt free of party obligation. A consistent supporter of President Roosevelt's policies—both foreign and domestic—the Senator had indicated during 1947 his growing unrest with President Truman's shifts.

In late 1947 Taylor had made the front pages with a blatant publicity stunt—an attempted coast-to-coast horseback ride. According to the Senator, he had undertaken this jaunt with a dual purpose in mind: publicizing what he termed the "drift towards war" with the Soviet Union and at the same time attempting to discover public opinion on this vital matter. Taylor sensed that by employing this device he was making it impossible for even the most hostile newspapers to ignore his tour completely. This ambitious plan, however, had been cut short by a special session of Congress in November. Back in the Capital, Senator Taylor had been in close contact with both Senator Pepper and Wallace. The three were of a like mind about the need for altering the administration foreign policy, lest it lead the nation into World War III.

Publicly sympathetic to the Wallace views, Senator Taylor had been prominent in much of the third-party speculation that preceded the ultimate decision. Shortly thereafter he was informally offered the candidacy. Considerable self-searching ensued. The Senator's administrative assistant, J. Albert Keefer, was dispatched on a sounding expedition to Idaho. He returned with the advice not to run, suggesting that Taylor would be committing political suicide if he accepted the offer. Still, a principle in which Taylor believed was at stake.

For more than a month the Senator stayed on the fence. Finally, however, at the behest of friends, advisers, and family, he decided to decline the offer. In his own words:

I wrote out a letter of refusal, put it in my pocket and went down to the office next morning, intending to release it to the press. But when I reached my desk, the first thing I saw in the morning paper was that President Truman had fired another good man—another leading New Dealer— Jim Landis, from the Administration. When I saw that, and started to think of all the other recent Truman dismissals and appointments, I got so disgusted I changed my mind, tore up the letter I had written, and decided to run with Henry Wallace.[1]

Plans were laid for a radio declaration of formal candidacy some weeks later. Referring to a 1940 speech of

[1] On the eve of the expiration of Mr. Landis' term of office, President Truman had announced that he would not reappoint him. Although the President failed to announce any reasons for his action, some circles felt that he had been influencd by air-line operators who had reportedly been angered by Mr. Landis' "overstrict" enforcement of safety rules. See *New York Times*, January 1, 3, 4, 1948.

Roosevelt's warning the Democratic Party against political suicide if it should "nominate conservative candidates . . . on a straddlebug platform," Senator Taylor said in his acceptance speech:

> I am not leaving the Democratic party, it left me.
>
> I, no more than Roosevelt, could remain in the party which has betrayed the principles in which I believe . . . .
>
> I am going to cast my lot with Henry Wallace in his brave and gallant fight for peace.
>
> I received a mandate from the people of Idaho to carry out the policies of President Roosevelt in the Senate. I pledged myself to support a world organization to promote peace. Our foreign policy of supporting reaction all over the world on a unilateral basis has weakened and undermined and almost destroyed the United Nations. I would be untrue to the people who elected me if I took any action other than the one I have chosen.
>
> I believe the American people will rise to the heights of faith and sacrifice demanded at this most demanding moment of all time . . . . We dare not falter because a few steps farther down the road we are presently traveling lurks oblivion. Not just another war—atomic and bacteriological oblivion.[2]

Thus was formed the team to spearhead the "fight for peace"—the team of Henry A. Wallace and Glen H. Taylor. Behind one a long career of governmental service, behind the other a background as a cowboy minstrel; behind one a family fortune augmented by personal discoveries in scientific agriculture, behind the other a history of early want and one-night stands; this was a team to behold, even on the

[2] Text of Senator Taylor's Address, *PM*, February 24, 1948. (*PM* was a short-lived, liberal-viewed daily newspaper which was published in New York City from June, 1940 to June, 1948.)

American scene—a team whose members warrant more
careful scrutiny than that afforded them by the contemporary
press.

I believe in God.
I believe in progressive capitalism.

Thus Henry A. Wallace prefaced his remarks on the occasion of his "only meeting with known Communists" in the
course of the campaign. Completely comprehended, they portray graphically this man who had been Secretary of Agriculture, thirty-fourth Vice President of the United States, and
Secretary of Commerce and was now the presidential candidate of a new party of foreign policy dissent.

So frequently stereotyped as paradoxical by press and
quasi-biographers alike, Wallace himself has provided the
most important clue to his actions—the primacy of his emphasis upon religion, upon spiritual and moral values.

An incident which happened while Wallace was Secretary
of Agriculture is illustrative of both his rectitude and the difficulty of many in understanding one who practices daily his
religious tenets. In a departmental conference, the Secretary
had terminated the arguments of a special interest pleader
by informing him that "unless we learn to treat each other
fairly, this country is going to smash." Paul Porter, a Wallace
aide at the time, turned to a colleague and remarked in tones
of both amazement and revelation, "Don't it beat hell? He's
a Christian." [3]

Accepting this one basic fact—the fact of thoroughgoing
Christianity, the myth surrounding Wallace tends to vanish,
the paradox to clear. Henry A. Wallace's political philosophy
was rooted firmly in the precepts of the Sermon on the

[3] As related by Russell Lord, "MacDonald's Wallace and the One
I Know," *New Republic*, 118 (March 1, 1948).

Mount—the fundamental dignity of the individual and the inherent value of human life. Equally basic in Wallace's concepts was the corollary that all possible should be done to improve the individual's brief stay on earth. As he phrased this belief:

> We must invent, build and put to work new social machinery . . . that will carry out the Sermon on the Mount as well as the present social machinery carries out and intensifies the law of the jungle.[4]

What were the Wallace policies stemming from this belief? First, peace was an absolute essential. Without lasting peace, an overwhelming percentage of the world's raw materials, its man power, and its precious time would go into weapons of destruction. As Wallace put it, "A quart of milk is cheaper than a quart of blood." With lasting peace, the world could turn to constructive activities, creating a better place in which to live and assuring everyone—even the most common of men—of an adequate share in the fruits of their own labor. "Peace," Wallace said, "must mean a better standard of living for the common man not merely in the U.S. and England but also in India, Russia, China, and Latin America— not merely in the United Nations, but also in Germany and Italy and Japan."

Second, Wallace persistently exhibited a concern for the common man—the man of whatever race, whatever religion, who has found himself, through no fault of his own, unable to achieve all the goals of a fuller life. As Wallace defined him:

> . . . The common man is the forgotten man—the man who is as good as anybody else but who never had a break

[4] Henry A. Wallace, *New Frontiers* (New York: Reynal & Hitchcock, 1934), p. 11.

because of being born in the wrong locality and having little education, poor food and no money—landless, jobless and working for $30 a year in the Orient . . . . This is the man whom Jesus put at the very heart of his gospel —blessed are the meek and poor in spirit. Now as Jesus and the prophet Amos foresaw so long ago, those who have been rejected are striving to come into their . . . [own].[5]

These barriers, these road blocks, Wallace felt, must be removed or at least smoothed out, with the welfare state providing a means to such an end, as could a "progressive capitalism."

. . . Ever since 1929 the western world has been totally unable to bring about full employment except by war or getting ready for war. Old fashioned capitalism has been replaced by the welfare state for the simple reason that private capital was too timid to flow in sufficient volume. The welfare state is not socialism . . . . But it does involve planning to serve human beings both in the U.S. and in the world as a whole.[6]

Thus to reconcile the Wallace combination of vision and realism—a man independently wealthy through his own efforts and discoveries in agricultural experimentation and yet a man advocating "a quart of milk for every Hottentot"—it is necessary to look only into underlying religious concepts which were his—the practice of long-lived though seldom used ethical principles.

In addition to these moral feelings expressed so frequently

[5] From speech "Where I Stand," delivered at Brooklyn Jewish Center, January 2, 1951 (supplied by Mr. Wallace).
[6] From speech "A Century of Blood or Milk," delivered by Mr. Wallace at the Community Forum, New York, N.Y., November 12, 1950. (Mimeographed.)

with a complete lack of self-consciousness, there were other traits to be observed—traits stemming in part from Wallace's early environment in Iowa, traits to be kept in mind if the former Vice President is to be more clearly understood.

Henry A. Wallace was raised in a typical midwestern Protestant environment—God-fearing, xenophobic, and not too tolerant of dissent. This upbringing affected his social outlook vitally, bringing this "Man of Good Will" perilously close to the brink of intolerance. Wallace stated bluntly his view that Americans "don't want communism, Catholicism, capitalism or colonialism to conduct themselves in ways which provoke war." At the same time he noted that "those who profess the old-fashioned, common sense American religion . . . are increasingly suspicious of the efforts of the four C's to dominate the world." [7] Another facet of this outlook may be found in Wallace's remark that the common man "has been marching fast ever since America was discovered and the Protestants insisted on going to God direct instead of through priestly intermediaries."

This same background emerges in the overtones of isolation found in many of Wallace's comments on the British. The Anglophobia common to much of the Middle West had its impact, even though Wallace channeled his public protests primarily against "British imperialism."

Along with Protestantism and anti-imperialism, the ties to the land of Wallace's Iowa days instilled in him an innate conservatism quite contrary to the radicalism regularly attributed to him. Along with certain religious and international attitudes, Henry A. Wallace also acquired an abhorrence of both waste and radical change. The way to cure an ill, to correct an evil, was not by destroying and building anew, but rather by improving the old and tested. Thus capitalism was not to be discarded completely, with all its proven

[7] Address to the Community Church of New York, reported in the *Baltimore Evening Sun,* December 5, 1949.

merit, but rather to be improved upon—to be made "progressive" to serve more effectively the common man.

An understanding of some of the seemingly contradictory Wallace policies of New Deal days—the "plowing under of the little pigs"—is aided by a reference to those same traits of frugality and conservatism. Wallace's writings demonstrate unchanging principles despite such apparent inconsistencies of policy. To him the slaughter program was essentially an emergency measure necessitated by earlier failures to solve farm problems.

> . . . To have to destroy a growing crop is a shocking commentary on our civilization. I could tolerate it only as a cleaning up of the wreckage from the old days of unbalanced production.
>
> The paradox of want in the midst of plenty was constantly in our minds as we proceeded with schemes like the emergency hog slaughter . . . . To many of us the only thing that made the hog slaughter acceptable was the realization that the meat and lard salvaged would go to the unemployed.[8]

Nor were these temporary expedients ever accepted as long-range policies. For Wallace's earlier experiments with hybrid corn and his later ones with poultry were both directed toward the goal of increasing low-cost production for the hungry and impoverished areas of the globe—but not at the cost of the American farmer's living standards.

Yet despite his conservatism, Wallace understood the preservation of the old order to be dependent upon a willingness to make concessions, to adjust time-honored patterns to fit current needs. He foresaw that a continued stubborn resistance to change can lead to but one result—the use of violence either to defend or overthrow the system. As Wallace noted on one occasion:

[8] Wallace, *New Frontiers,* pp. 174–75, 183.

The trouble with most reactionaries is not that they are evil men, but that they are so stiff minded that they do not adapt their actions to a changing world. Therefore they rely on force . . . .[9]

With his basic belief in capitalism as a system potentially offering much more to the common man both in freedom of action and in superior incentives, Wallace's fight was for the improvements that would enable a "progressive capitalism" to endure. His was an approach best interpreted as enlightened conservatism—making the necessary adjustments in the established system rather than making communism or socialism inevitable by a stubborn refusal to reform.

Since laboratory experiments and controlled social systems were out of the question as long as people—common and uncommon—were involved, it would be necessary to be constantly willing to tinker, for only from life-size experiments would come the necessary innovations. Wallace's pleas were for flexibility, for open-mindedness. As he pointed out in 1934:

. . . It is important to remember that the supremely important development [toward a new world] is not any particular plan, but the willingness, from a social point of view, to modify the plan as often as necessary.[10]

Out of his Iowa background came Wallace's conviction that in this experimentation the common man himself must bear the brunt of the burden. He must be assisted, it is true, but his self-reliance must be both depended upon and strengthened in the process. Thus to Henry A. Wallace it was

[9] "March of the Common Man: Constructive or Destructive?" Speech to the Community Church of Boston, Mass., January 21, 1951. (Mimeographed.)

[10] Wallace, *New Frontiers,* p. 201.

the task of government to do no more than to remove those obstacles large enough to be unyielding to the earnest efforts of even the most self-reliant.

These, then, were some of the principles and policies upon which Henry A. Wallace hoped to found a new American political party—a party which would become a broad party of the people and which would in time supplant the Democratic Party as the standard-bearer of the common man in a more meaningful two-party system of the future.

But Wallace also brought to the new party—for better or for worse—his own special leadership attributes. One of his chief characteristics—a strength as well as a weakness— was his willingness to take a stand that might prove unpopular. Wallace's position was never characterized by the apocryphal remark: "There go my people. I must follow them, for I am their leader." With Wallace it was, in fact, nearly always the reverse. Quite consistently, he moved so far ahead of his followers that he left them completely behind. President Franklin D. Roosevelt, possessed of considerably more political caution and acumen, made good use of Wallace's trait. Throughout the New Deal period, the Secretary of Agriculture was regularly assigned to exposed positions—number one target for press attacks on "radical" proposals. Notwithstanding the venom of the assaults on him, Wallace's willingness to take a positive stand on new, untried proposals brought him a considerable measure of acclaim, both among the general public and privately—even among the most vitriolic of his Washington assailants.

And yet, by comparison with the great political leaders of American history, Henry A. Wallace's qualities did not place him in their forefront. Indeed, he admitted both his own shortcomings and the fact that he "never felt at home in a political atmosphere." He laughingly referred to the last-minute attempts to build him up as a political operator at the 1940 Chicago Convention, when, he related, he was conducted on a table-to-table tour of the Democratic big city bosses by the late Harry Hopkins. The most lasting result, Wallace noted wryly, was a series of photographs intended to convince party faithfuls that he was really one of the boys.

The contrast between Wallace's outstanding success as an administrator in the largest peacetime department of the government as Secretary of Agriculture—a success acknowledged even by anti-Wallace Washington observers—and his failure to oversee adequately the organization of his New Party seem explicable only in terms of this lack of interest. Wallace himself admitted to being "just not interested in political organization."

Coupled with this general lack of interest in party maneuvering was a tendency to leave his own fortunes in the hands of chance, of friends, or even of strangers. These traits proved fatal to his vice-presidential hopes and led to the delegation of the party organization tasks to a campaign manager, the personal choice of the candidate, who was to prove almost equally deficient. And this became a handicap from which the party was never to recover fully.

Wallace's qualities were to emerge in the campaign as those of a religious rather than a political leader. As Dorothy Thompson once observed, long before the 1948 campaign, "There is a hard clear streak of biblical righteousness in Henry Wallace . . . . With it goes humaneness and mercy." The concept which Wallace entertained of himself as a crusader was not far amiss. While his designation of his band of followers as a "Gideon's Army" was contradicted by his expressed hopes that the new party would rapidly become a mass people's movement, the religious overtones remained evident throughout his campaign addresses. The "fight for peace" was to become a crusade—a quixotic crusade—with Henry A. Wallace in the role of Crusader for the Common Man.

In addition to this major defect, several other traits that undoubtedly cost him votes were to emerge in the course of the campaign. Despite his years of political activity, Henry A. Wallace remained a man *for* the people, rather than *of* the people—with a liking for them in the abstract rather than as individuals.

Reticent by nature, Wallace was far from the cold person portrayed by so many journalists; rather he was almost completely lacking in both the ability and the desire to engage in small talk. Moreover, he seemed little aware of, and even less concerned with, the lack of this trait which is so helpful to a candidate in almost constant campaign contact with the reporters covering his activities. Making few attempts to conceal his boredom with things he considered trivial, Wallace could become almost eloquent when the conversation turned to those subjects near his heart. Still another handicap was the Wallace tendency to think in spurts, with periods of intense concentration followed by times of near-lassitude and resting, coasting, or wandering attention. Such characteristics did not endear him to an already antagonistic press corps.

Then, too, Wallace had at one time or another been interested in a broad range of experiments from plants and poultry breeding to dietary tests, from his more publicized corn and chicken work to vegetarian and fat-tailed sheep diets. Couple with this the streak of mysticism underlying Wallace's basic Christianity, and some light may be cast upon the former Vice President's reported excursions into areas of strange and exotic religious beliefs. Wallace may indeed have written, as Westbrook Pegler alleged, the so-called "Guru letters"—notes in which, it was claimed, Wallace had sought the advice of a Hindu mystic. True or not, these claims of "deviant behavior" were seized upon and set forth in great detail by the press.

Moreover, a lack of caution cropped out in many of Wallace's press conferences, where he displayed a frequent tendency to go off the deep end in off-the-cuff responses to unexpected questions. This behavior of the former Vice President was not unlike that of his Democratic adversary President Harry S. Truman.

Wallace's press relations were made even worse by his transparent impatience with those unable or unwilling to get his views straight. Numerous jousts with reporters ensued as a result of their insistence that Wallace repeatedly answer the same old questions, such as his stand on acceptance of Communist support. He finally resigned himself by carrying in his wallet a prepared statement which pointed out that he "was not, had never been, and did not expect to ever become" a Communist, but that he was willing to accept the support of anyone who did not advocate violent overthrow of the Constitution of the United States.

The sophisticated distinctions between Liberal and Radical, or indeed between Conservative and Liberal, are seldom to be found in the hurried stories of a political campaign from harried reporters. And from his early days in Agriculture, the Secretary, as New Deal philosopher-advocate, had been considered fair game by opposition forces far more concerned with destruction than accurate portrayal. Wallace was much less concerned with press reaction than with the response of future generations, an outlook not particularly helpful to a political candidate.

Perhaps the best expression of Wallace's long-range philosophy—of this concern for the future—is to be found in *New Frontiers,* written long before he was to become a candidate. Therein he had noted:

> For those who see now that the men who led us into chaos have nothing to give except another selfish fling and

more chaos, new frontiers beckon with meaningful adventure.

. . . . .

To build new social machinery requires economic engineers . . . to subdue the social wilderness . . . today [a new world] has to be discovered, and when it is discovered it must be held onto. The problem is largely one of spirit, but it is also one of hard facts and definite action continually accompanying the unfolding of the spirit.

. . . . .

What we approach is not a new continent but a new state of heart and mind resulting in new standards of accomplishment. We must invent, build and put to work new social machinery.[11]

Or, as Wallace put it so succinctly a year after the campaign, "I am not greatly concerned with the history of the past. What I am interested in is that which still lies ahead."

In summary, Henry A. Wallace's shortcomings as a political leader stemmed from those same traits that lent him strength as an ideological leader—the moral note of religious faith and even the quixotic willingness to tackle the impossible. These were things that made up this self-appointed Crusader for the Common Man.

But what of his prospective running mate, Senator Glen H. Taylor? Like Wallace, Taylor had been subjected to harsh treatment at the hands of a conformist American press. Whereas Wallace had been portrayed as the fuzzy-minded, idealistic, impractical visionary, Taylor was depicted as the simple-minded buffoon, a sort of "Pappy O'Daniel on horseback," an uneducated and hence ignorant cowboy singer, a "Left Wing Minstrel." However, the power of the press had

[11] Wallace, *New Frontiers,* pp. 11, 281, 283.

failed to keep Taylor from election in Idaho, and he had adopted the showman's attitude that "any publicity is good publicity; it's only when the newspapers ignore me that I begin to worry."

Glen H. Taylor was, for the mid-twentieth century, a unique member of the Senate in that his formal education had extended only to the age of fifteen and in that he had come to that august body from the world of entertainment— from show business. Without the confining doctrines of either professor or machine politician, Taylor had come up with a working philosophy of politics and life both homespun and penetrating, as well as distinctively his own—something of a throwback to pioneer days in the West.

Born and raised in Idaho as the son of an itinerant evangelist, the Reverend Pleasant John Taylor, the Senator, like his running mate, had been exposed in early years to a combination of self-reliance, religion, and the realities of life. On his own at an early age, Taylor found himself during the depression days of the late 1920's and early 1930's at the head of a small touring cowboy troupe. Frequently unable to obtain bookings in even the most humble theaters, they often found themselves miles from the nearest hamlet with only their truck for a home and a jack-rabbit stew for supper. "In fact," remarked Senator Taylor, "had it not been for those jack rabbits, we might well have starved to death. But we sure did get sick and tired of them as a steady diet."

Throughout all the traveling, this itinerant minstrel was constantly reading—working on his own to make up for the deficiencies of his abbreviated formal schooling. Covering a broad range from Plato and Aristotle to John M. Keynes and Stuart Chase, he found himself attracted to economic matters in general and the works of the latter in particular. Out of his studies and his own depression experiences, Taylor ultimately arrived at a confirmed point of view.

Moreover, in the course of his reading, the Senator came

upon a phrase that stayed with him: "The ultimate object of all knowledge is action." As he toured the mountain ranges singing for his supper, he began casting about for some practical use for his self-acquired learning. Finally, one night, standing in the rear of a small theater where he was to appear the next day, he found this same thought running through his mind as he watched the performance of another touring troupe whose goal was the election of a state governor. Observing the politicos with a professionally critical eye, Taylor concluded that the arts of acting and stagecraft played no small part in their appeal to the audience. He reasoned, "They're little more than amateurs who spend only part of their time before audiences. Why shouldn't I, a full-time professional performer, be able to do as good or better a job?"

The thought was father to the action. With no little trepidation, the Senator has admitted, he entered his name as candidate for the Democratic congressional nomination in his home district in Idaho. In the ensuing campaign Taylor introduced the idea of rounding up votes with a cowboy band. "Give the people a little entertainment," he reasoned, "and the political pill goes down a lot easier."

But for Taylor the hour of victory was still in the future. In this baptism of political fire (this was 1938), he ran fourth in a field of nine for the congressional nomination. "But at least," he consoled himself, "I had found out that some people would actually vote for me. And that was a big step forward."

Two years later, undaunted by the first failure, the Taylor caravan again took to the road, this time in pursuit of the senatorial nomination. "And this time," the Senator relates, "we really went back into the hills. Not only the one-horse towns, but the places where the people were too poor to have even a horse. We got into places where no candidate for any office, let alone for the U.S. Senate, had set foot in the last fifty years. And this paid off on the primary election day.

When the first city returns came in, I was trailing. I picked up a little in the smaller villages, but it was only when the returns from the 'backwoods' came in that I finally pulled up even and was eventually nominated by a few hundred votes."

But because he had won the Democratic nomination over the machine candidate, the party State Central Committee proceeded to drag its feet, reasoning that the easiest way to get rid of this "maverick" was to let him go down to defeat at Republican hands in the general election.

But the defeat, not long in coming, failed of this purpose. For so close had he come that Taylor was irretrievably bitten by the political bug. Two years later he entered the 1942 campaign. Again his tactics gained for him the Democratic senatorial nomination without machine endorsement, and again he was defeated in the general election. Undaunted, he returned a third time, again triumphing over the machine candidate in the primary. This year—1944—aided by Roosevelt's presence on the ballot, the erstwhile cowboy singer was not to be denied—even by a reluctant state leadership. Glen Taylor triumphed with the same 5,000 vote margin by which Roosevelt carried the state. Again the hill people had responded to the Taylor appeal, and their votes—with an assist from F.D.R.—had proved decisive.

Thus the newly elected Junior Senator from Idaho arrived in Washington with the feeling that he was under "obligations to no one, least of all to the Democratic state committee" or to the professional politicians who had never given him better than halfhearted support. The target of every newspaper and every important industrial interest group in the state of Idaho, he owed no debts there. Instead, he claimed, the only people to whom he was beholden were those whose votes had elected him—above all, the people back in the hills.

Senator Taylor's voting record in the subsequent six-year period became one of the best measures of his independence. His mission, as he interpreted it, was to carry out the mandate given him to support the policies of Franklin D. Roosevelt and the New Deal in both domestic and foreign affairs. In the early years of his term, Taylor's record of support of Democratic administration measures was one of the highest in the Senate—an over-all average of 92 per cent from 1945 to 1947. It was only with the Truman foreign policy shift that the Cowboy Senator began to vote against the administration in these areas, feeling that the Roosevelt policies were being abandoned. His votes on domestic matters continued to be strongly Fair Deal–New Deal and apparently free from special interest pressures. Only one measure of significance throughout his career indicated any unusual response to local groups. In his last Congress, Senator Taylor veered away from the official Democratic position to join a "potatoes for soy beans" coalition on a farm bill vote.

This, then, was the political background and ideological orientation of the third party's vice-presidential nominee. As far as personal characteristics, Glen Taylor presented a marked contrast to the more reserved Wallace. Unlike the presidential nominee, the Senator had gone hungry; he had earned his living by the sweat of his brow—first in show business and later as a welder in a California airplane factory. Such experiences, coupled with his warmer personality, gave Taylor a closer and more direct link to the common man. Unlike Wallace, Taylor was a man *of* the people, as well as *for* the people.

Also unlike Wallace, a philosopher first and only secondarily a politician, Taylor was aware at every step of political actuality, reality, and the need for organization; his thinking processes tended to be incisive rather than philosophical. One of his striking abilities was that of putting complicated ideas across to the average citizen in personal terms—as in the lucid, simple phrase: "I just don't want my sons dying on some Siberian steppe in any war that I can do anything to prevent."

Coupled with an innate warmth and a liking for people as individuals as well as abstract concepts, Senator Taylor's stage presence allowed him to capitalize on his assets to the utmost. Nonetheless, Taylor, like Wallace, often exhibited the same overwhelming concern with broad problems of world affairs that on occasion made it difficult for him to engage in small talk.

Perhaps one of the most unusual demonstrations by Taylor in Washington—more spectacular, even, than his horseback ride up the steps of the Senate Office Building—was his willingness to admit quite frequently that he just "didn't know." Indeed this may have been a deliberate device to capitalize on his self-professed ignorance. "I'm all confused by this complex issue," he would tell his Idaho constituents, "I just don't know what to do. I need *your* advice, I want *your* decision. What do *you* want me to do?"

In short, the Senator claimed to base his representative theory on an advocacy of the people's wishes rather than on his own views. "I was elected from Idaho as a Democrat," said Taylor after the 1948 election, "and I sit in the Senate as one." And yet, when the chips were down in early 1948, the Senator struck out on his own. In spite of clear indications that the people of his state were "not interested" in the peace issue, faced with the imminent danger of losing the "best job he ever had," Glen H. Taylor cast his lot with Henry A. Wallace. To him it was a matter of conscience; it was his duty to warn the American people, to do everything within his power to halt the "increasing drift towards a disastrous war and domestic fascism"—the inevitable result, he feared, of administration policies at home and toward Russia.

In spite of tremendous pressure, he remained steadfast in his conviction that a third world war was simply "unnecessary" and that American as well as Russian policies were dangerous to world peace. Even after his reconciliation with the Democrats had been effected in September, 1949, with a visit to the White House, Taylor remarked publicly, "I wish I could go along with the President [on his foreign policy]. It would be much more pleasant."

And on the eve of his departure from Washington following his defeat in the 1950 primary, Glen Taylor remained convinced that his and Wallace's position had been correct, even if the public had failed to rally to their support. As the Senator put it, he had "done everything [he] possibly could to avert the drive to war." And, despite the "slowness of public opinion to react," despite the "misinformation of the press," he still retained his "basic faith in the ultimate good judgment of the [American] people." Despite the fact that his reliance on the courage of his convictions had, at least in the short run, proved disastrous, Taylor retained his faith in the ultimate common sense of the common man.

Given their backgrounds, philosophies, and fundamental beliefs, what were the views shared by the Wallace-Taylor team with respect to the specific problems facing the United States in 1948? What were their hopes for their New Party?

First, and most important, was the view that the best interests of the common man, throughout the world as in the United States, could be furthered only by a lasting peace between the U.S. and the U.S.S.R. Both men were convinced that the drive to war would deprive the people of most of their recent social advancements and would slow up or halt future improvements. As Taylor put it, "We stand at the most terrifying and cataclysmic instant in all history."

In line with this, both Wallace and Taylor felt that everything possible should be done to strengthen the United Nations, which they both viewed as the world's best—and perhaps its last—hope for peace. Both felt that the Truman administration was betraying, if unwittingly, the U.N., the doctrines of Franklin Roosevelt, and the American people by its get-tough-with-Russia policy.

As for the party, unlike those Communist participants who viewed the movement as beginning the breakdown of the two-party tradition—the beginning of a multi-party system in which they might possess the balance of power—both Wallace and Taylor thought of it as an organization which would attain major status, supplanting an old party which had failed to serve the interests of the American people. As Wallace observed, the third party was a "long range venture. Neither old party stood for anything definite." He felt that "both stood for an unrealistic foreign policy. There was a need for the people to have choices on the basis of issues, not personalities. Both old parties were composed of elements that couldn't act." A new party based on issues and composed of elements that *could* act would provide the answer.

Senator Taylor was in wholehearted accord with Wallace's views on the need for party realignment. Although he differed in feeling that this change was bound to come eventually, if not through a new party, then through a realignment of the existing parties, he agreed that a completely new organization offered the best opportunity to be free of the dual millstones so long around the neck of the Democrats—the big city machines and the reactionary southerners.

Thus it was that these two persons, so divergent in their personalities, found themselves linked in their basic principles and policies—in their sympathy for the common man, in their advocacy of a reform program, and in their belief in the necessity of peace for the attainment of a true welfare state. They were joined in their visions of a better world and in their concept of a new party that could present a positive program "for a better world right now."

CHAPTER 4

# "The Fight for Peace" — Spring Campaign

UNLIKE THE usual preconvention campaigns of major parties with their routinized minuet patterns, the Progressives' spring campaign was not devoted to formalized advances and retreats of hopefuls with their mincing steps toward the prize they must seemingly not covet. Nor was it a time of maneuvering over issues for the fall campaign—a time in which divisions of disputing factions might be aired, then buried in anticipation of the compromises necessary for a party platform.

For the Progressives, such matters had already been clearly defined as they rallied to their self-declared presidential candidate with his openly avowed platform planks. Instead, their problems were an atypical lot—a series of national tours by candidates already decided upon; attempts to relate incidents, not always of their own making, to their newly adopted campaign slogan, "Peace, Freedom and Abundance"; as well as the multitudinous tasks of building and financing a new party, of obtaining for it a place on the ballots of the forty-eight states. The story of their "fight for peace" became a story of alternate hope and disappointment, coupled with an engulfing tide of events far beyond their control—or even their comprehension at the time.

63

The first blows came in New York State, where the American Labor Party—its decision to support the Wallace candidacy imminent—was faced with the withdrawal of its largest union—the Amalgamated Clothing Workers of America. Following closely upon this, the State Executive Board of the Congress of Industrial Organizations met to consider its relations to the third party and by a three to two margin called upon all CIO unions to quit the American Labor Party once it endorsed the Wallace candidacy. Calling the movement a "piece of political adventurism which can lead to nothing but disastrous consequences to all the American people," the State Board in its action clearly forecast the coming decision of the National Board. And the vote, closely following the existing left-right cleavage within CIO ranks, indicated that all the major national unions except the United Electrical Workers were lined up in opposition to Wallace.

Some two months later, in March, the New York State Board took action by an even more decisive two to one margin to create a state-wide Political Action Committee to oppose both the American Labor Party and the Greater New York Council of the CIO, which was favorable to the Wallace drive. Thus the division in state CIO ranks was solidified, and Wallace's organizational support neutralized.

But what of the national scene? While substantial backing from the American Federation of Labor had never been indicated, and the course of the CIO's Political Action Committee had veered away sharply before the December decision, there had remained hopes of strong organized support from the so-called leftwing unions. Even after the CIO's National Board, in late January by a vote of thirty-three to eleven, had repudiated the third-party movement as inimical to the best interests of labor, several dissenting union heads had seemed determined to invoke the "autonomous rights" of their unions and endorse the Wallace candidacy. It was generally anticipated that the ten unions represented on the board minority would bring their organizations formally under the banners of the New Party.[1]

Now, however, strong pressure was brought to bear on these leftwing leaders—the pressure of Phillip Murray, Jack Kroll, Walter Reuther, and others—to disavow the Wallace candidacy. CIO President Murray, while acknowledging the legal correctness of their position on autonomy, reminded them that they had a "moral obligation to back the executive board's . . . decision." Informed of this, Harry Bridges, leader of the International Longshoremen's Union and CIO regional director for Northern California, foresaw the future accurately: "I think that there will be punitive measures attempted and forms of compulsion resorted to that will be resisted by our union." Within a few weeks, he found himself forced to relinquish his post as regional director. His union joined the resistance.

Moreover, the attempt of the New York Industrial Council and of some California Political Action Committee groups to remain neutral by neither endorsing nor condemning a third party soon became the subject of a crackdown by the parent CIO Political Action Committee. Warned director Jack Kroll, "There can be no neutrality in fighting the idea of a third party." He went on to threaten that unless the national policy of repudiating the Wallace candidacy were followed, steps would be taken to remove or discipline the officers involved.

Nor were these the only methods of persuasion employed

[1] The ten unions represented in the vote were: United Electrical Workers (2 votes); United Office and Professional Workers; International Longshoremen's and Warehousemen's Union; Food, Tobacco and Agricultural Workers; United Furniture Workers; Marine Cooks and Stewards; Fur and Leather Workers; United Farm Equipment and Metal Workers; Transport Workers Union; and National Maritime Union (1 vote for, 1 against the third party). Two unions—the Mine, Mill and Smelter Workers and United Public Workers—abstained from voting. See the *New York Times,* January 23, 1948.

to prevent labor endorsement of the Progressive Party. Reports were soon circulating that the United Auto Workers, under the energetic Walter Reuther, was planning a campaign to take over locals and members of some of the leftist unions. The United Electrical Workers, the United Farm Equipment and Metal Workers, the Transport Workers Union, and the Mine, Mill and Smelter Workers were the announced targets. Despite the fact that CIO President Murray sent a letter to Reuther reminding him that the "CIO never condones 'raiding,'" there was a strong threat of just such action. Nor did the threat appear an idle one, as a Hartford, Connecticut, local of the United Electrical Workers was actually won over to the United Auto Workers.

In the face of these tactics, some leaders were unable to secure the Wallace endorsements expected from their own unions. For example, even though Albert Fitzgerald and Julius Emspak of the United Electrical Workers withdrew their union from the Political Action Committee to form an independent committee for Wallace and Taylor, they found it inadvisable to seek outright board endorsement for the Progressive Party. The United Office and Professional Workers Association also failed to take an official stand in support, although it did pass a resolution praising Wallace and condemning both Republicans and Democrats, as well as reaffirming the "right of members and local unions to make their own decisions."

While one half of the dissident unions—the Fur and Leather Workers, the Longshoremen, the Mine, Mill and Smelter Workers, the United Farm Equipment and Metal Workers, the Food, Tobacco and Agricultural Workers, and the United Furniture Workers—proceeded with formal endorsements, the combined total of their membership was less than that of the single powerful United Electrical Workers.

Meanwhile, the rightwing unions were not content to stop with board action, pressure tactics, or a positive stand for

President Truman. Instead, the two largest—Phillip Murray's Steelworkers and Walter Reuther's Auto Workers—voted overwhelmingly to oppose actively the Wallace campaign. The smaller unions, in an approximate three to one ratio, followed their lead.

At about the same time American Federation of Labor President William Green, never receptive to the third-party idea, publicly recorded his opposition to the venture as "a great political mistake." The trend became a landslide when the same Brotherhood of Railway Trainmen which in 1946 had been promising a "million-dollar slush fund" to defeat President Truman now voted to raise money for his re-election.

Nor was there any significant counterbalance to the loss of labor support; no important new groups indicated any inclination toward the Wallace banners. Negro organizations continued to veer away. Even some of the local Townsend clubs indicated that they might not follow their leader, Dr. Francis Townsend, who seemed certain to endorse the Wallace ticket.

But in the midst of all these gloomy portents there came a ray of hope—the victory, following an uphill battle, of Leo Isaacson in a February special election in New York's Twenty-fourth Congressional District. Here the Democratic incumbent, Benjamin J. Rabin, had resigned to accept a judicial post, and Governor Thomas E. Dewey had called a special election. While the Twenty-fourth had always gone Democratic in past elections, it had also constituted one of the strongest American Labor Party areas in the city of New York. In the 1946 election the ALP candidate had run a fairly good second in a four-cornered race, garnering some 27 per cent of the vote.

This 1948 special election was given advance interpretation by both sides as a significant test of over-all ALP strength and hence of Wallace support, since the party provided his

vehicle in the Empire State. Some expected that the ALP
would be hard pressed to equal its earlier performances. As
the *New York Times* remarked (January 15, 1948):

> While these [1946] figures indicate the virtual certainty
> of the election of the Democratic nominee . . . the ex-
> pected decrease in the vote for the Labor party candidate
> in the Congressional district generally will be accepted as
> an indication of the measure of the loss of Labor party
> votes caused by withdrawal of the anti-Communist unions
> from affiliation with the Labor party.

On the other hand, John K. Weiss and Tom O'Connor,
writing in *PM* (January 17, 1948), pointed to a number of
offsetting factors.

> Most of the voters in the district are low-income families.
> Roughly 40 per cent are Jewish and 25 per cent Negro and
> Puerto Rican. Wallace's popularity with minority groups
> —presumably enhanced by his recent trip to Palestine and
> his tour of the South speaking before non-segregated audi-
> ences—is counted upon by the ALP to weigh heavily.

They also noted the ability of "left wing and labor groups
[to] make a much better showing in a special election than
in a regular election," citing the 1946 ALP candidacy of
Johannes Steel in the New York Nineteenth District. Here,
despite a three to one Democratic enrollment, Steel had lost
by a narrow 4,000 vote margin to the joint Democratic-
Liberal candidate Arthur O. Klein. "There was general
agreement," they concluded, "that the extraordinary ALP
showing could be credited to a new political technique; concentrating experienced political workers from the entire City
in one district."

This same technique was again employed in the Twenty-fourth. According to Morris Goldin, New York County ALP strategist responsible for the planning, there was, at the height of the campaign, a total of some 7,000 individuals working in the district for the Wallace candidate. Recruited from the ranks of the Progressive Citizens of America and from the trade unions, as well as from the ALP itself, these volunteer crusaders turned in a performance that put Democratic boss Ed Flynn to flight. Working nights, moving steadily from door to door, they played up the issues most appealing to voters in the district. To Jewish constituents they talked Israel and rent control, to Negroes and Puerto Ricans, problems of racial segregation and minority rights.

While the Democratic mobilization approximated the ALP aggregation in numbers, it lacked the latter's spirit and drive. Many Democratic workers did little more than go through the motions, with the result that they were unable to keep their pledges in line on election day.

Both sides were lavish in their importation of name speakers to support the actual contestants. For the Democrats, Mayor William O'Dwyer and Mrs. Eleanor Roosevelt led the appeals for "continuing the New Deal tradition" with the Democratic candidate, Karl J. Propper. On the ALP side, Henry A. Wallace was the leading figure, assisted by Representative Vito Marcantonio and singer Paul Robeson. Their primary theme was the attack on Truman foreign policy and —particularly in the Twenty-fourth—on its inconsistency in dealing with the Palestine issue.

Relatively little thought was paid the other two contenders —Liberal and Republican—who had made the field a four-cornered one. The Liberals had advanced one of their strongest vote getters, former gubernatorial candidate Dean Alfange, but the Republicans did little or no active campaigning for their candidate.

The results from the polls on February 17 showed, in the words of the *New York Times,* a "sweeping victory" for the

Wallace candidate, Leo Isaacson. Not only had he defeated his Democratic opponent, but he had also received a clear-cut majority, nearly 56 per cent of the votes cast, as against 31 per cent for Mr. Propper. The Liberal candidate was a poor third, and the Republican nominee, Joseph A. De Nigris, also ran.

Warren Moscow, writing in the *New York Times,* noted that

> The result was an upset with definite national political connotations. In political circles, Mr. Isaacson never had been considered to have a chance to win, but the percentage of the votes given to the third party forces was to be regarded as an indication of the potential Wallace strength in November.
>
> . . . The result was regarded as certain to strike at Democratic hopes for Presidential victory and to bring gloom to the Truman high command.[2]

Elation in third-party circles equaled the gloom and depression in Democratic quarters. The results offered evidence that political miracles were not impossible and that Henry A. Wallace's candidacy could be a major force in the presidential campaign. C. B. "Beanie" Baldwin, Wallace's campaign manager, was quick to hail the election as "proof—as Mr. Wallace has been saying for months—that the people demand a new party, a third party led by Henry Wallace, dedicated to achieving peace, security and abundance." Isaacson interpreted his victory as a "resounding repudiation by the people of the policies of the Truman administration, policies which are leading down the road to war."

Actually, as both James Reston and Arthur Krock of the

[2] *New York Times,* February 18, 1948. The numerical totals were: Isaacson (American Labor Party), 22,697; Propper (Democrat), 12,578; Alfange (Liberal), 3,840; De Nigris (Republican), 1,482.

*New York Times* were now quick to point out and as Weiss and O'Connor had noted a month earlier, the Twenty-fourth District was a rather special case. In the first place, the area issues had been virtually tailor-made for the American Labor Party. Discontent with administration fumbling and back-tracking on the question of Israel was strong in a section so predominantly Jewish. Moreover, this was a low-income, large minority group area to which the domestic program of the former Vice President was bound to appeal.

Secondly, the American Labor Party organization had functioned smoothly both in getting out the vote and in keeping its pledges in line. It had mobilized effectively for the task and had been able to get its issues across by dint of doorbell ringing and house-to-house canvassing. On the other hand, Ed Flynn's Bronx machine had fallen down on the job. He had failed both in getting out the vote and in holding those who did turn out. A staff writer of the *Baltimore Sun* suggested only half in jest that Mr. Flynn "had better stop writing pieces explaining the mysteries of his esoteric craft and go back to bossing."

But, making all due allowance for the special factors involved in the special election, the victory for the Wallace forces was truly a sweeping one, and a very bright ray of light in their preconvention campaign. They had scored at least one battle victory in the "fight for peace."

In spite of this triumph, speculation still continued about whether Henry A. Wallace would actually go through with the 1948 campaign or would, instead, abandon the fight at some strategic time prior to the election. Arthur Krock, writing in the *New York Times* just after Wallace's December declaration, had observed:

> The possibility exists that Mr. Wallace may withdraw his candidacy before or just after the conventions of the two major parties . . . . Even if . . . a third party

nominating convention is held, and Mr. Wallace enters on
a vigorous campaign, he still is capable of finding it expedient to withdraw "before the election."

And now, close on the heels of the Isaacson victory, such
speculation was increased by a second open radio bid on the
part of Senator J. Howard McGrath, Democratic national
chairman, for Wallace's return to the fold. Even before the
December declaration of candidacy, McGrath had proferred
a series of tentative bids for the support of the former Vice
President, saying that "if Mr. Wallace decided to support 'the
Democratic candidate' this support would be 'received and
welcomed.' "

Wallace's reply to the renewed offer was brief and to the
point: "Whenever the Democratic party proves that it is the
peace party and Truman gives up his ideas on military training, I'll consider it. At the moment I see little prospect."

Rumors of the prodigal's impending return to the Democratic fold continued throughout the spring campaign, but
no concrete offers of compromise on foreign policy were ever
actually made by the White House. According to Wallace, all
the "peace feelers" were based on his acceptance of the administration's foreign policy as it stood. As such, they never
received serious consideration from the Vice President. For
the most part, the sources of these rumors were difficult to
locate, their sincerity even more problematical, since they
may have been plants of Democratic strategists attempting
to discourage voters from supporting a "temporary" Wallace
party.

But what of the course of events both in the U.S. and
elsewhere during the spring of 1948 that so vitally affected
the "fight for peace"? Three incidents stood out in the preconvention campaign period. The first, over which the Pro-

gressive Party exercised no control, but which affected its fate strongly, was the Communist coup in Czechoslovakia. The second was Henry A. Wallace's open letter to Marshal Josef Stalin of the Soviet Union; and the third involved Senator Glen Taylor's brush with the police of Birmingham, Alabama, over racial segregation.

To many the existence in Czechoslovakia of a postwar coalition government in which Communists and non-Communists could work side by side demonstrated the feasibility of similar cooperation on an international scale between East and West. This Czechoslovakian bridge accorded with the Progressive Party's basic contention about peaceful coexistence and served to demonstrate the practicality of their peace plank for lessening world tension.

Consequently, it came as a tremendous blow when, in February, 1948, the Communist Party in Czechoslovakia staged a *coup d'état* whereby the hitherto democratic government fell under a party dictatorship. Many who had felt it possible for the U.S. and U.S.S.R. to live as peaceful, tolerant neighbors in a shrinking world were now convinced that Russia, shelving her wartime alliance of expediency, had resumed her long-range plans of world conquest, utilizing in Czechoslovakia the same force and fifth column methods employed earlier by Hitlerite Germany.

Viewed in this new light, the Progressive Party's proposals for a peaceful resolution of Russo-American differences seemed futile to many—a disastrous form of appeasement to others. Potential supporters who never could have been dissuaded by American Red-baiting tactics and anti-Communist hysteria found these international facts of life persuasive and compelling. Numbers who had already joined now left the third party; many who were previously undecided now stayed away.

There was no way of gauging precisely the ebb tide resulting from the Czech coup. But, judging by the polls at the time, the defections were sizable. Although no clear-cut before-and-after surveys were made, a January Roper survey had indicated that Wallace would receive 11 per cent of the popular vote. By June, the figure had fallen to 6 per cent.

Coupled with the effects of the incident itself—so shattering to Progressive hopes—came the reaction of presidential candidate Wallace. His first impulse, in a speech at Minneapolis, had been to adopt a logically defensible position that:

> The Czech crisis is evidence that a "get tough" policy only provokes a "get tougher" policy.
>
> What is happening in Czechoslovakia is not a tempest in a vacuum. There is a clear pattern of cause and effect— a triangular pattern connecting Moscow, Prague and Washington.
>
> Every act under the Truman Doctrine is clearly labeled anti-Russian. The men in Moscow from their viewpoint would be utter morons if they failed to respond with acts of pro-Russian consolidation.
>
> The Czechoslovakia story will repeat itself so long as our gun and dollar policies in Greece, China and elsewhere on Russia's doorstep are continued.[3]

However, a few weeks later in a New York press conference Wallace put himself out on a limb when asked about the Czech situation. In response to a reporter's question, he said he had commented on the Czech crises before he "knew what Steinhardt [U.S. Ambasador to Czechoslovakia] had been up to, before the rightists staged their coup." Queried further, Wallace implied that Ambassador Steinhardt's actions supporting the rightist cause had provoked the Communist intervention—that the Communists had acted in self-defense to prevent a *rightist* coup. The press conference was a tumultuous one, and it may have been that Wallace was

[3] *New York Times,* February 28, 1948.

prodded farther than he intended to go. But, to many of his earlier sympathizers, his remarks indicated that the extreme leftists among his advisers had gained his ear too well.

The end result of both the incident and the Wallace reaction was a marked weakening of the peace plank's appeal. If, as some charged, the Wallace Progressive Party was nothing more than the American branch of an international Communist conspiracy, it had received a tremendous jolt from its home office. For years the Stalin tactics shattered most hopes of peaceful coexistence between the two major powers.

Two months later the second incident involving the peace issue had a much different orientation, with American origins, and reflected a newly changed Moscow view with respect to the desirability of propagandizing her "peaceful" intentions in America. The idea of addressing an open letter to Russian Premier Josef Stalin originated at a midwinter conference attended by Michael Straight, publisher of *New Republic,* Henry Wallace, editor of the magazine at the time, and Lewis Frank, Jr., editorial aide and later chief speech writer for the candidate. While no immediate action was taken, the idea took definite shape some months later, prior to a major address scheduled for May 11. According to Wallace himself, "I had been thinking about it for some time and when I got up to the farm I decided to go ahead. Actually I wrote part of it at the farm and I finished it on the train coming in from South Salem."

Early in the morning on the day of the scheduled speech, the story broke about an exchange of notes between U.S. Ambassador to Moscow Bedell Smith and Russian Foreign Minister Molotov—an exchange interpreted by many as indicating a more conciliatory attitude on the part of each nation in seeking new paths to a settlement of their differences. Wallace felt that the incident made propitious the publication of his letter. Despite contrary advice, he delivered in his speech that night an open letter to Stalin. Before an audience of 19,000 which jammed Madison Square Garden, he outlined the letter's six-point program for terminating the cold war between the U.S. and the U.S.S.R.

1. General reduction of armaments—outlawing all methods of mass destruction.

2. Stopping the export of weapons by any nation to any other nation.

3. The resumption of unrestricted trade [except for goods related to war] between the two countries.

4. The free movement of citizens, students and newspapermen between and within the two nations.

5. The resumption of free exchange of scientific information and scientific material between the two nations.

6. The re-establishment of a reinvigorated United Nations Relief and Rehabilitation Administration [UNRRA] or the constitution of some other United Nations agency for the distribution of international relief.

Having examined some of the problems creating friction between the two nations, such as the German and Japanese peace treaties, control of atomic energy, and the "ideological competition between communism and capitalism," Wallace concluded:

There is no misunderstanding or difficulty between the United States of America and the Union of Soviet Socialist Republics which can be settled by force or fear and there is no difference which cannot be settled by peaceful, hopeful negotiation. There is no American principle or public interest which would have to be sacrificed to end the cold war and open up the Century of Peace which the Century of the Common Man demands.[4]

[4] For complete text of the Address, see *New York Times,* May 12, 1948.

The delivery of the speech itself created little stir in the American press. Although the *New York Times* published the full text, the Associated Press and other news services carried only brief résumés. The entire episode would undoubtedly have been quickly forgotten, consigned to obscurity as just another campaign speech, had it not been for Stalin's decision to respond. Less than a week later, the Soviet Premier broadcast his answer, declaring that the letter constituted a "good and fruitful" basis for discussion between the two nations. Although he did not indicate acceptance of all the Wallace proposals, Stalin labeled the six-point plan a "serious step forward" from the Smith-Molotov notes and called it a "concrete program for peaceful settlement of the differences between the U.S.S.R. and the United States." Moreover, concluded Stalin, ". . . The U.S.S.R. Government considers that despite the differences in their economic systems and ideologies, the coexistence of these systems and a peaceful settlement of differences between the U.S.S.R. and the United States are not only possible but also doubtless necessary in the interests of a general peace." [5]

The furor created by this reply was immediate and lasting. Wallace, apprised of the news just before a campaign speech at Oakland, California, was elated and remarked, according to Howard Norton in the *Baltimore Sun,* "If my letter has served and can still serve to further international understanding of the issues and the practicability of peace, I consider that this past two years' work has been truly fruitful."

The reaction in Washington was markedly different, however. As had been the case a year earlier on the occasion of Wallace's European tour, there were congressional calls for prosecution for violation of the Logan Act of 1799. This time it was Senator Owen Brewster (Republican, Maine) who alleged that the Progressive nominee was guilty of violating the Federalist injunction against a private citizen's interfering in the relations between this nation and a foreign power.

[5] *New York Times,* May 18, 1948.

Of more lasting import was the administration's reaction. Although his scepticism regarding Stalin's sincerity may have been well grounded, President Truman's failure to follow up meant that the offer was destined never to be tested. Once again the administration laid itself open to charges of having failed to explore a possible avenue to peace uncovered by a political rival. As the pro-Truman *Washington Post* ruefully editorialized, "How much capital Henry Wallace collected out of the Administration's maladroitness of last week is anybody's guess. But we feel it was plenty."

Moreover, it is probable that this abrupt end to the "peace scare" closed the door completely on any possible *rapprochement* between the Progressives under Wallace and the Democrats led by Truman. To many this was convincing evidence of Wallace's accuracy in his contention that Truman was absolutely opposed to even the slightest compromise on foreign policy, and that only the third party offered an opportunity to protest the bipartisan get-tough-with-Russia program. If the "fight for peace" was to continue, there was only the Progressive Party to wage the battle.

But once again the potential appeal of the coexistence theme was undercut as soft Russian words gave way to hard Soviet actions. This time it was Berlin. Following a series of moves and countermoves linked to German currency reform, the U.S.S.R. began early in June to place increasing restrictions on Western supply lines through East Germany into Berlin. The pressure increased until on June 24 all rail traffic was halted by their inspectors. It became intolerable when, on June 25, all food shipments were stopped. Western reaction was both immediate and vigorous, and on June 26 President Truman ordered planes mobilized to supply the beleaguered city by air. Thus began the famous Berlin Airlift which was to become a monument to Western determination, and the tombstone for Progressive hopes of an immediate response—by either Soviet leaders or American voters—to the Wallace proposals for lessening tension.

A third incident of the preconvention campaign saw the spotlight of publicity focused on the other member of the Wallace-Taylor team. This time their second issue—freedom and the protection of civil rights—was involved in the Birmingham arrest and conviction of Senator Taylor.

Although the formal charge was disorderly conduct, the actual question clearly concerned racial segregation at public meetings. Taylor was scheduled to address a meeting of the Southern Negro Youth Congress—an organization listed by the Department of Justice as Communist-inspired, according to the *New York Times*. The Negro group had encountered difficulty in finding a meeting place after Birmingham City Police Commissioner Eugene ("Bull") Connor had threatened, "There's not enough room in town for Bull and the Commies." Eventually, arrangements had been made to hold meetings in a small Negro church, but, on the afternoon of Senator Taylor's scheduled speech, four of the convention's leaders had been arrested on charges of permitting unsegregated meetings. Following this arrest, temporary barriers had been erected to separate the races, and police officials had designated separate "white" and "Negro" entrances to the church.

When Senator Taylor attempted to enter the church through the "Negro" entrance, he was taken into custody. At this point reports differed concerning whether the Senator attempted to resist or whether the arresting officers decided to rough him up a little, but the fact remained that the Senator arrived at the police station in a disheveled condition. There he was booked and posted bail for a court appearance.

At a hearing held later the same week, Taylor was convicted of disorderly conduct, fined fifty dollars and costs, and given a suspended jail sentence of 180 days. Police Court Justice Oliver Hall, according to the Associated Press, "gave Taylor a profound tongue lashing for 'introducing' the racial issue into the case," ascribing the matter to publicity seeking and an "outside influence attempting to create disturbances between the white and Negro races in the South."

The Senator immediately announced his intention of appealing the case all the way to the Supreme Court, if necessary. More than a year later the Alabama State Appeals Court upheld the conviction. The United States Supreme Court eventually declined to review the case, with Justices Black and Douglas dissenting, being of the opinion that Taylor's petition for a writ of certiorari should have been granted. Birmingham officials then pressed for the Senator's extradition to serve out the jail term, but Alabama Governor James Folsom refused to seek his return, and the case was finally abandoned.

While other similar incidents occurred during the spring campaign, such as the Baltimore tennis courts case, obviously planned to invite arrest for the purpose of testing the validity of segregation ordinances, none received the same nation-wide publicity. While the freedom issue was thus emphasized, its net vote-winning impact was highly questionable, with many anti-segregationists deploring such "publicity-seeking opposition."

Although spectacular incidents and issues played a large part in the preconvention campaign, the main device employed by the Wallace-ites to link together their party organizational and publicity work was the traditional campaign tour. These tours became a means of arousing interest in the various state founding conventions, of attracting prospective party workers, of spurring the drives for a place on the state ballots, and of providing the focal stellar attractions for the fundraising, paid-admission rallies.

Beginning in February with a blizzard-swept tour of Minnesota, timed to coincide with the attempt to capture the Democratic Farmer-Labor nomination in that state (to be discussed in the next chapter), presidential candidate Wallace was almost constantly on the road. Despite the fact that he "hated campaigning, and hated to get into it," the third-party nominee began the tours that were to set a new record, as of 1948, for mileage covered by any candidate in American history.

February witnessed, in addition to stops in the Midwest en route to and from Minnesota, a junket to Florida, where the deadline for ballot qualification came early, and a series of speeches in the New York State Twenty-fourth Congressional District. March was comparatively quiet, with the high point a Pennsylvania Progressive Party Founding Convention at York. But the end of the month witnessed the beginning of a New England tour timed to coincide with organizational drives in Connecticut and Massachusetts. This was followed in April by a second trip into the Midwest, which included the Chicago Founding Convention (to be discussed in the following chapter), as well as several speeches in Indiana, where the Progressive organization was being perfected.

May, however, witnessed the peak of the spring campaign. Kicking off with the Madison Square Garden speech at which the open letter to Stalin was unveiled, Wallace embarked on a transcontinental tour via chartered air liner that took him four times across the continent in the space of two weeks. After a brief stop in Detroit, where he marched with the picket lines around the strike-bound Chrysler Corporation plants, Wallace arrived in Los Angeles, spent two days in that area, thence continued to San Francisco, Oakland, and south again to San Diego. The Pacific Northwest was next. Arriving in Oregon in the midst of the torrid Dewey-Stassen Republican presidential preference primary, the third-party candidate assailed both contenders. Continuing through this area, Washington and Idaho were covered before Wallace interrupted his tour temporarily, flying back to Washington to testify before a Senate committee considering the Mundt-Nixon proposals for subversive control.

Returning once more, the candidate continued throughout the Mountain States and the Southwest, appealing in Denver for a broadly based state organization and speaking in Spanish before Mexican-American audiences in New Mexico and Arizona.

Finally, after twenty-five days in which he had covered some 25,000 miles, Wallace wound up the tour and returned to his South Salem, New York, farm for a brief rest before embarking on a second New England tour that immediately preceded the Philadelphia Convention.

Throughout all of his speeches in these different states and cities there was one unchanging theme: Only the Progressive Party offered Americans a chance to vote for peace—to vote in opposition to the bipartisan drive of both Republicans and Democrats toward a new world war. The third party was the people's weapon in the "fight for peace," its candidates their leaders.

There were, of course, many issues of national concern dealing with a third plank: "Abundance"—an end to inflation, economic planning to prevent a new postwar depression, and Federal aid for health, for education, and for housing. And in every locality there were particular vital issues of local concern: irrigation proposals in the arid Southwest, racial problems in Mexican-American country, and power development and flood control in the recently devastated Columbia River Valley.

Thus the Progressives' candidate attempted to relate the main issue to his audiences—to link their immediate, closely felt needs to his third-party platform—to demonstrate that their solution was dependent upon solving the overriding issue of peace. Foreign policy remained the dominant theme, since all these public projects, works, and improvements necessitated peace for their completion—a peace which Henry A. Wallace alone of the presidential possibilities was pledged to work and fight for.

Meanwhile his running mate, Senator Glen H. Taylor, was

concentrating his endeavors in the nation's Capital and throughout the South. Unremarked by the press, save for the Birmingham incident, the Senator's tours were run on a similar basis. Organizational meetings in North Carolina, ballot drives in West Virginia, and fund-raising rallies everywhere—these were the skirmishes in the Taylor portion of the crusade.

Almost everywhere he went, Taylor cast down the antisegregation gauntlet. Refusing to speak to audiences separated by the color of their skins, Senator Taylor conducted his southern tour to the accompaniment of a series of incidents paralleling the Alabama case. The major exception came in Macon, Georgia, where the issue arose at the Progressive Party State Founding Convention. With both white and Negro delegates and the customary municipal ordinance forbidding mixed public gatherings, the party found it expedient to bar the public, thus making the meeting technically private.

Although Senator Taylor's preconvention campaigning reached as far west as California and included northern and midwestern states, this southern tour was his most significant contribution outside the Halls of Congress. Inside the Senate Chamber, however, he did much to publicize the party's stand on both foreign and domestic issues. An open letter to President Truman demanding the ouster of James Forrestal as Secretary of Defense exemplified the Progressives' attack on the Wall Street–military team which, they alleged, controlled both course and conduct of American foreign policy.

Perhaps the most noteworthy congressional action revolved around Senate consideration of the peacetime draft. Joined by Senator William Langer (Republican, North Dakota), Taylor undertook an eighteen-hour filibuster against the appointment of Senate conferees on the measure. Doomed from the outset, this two-man delaying action provided a dramatic means of highlighting the Progressive Party position on the issue.

Congressional testimony also offered a vehicle for Progressive Party publicity as their presidential nominee appeared before numerous committees. In February, Wallace testified before the House Foreign Affairs Committee, opposing the European recovery program "as constituted." Despite a ruling by Chairman Eaton (Republican, New Jersey) barring newsreel, sound-recording, and television men from the hearings, press coverage of Wallace's counterproposals was extensive although not very detailed.

Noting his earlier support for economic aid to Europe as a "lend-lease program for peace," Wallace ascribed the reversal of position to his view that Europe was now being handed a "blueprint for war." In the face of hostile cross-examination, he defended strongly his eight points, which he felt constituted a plan to end "the gnawing fear of war and destruction." Keystone of the Wallace proposals was a fifty-billion-dollar reconstruction fund to be administered by a United Nations agency—rather than by any single nation or its big-business groups—and to be supported by those nations "with appropriate means." He felt that aid should be based on need, not political belief—available for *all* war-devastated nations, with no strings attached (such as prohibitions against usage for nationalization of industry) save to prohibit their employment in purchasing implements of war and destruction. Moreover, the United Nations should set up a world-wide ever-normal granary both to prevent famine and to support world grain markets, thus aiding the American farmer. Finally, Wallace envisioned joint supervision of the Ruhr industrial potential by Britain, France, Russia, and the United States to insure that "its resources [would] be used to reconstruct Europe."

While unsuccessful in convincing the committee that the Marshall plan was little more than an extension of the earlier Truman doctrine, Henry A. Wallace had, in the view of some observers, emerged as one possessed of a clear and concrete counterproposal which might serve as a basis for modifying the original administration plans. Although the unwarranted action of the committee in barring full press coverage of the hearings occasioned considerable protest, it curtailed public awareness of his points.

Wallace's second opportunity came some two months later before a Senate Armed Services Committee considering the peacetime selective service—universal military training proposals of the Truman administration. Ascribing a series of "deliberately created crises" to the President, Wallace called for a reversal of American policies that, in his opinion, were helping to breed a new war.

> Our country is in danger. But the danger comes from our own policies which will bring war—unnecessary war —upon our country. The crisis lies in the war fever itself, not in the real threats of invasion, but in the synthetic "threats of invasion" pumped out to support the arms program.[6]

If a "peaceful foreign policy" were resumed, said Wallace, there would be no need for either inflated military budgets or armed forces built up beyond a point attainable with voluntary enlistments. Once more, the consensus of opinion was that the former Vice President had changed few minds in Washington but that he had obtained a public forum for the third-party position.

The third opportunity came with Senate Judiciary Committee hearings on the Mundt-Nixon subversive activity control bill. Dramatically interrupting his far-western tour, Wallace flew back to Washington to testify that the proposed legislation was both ill-advised and undemocratic. It was contrary to traditional American freedom of expression, he said, and sought to impose restrictions on political

[6] As quoted by C. P. Trusell in the *New York Times,* March 31, 1948.

thinking and ideas—even going so far as to outlaw his new party.

> As the bill is framed, its penalties can be visited upon every organization which espouses the cause of world peace and progress—every organization which opposes the basic tenets of the bipartisan program.
>
> In the name of fighting foreign totalitarianism [the Mundt-Nixon bill seeks] to impose domestic totalitarianism. In the name of saving the constitution, the constitution is destroyed.[7]

But while the party thus received a ready-made, if specially muted, national sounding board, it was changing few minds, swaying few votes; for the crusade was under way in a milieu which increasingly insisted upon conformity—a climate of opinion learning to label as subversive all dissent and to demand punishment for the dissenters. Violence, slanted press coverage, and attempted intimidation all became a part of the "fight for peace." The first actual bloodshed came as a Wallace organizer was stabbed to death, apparently for his third-party activities, in Charleston, South Carolina. The drive for the petition signatures in West Virginia witnessed gunplay, midnight auto pursuits, and threats of bodily harm for organizers, although fortunately no actual bloodshed was reported.

Nor could all of this un-American display be attributed to extremists or the uneducated. Violence of a different sort —intimidation to remain silent or risk losing one's job— broke out in an appalling number of colleges and universities across the nation. At Evansville College in Indiana, Professor George Parker was summarily dismissed for acting as chairman of a local Wallace rally and introducing the third-

[7] As reported by Rodney Crowther in the *Baltimore Sun*, May 30, 1948.

party presidential candidate. College officials frankly admitted that the reason for the dismissal was "Mr. Parker's political activity, both on and off the campus." At the same time they claimed, according to the *Baltimore Sun,* "The college fully subscribes to the principle of academic freedom but believes that the individual who exercises the privilege must assume the responsibility for his utterances and actions when they destroy confidence and faith in the institution of which he is a member."

The following month a Bradley University professor, Dr. W. V. Lytle, introduced Mr. Wallace to a Peoria, Illinois, rally over the protests of university officials and soon found that his contract would not be renewed. Although he did not actually lose his position, it was reported that pressure was exerted on Professor Curtis MacDougall by his university (Northwestern) in an unsuccessful attempt to force the withdrawal of his name as Progressive senatorial candidate in Illinois.

In the South, pro-Wallace activities were the cause for the dismissal of four instructors at two other institutions. The University of Georgia fired Assistant Professor James Barfoot, proposed Progressive gubernatorial candidate, on the grounds that "his political activities had become so extensive and involved that his effectiveness as a teacher was impaired." And the University of Miami in Florida conducted a wholesale purge, releasing three instructors who dared support the Wallace candidacy.

At the University of New Hampshire, Professor John Rideout, who had served as chairman of the state Progressive Party, suddenly found it advisable to move to Idaho, despite the fact that his contract had another year to run. A second Wallace-supporting New Hampshire professor who had seen promotion denied him because of his political activities remarked that he might "be forced to resign to save [his] career." As a result of its actions in these cases, the University of New Hampshire found its application for a Phi Beta Kappa charter tabled for three years.

Despite sanctions such as this and reprimands from the American Association of University Professors, the toll in academic freedom ran high—far higher than the reported firings. On too many campuses traditional American free speech fell victim to short-sighted administrations and witch-hunting boards of trustees.

Progressive campaigners found it increasingly difficult to secure either auditorium or hotel accommodations in many cities. The Birmingham incident involving Senator Taylor was typical of the difficulty in finding a forum. Scheduled to deliver speeches, Wallace and Taylor would find themselves deprived of a meeting place with little or no notice. Registering at a hotel, they would find their reservations had been mysteriously canceled. And again, it was not only a case of political machines denying the use of municipal facilities. University administrations which had in the past permitted the presentation of divergent political views now found it inexpedient to permit the voice of a third party. Thus Wallace found himself barred from campus facilities of the University of California at Berkeley, the University of Missouri, the University of Cincinnati, and Syracuse University, to mention only a few.

At the University of Washington, Wallace found himself in strange company as officials there simultaneously excluded both him and Republican contender Thomas E. Dewey from the campus, notwithstanding the fact that President Truman was scheduled for later delivery of a "nonpolitical" address.

And in those more enlightened institutions where free speech was sustained as more than a theoretical concept, it often became impossible for third-party speakers to make themselves heard above the clamor of hecklers unversed in or unwilling to abide by the American tradition of freedom to present all points of view.

The most damaging impact of all this was not upon the Progressive Party itself, but rather upon the whole of American society. As the campaign progressed, the pressure for conformity and the unwillingness to permit any expression of dissenting opinion increased rather than abated.

As John Stuart Mill had warned a century earlier:

> . . . It is not the minds of heretics that are deteriorated most by the ban placed on all inquiry which does not end in the orthodox conclusions. The greatest harm done is to those who are not heretics, and whose whole mental development is cramped and their reason cowed by the fear of heresy.
>
> . . . . .
>
> . . . There is always hope when people are forced to listen to both sides; it is when they attend only to one that errors harden into prejudices, and truth itself ceases to have the effect of truth by being exaggerated into falsehood.[8]

There was still another facet of the spring campaign which made it increasingly difficult for the American people to listen to both sides—the scanty coverage accorded the third party by both press and radio, save in a few metropolitan centers. Although large numbers of reporters accompanied candidate Dewey on his western preconvention jaunt and throngs of commentators traveled with the Truman "nonpolitical" campaign train, only three newspapers saw fit to give full coverage to Wallace's spring tours. And the objectivity of coverage by these three, the *New York Post,* the *Baltimore Sun,* and the *St. Louis Post-Dispatch,* suffered considerably by comparison with their handling of the major party campaigns.

Perhaps the most glaring examples, in the light of reputed

[8] John Stuart Mill, *On Liberty* (New York: Liberal Arts Press, Inc., 1956), pp. 41, 63.

fairness and expected full coverage, were the *New York Times* and the *New York Herald Tribune*. Although the *Times* did report in greater detail than other papers those incidents occurring in New York City (such as the Wallace letter to Stalin), it clearly allowed its editorial view that the American Labor Party was "Communist-dominated" to permeate its news columns. This bias emerged particularly in its coverage of the Isaacson campaign, for which objective treatment by the anti-third-party *PM* offered a basis of comparison.

Vice-presidential nominee Taylor was given even more pronounced silent treatment by the press than was Wallace. Only the Birmingham incident, played up for its sensationalism, showed that journals across the nation were even aware of his candidacy.

A few papers demonstrated even greater zeal—going so far as to attempt the intimidation of voters who had dared sign Wallace nominating petitions. The *Pittsburgh Press,* as will be described in a later chapter, was the leader in this respect, and journals in Boston, Milwaukee (the *Milwaukee Journal*), and Cleveland, as well as others of the Scripps-Howard chain, were guilty of similar practices, according to party officials.

While radio commentators were on the whole scarcely more objective in dealing with the Wallace Progressive Party, the national networks, until the time of the Philadelphia Convention, provided considerable free time for the party's speakers. Thus the Taylor acceptance speech, Wallace's reply to an intemperate Truman attack on the party as a "Communist front," and several other major preconvention addresses received full airings.

But on the whole, the American mass media did little in this preconvention campaign to disprove Senator Taylor's comment that "our modern means of communication do not necessarily mean that the American people are the best informed in the world, only that they have greater access to larger amounts of information and possible misinformation."

As a first round in the "fight for peace," the spring campaign proved a losing one for the Wallace forces. Preaching the virtues of peaceful coexistence, they watched the Czech coup destroy their only successful model, taking with it the appeal of their peace issue. Successful in a congressional contest where the Palestine problem was foremost, they saw the Truman administration shift to a more consistent pro-Israelite position. Still hopeful of Labor and Liberal support, they witnessed a pronounced trend to the left as President Truman, aided by the Americans for Democratic Action, strove to muster the New Deal remnants into a Fair Deal army. Their arguments for abundance became less persuasive as the Democratic Party once again took on its Roosevelt image as the party of the people. And before long their freedom issue was to be undercut by the victory of the Humphrey-led integrationist forces at the Democratic National Convention and by the subsequent defection of the Dixiecrats.

Thus the Progressives had not only lost the first battle in the "fight for peace," but their arms—"Peace, Freedom and Abundance"—had been captured by the enemy as well. For the first time in American history, the thunder of a party of discontent had been stolen, neither four nor forty years later, but in the very midst of the campaign.

# CHAPTER 5

# *Building a New Party*

ALTHOUGH THE campaign tours of the candidates, the New York City by-election to fill the Bronx vacancy, and the inexorable press of events—both at home and abroad—formed the major features of the 1948 spring campaign, they were far from the only battles in the "fight for peace." But the Wallace crusaders were faced with the multiple tasks of building a new party. Three major problems confronted them—organizing party machinery, obtaining a place on the ballots of the forty-eight states, and securing adequate financial support. From the standpoint of both importance and timing, all three were integrated, all three were independent. They form the subject of this and the two following chapters.

If this was to become a true party of the people, organization was the first need—to build a machine possessing a breadth of support, depth of organization, and endurance for the future. As L. B. Wheildon had concluded in *Editorial Research Reports* the preceding July, "Established party machines can be overthrown, if at all, only by new machines. Electoral votes are created out of the votes in precincts, wards and districts."

It was to the precincts, wards, and districts that the Wallace followers now turned their attention. And here, it soon became apparent, there was not the same general degree of agreement that surrounded the "Peace, Freedom and Abundance" issues already discussed. Of the three questions raised—whether the party was to seek "breadth or narrowness," whether the primary target was the 1948 or the 1952 campaign, and whether or not an attempt should be made to build from the ground up—there was general agreement on only one. Whereas the divergent groups in the party accepted most Wallace policy decisions, they were unable to agree on his organizational views.

The first ideological cleavage developed over the question of securing breadth of support for the New Party. Wallace himself was very much aware of the importance of this factor. In an April speech to the New York State Wallace-for-President Committee he warned:

> I urge elimination of groups and factions in this new party movement. This movement is as broad as humanity itself. I urge that we accept all people who wish for a peaceful understanding between the United States and Soviet Russia . . . . We can get the support of these people if they realize that we do not represent one group.
>
> If we are going to be a party of 20 million, there are going to be many kinds of people in that party. Keep the door open.

On the other hand many within the party looked upon it as more of a pressure group for their particular viewpoint. They were anxious to keep its organization narrow so that it might express those views more vigorously. For example, some of its labor leaders urged that the party de-emphasize the international relations aspect, and play up Taft-Hartley as the main issue of the campaign. Then there were those of Communist leanings who felt that all pretense of breadth should be abandoned and a closely knit "cell-type" structure established.

Closely related was the question of whether to build for

the 1948 campaign alone, or for the future. The immediate need for haste if election deadlines were to be met was in the back of everyone's mind. But those who favored a narrow organization argued that theirs would be the only type with sufficient cohesiveness to endure. Again their premise was based upon the idea of a small band of well-disciplined, loyal workers whose continued support could be relied upon. Wallace rejected this idea as well, telling the Colorado Progressive Party:

> People who want the party narrowly based say that a broad base won't work. They want to go ahead with the idea of winning not in '48 but in '52 . . . . But it's a hard fact that we can't win the necessary votes in *either* year unless by a crusade among the principal groups of our people . . . the women's groups, the church groups, and the young people in our schools and colleges.

The only organizational matter upon which there was agreement in the ranks was the necessity of a strenuous attempt to establish machinery down to the ward and precinct levels all across the nation. This, it was realized by all, was the only way to attract any sizable number of voters into the Progressive camp and to turn them out on election day.

Despite the fact that this was a new party, there existed, even prior to the Wallace declaration, considerable nationwide machinery. The most important was that of the Progressive Citizens of America. The origins of PCA could be traced to a series of political maneuvers in the 1944 presidential campaign. In that year the Political Action Committee of the CIO had formed the National Citizens Political Action Committee in the attempt to broaden its appeal outside the labor sphere. The National Citizens Political Action Committee operated on a national basis in the 1944 campaign to raise funds for the Roosevelt-Truman ticket. In the spring of the same year a New York City group led by Mrs. Elinor S. Gimbel, Quentin Reynolds, and others, feeling that Tammany Hall was not sufficiently active for the Roosevelt candidacy, had formed the Citizens' Action Committee. This group of political amateurs, primarily Democratic but with a sprinkling of Republicans, desired to work on the local level, ringing doorbells and speaking to small groups, thus actively entering into practical politics.

Shortly after the Democratic National Convention still a third group came into existence, the Independent Citizens' Committee of the Arts, Sciences and Professions. An outgrowth of the earlier (1940) Independent Voters Committee, the ICC-ASP had a much different orientation, according to Miss Hannah Dorner, its director. Its members—from the stage, from the academic world, and from professional life generally—were more interested in pressure group activities, such as pressing for promotion of a National Science Foundation. But, here too, there were some seeking a broader political outlet for their specialized talents—from playwriting to stage lighting.

The first joining of forces came when the Citizens' Action Committee merged its local New York City activities into the broader National Citizens Political Action Committee during the 1944 campaign, thus bringing together the well to do, the middle class, and the labor segments of the original groups. Two years later, prior to the 1946 congressional campaign, the two main bodies, NC-PAC and ICC-ASP, merged to form the Progressive Citizens of America. With similar interests and backing it was felt that a combination would effect greater strength and greater efficiency. However, once inside the PCA, many of the ASP members who had favored pressure-group activity alone began to feel ill at ease. Many walked out when the PCA became the vehicle for the Wallace third-party candidacy.

As noted in an earlier chapter, both NC-PAC and ICC-ASP had supported the Wallace position following the Madison Square Garden speech. In 1947, with the enunciation of the Truman doctrine, the PCA embarked upon a broad campaign of opposition to the administration's bipartisan foreign policy. Although Wallace was not a member, he became PCA's principal speaker at a series of rallies and meetings across the nation.

At this time, C. B. "Beanie" Baldwin, who had served under Wallace in the New Deal days, was the executive vice president of PCA. He was already trying to kindle a third-party fire, despite Wallace's continued advocacy at that time of action within Democratic ranks.

Finally, with the prospective candidate increasingly receptive, in December, 1947, the executive board of the PCA had voted with only three abstentions and one dissent "to urge Henry A. Wallace to run as an independent candidate for the Presidency of the United States." What contribution was the PCA prepared to make to the "fight for peace"?

Organizationally, they possessed state and local chapters of varying degrees of strength in twenty-five of the forty-eight states. New York and Southern California branches were well established, but elsewhere there was merely a skeleton framework. But the PCA also promised a background of political know-how. As early as 1946, Lew Franks and Ralph Shikes had conducted studies and compiled a manual of political organization aimed at the proven house-to-house type of campaign. Moreover, the PCA had originated a "school for political action"—a Washington, D.C. seminar for political workers. This school was the forerunner of those later utilized by the CIO Political Action Committee, the

Americans for Democratic Action, and eventually big business itself.

In addition, the PCA had been perfecting new techniques for gaining financial support. Originating with the CIO Political Action Committee, the basic idea consisted of paid admissions and voluntary contributions at political rallies. To these rallies, the ASP group from Broadway had added staging, lighting, and dramatization. The resulting presentations had proved themselves during 1947, when the PCA garnered over one quarter of one million dollars from their series of rallies opposing the Truman doctrine and administration foreign policy.

Thus the PCA had already faced two of the three major obstacles in the path of the New Party at this time, and promised aid in both.

In endorsing the Wallace candidacy, the Executive Board of the PCA announced that it would submit its decision to the second annual convention of the body at Chicago the following month. The 500 delegates to this January assembly promptly ratified the board action in a resolution that permitted: (1) the state chapters to affiliate, merge, or cooperate with any Wallace party or committee, (2) delegates to represent the PCA at an April founding convention for a third party, and (3) the National Board to determine whether PCA should merge into or affiliate with the third party, subject to ratification by two-thirds of the state chapters. Thus the way was paved for the PCA to retain its identity or to become the nucleus of the third party.

It soon became apparent, however, that the new party would require a much stronger central organization than could be evolved from the semi-autonomous PCA branches. As early as March, a threefold split into right, left, and center groups was appearing among the Wallace committees. State and local organizations had proceeded pretty much on their own, and conflict with national policy began to emerge. For example, the Independent Progressive Party of Southern California had gone ahead with plans to oppose the re-election of the Liberal Democratic representatives Helen Gahagan Douglas and Chet Holifield on the basis of their support for Marshall plan aid to Europe. This was contrary to the policy announced by Beanie Baldwin of supporting incumbents with a predominantly *"good"* record. Baldwin, according to notes by Helen Fuller, in the files of *New Republic,* told the Chicago conference, "While we cannot and must not judge any sitting Congressman *by any single vote,* there are certain conditions . . . to receive our support . . . support of the UN . . . the full rights of organized labor . . . support of the constitutional civil rights of every person living within our borders." (Italics supplied.) Wallace, in a later letter to Mr. C. J. O'Donnell was even more specific. "Candidates will not be judged on the basis of their position on any single issue such as the Marshall Plan."

In the meantime, plans were being formulated for a 700-member National Wallace-for-President Committee, to be headed by a brain trust composed of Baldwin as campaign manager, Elmer Benson as chairman, and Angus Cameron as treasurer. Its first meeting was scheduled to coincide with the Chicago assembly called by the Progressive Citizens of America for April.

At this Chicago meeting the decision was reached to take over the Progressive Citizens of America machinery and incorporate it into the new party. For policy planning the third party, like the British Labor Party, would have an *annual* National Convention, with representation based on individual members and interest groups as well as state and local organizations. For interim meetings there would be a much smaller National Committee. Representation on the latter was to be primarily geographical, with the number of state committee members proportional to population, unlike the major party pattern of two for each state. A supplemental "functional representation" for labor and other groups was added later. Since it was expected that the large size of this National Committee would make it even more unwieldy than its major party counterparts, there were to be two smaller bodies—a National Executive Committee to meet every month and an Administrative Committee to carry out the day-to-day tasks of policy planning.

For the execution of third-party policy, a board of national officers was projected—a chairman and several vice-chairmen, as well as a party treasurer, secretary, and campaign manager. This panel would be responsible for carrying out over-all policy, for establishing lines of communication to the various state, local, and associated groups, and for insuring coordination in all the phases of a presidential campaign.

With a basic structure thus agreed upon, the delegates went on to plans for a first national convention, at Philadelphia in July. This summer assemblage would formally establish the organization, adopt a name for the New Party, ratify a party platform, and formalize the choice of the national candidates.

The national organization now faced its major problem— determining an organizational policy and transforming this policy into a machine that would be both comprehensive and enduring. The fundamental antagonism now began to emerge between right and left—between Wallace himself and those he later labeled the "Peekskill Boys." [1] The candidate felt that the actions of his more rabid followers of the extreme left would result in a base far too narrow for the party following of 20,000,000 which he anticipated.

---

[1] Wallace's description of his more rabid followers as the "Peekskill Boys" derived from the methods and tactics of leftists in the series of riots and disorders at a scheduled Peekskill, New York, concert by Paul Robeson, in 1949. Although not overt antagonists, some of the left-wingers displayed an attack-us-if-you-dare attitude.

Despite his strong views on the subject, Wallace remained aloof from the organizational problems of the party. Having delegated this function completely to Beanie Baldwin, he devoted himself to policy issues and campaigning—an action which was not solely the result of time pressures. Viewing political organization only as a means to an end, Wallace, in his own words, was simply "not interested." He left the vital organizational tasks almost completely in Baldwin's hands, and Beanie was under constant, almost irresistible, pressure from the New York City extremists opposed to Wallace's view that this be made a broad party of the people. When non-Communist leadership and talent failed to respond on the organizational level in adequate numbers, the left-wingers were able by default to take over to a considerable extent. As Wallace viewed the dilemma, "the broad mass is always slow to act, the narrow, rabid group *will* act, but by their very action, will keep the others away."

Coupled with the failure of old New Dealers and eastern Liberals to respond to the organizational demands of the New Party was a similar lack of response from the midwestern inheritors of the La Follette tradition. As Rexford Tugwell wrote in the *Progressive* a year after the campaign:

> If there had been a flood of Progressives [to the Party] —energetic, determined, dedicated—where would the Communists about whom we hear so much, have been? . . . They would have been lost as they were always lost when they tried to claim President Roosevelt, or . . . when they made approaches to old Bob La Follette . . . . The reason Communist workers were so prominent in the Wallace campaign was that the Progressives were . . . sitting it out; wringing their hands, and wailing.
>
> The real tragedy [was the] withholding of support [and] leadership by those who should have offered it.

Professor Thomas I. Emerson of the Connecticut People's Party citing the difficulty of determining who was and who was not a Communist, summarized the problem: "Communist workers were undoubtedly involved and did much of the work [of organization] . . . . There was a lack of non-Communist talent and leadership to submerge the Communists . . . [but] the Communists probably lacked the strength to take over."

Given the rift over organization and the failure of the moderates to respond in greater numbers, what sort of organization emerged? To what extent was there coordination of the various groups involved and integration of the various levels? The strategic design followed a pattern more closely akin to British than to American major party practice, with national headquarters assuming supervisory powers over those state and local organizations already in existence. In unorganized areas personal contacts were established or re-established by the campaign manager Beanie Baldwin, in an attempt to secure a complete coverage of the nation. Field organizers were dispatched from New York to assist in areas where local know-how was lacking or deficient. There were five of these trouble shooters, the chief of whom, Barney Conal, had received his training in a research and organizational post with the American Federation of Labor.

One of the most pressing problems was that of establishing adequate communications. If there was to be national-local coordination, a two-way transmission channel was a necessity so that local problems and policy could be forwarded to New York and the decisions made there in line with national strategy, then dispatched to the local groups for execution. Baldwin's remarks indicated that this formidable task was never accomplished satisfactorily. As campaign manager he was unable to get out into the field and had to remain in the New York office to receive the emergency calls from local chiefs. Time was so short and the local groups so pressed by their ballot deadlines that no regular system ever emerged. Chief reliance was placed upon reports of the field organizers and upon sporadic phone calls from local leaders.

Consequently, national headquarters remained poorly informed regarding developments and problems in the field. The lower echelons, in their turn, failed in many instances to receive adequate or timely tactical plans that accorded with over-all strategy.

In any evaluation of organizational work, the conclusion must ultimately be reached that the Progressive Party was not too successful. The policy determination split over the broad versus the narrow approach was never successfully resolved, although, as Wallace suggested, this was possibly a dilemma whose horns could not have been avoided. Deliberately or not, the party wound up with a fatal narrowness.

Although the national organization was able to establish broad lines of authority over its state and local groups, it failed to integrate them through any successful control mechanism. The major parties' ability to operate successfully without any strong chain of command appears to rest on the power of their local and particularly their state committees. These committees possess the ability to conduct effective campaign operations on their own. Being strong, they can afford to be individualistic in manner and even in direction. However, lack of central control in the Wallace party was magnified by the continued weakness of most of the Progressives' state and local organizations.

The Progressives had only one strong local party—the American Labor Party. Hence it was necessary for their weaker units to operate along parallel lines if they were to be at all effective. Central command was necessary to insure that strength of unity would be afforded their endeavors. Moreover, the weak links had to be located, so that they might be given reinforcement. Had it not been for the vigor and initiative of the individual trouble shooters, it appears there would have been almost a complete lack of policy coordination among state, local, and national bodies.

The details of organization on the state and local levels were as varied as the forty-eight states themselves. But out of this myriad array of varying problems, techniques, and degrees of success, an extremely broad classification of patterns emerges that may be examined through the activities in only five states.

First, there were the states where the party hoped to make use of existing party machinery—New York with its American Labor Party and Minnesota with its Democratic Farmer-Labor Party. Second, there were those where organizing had already begun during the previous year, such as California with its Independent Progressive Party and Illinois. Finally, there were the forty-four remaining states, where the task would be to start from scratch and build organizations to fight the petition battles for places on the ballots as well as in the election campaigns. Connecticut was a typical example of building from the ground up, and Colorado exemplified a complete and open rift along the lines of the broad-narrow right-left cleavage referred to above.

In New York State, the American Labor Party had been born of the 1936 campaign coalition of anti-Tammany Labor-Liberal sentiment mobilized for the re-election of President Roosevelt. In the ensuing years it had built for itself a strong, deep, and durable machine on the sidewalks of New York. Never able to attract any substantial following upstate—even in the industrial cities of the Mohawk Valley and Lake Ontario Plain—the ALP's power in the metropolis was such that it could regularly turn out some 400,000 votes in every state-wide election.

What were the foundations of its metropolitan machinery?

First, there was, in the Eighteenth Congressional District, the personal following of Representative Vito Marcantonio. In an area predominantly populated by low-income groups of Italian, Jewish, Puerto Rican, and Negro lineage, Marc had employed an orthodox if modernized ward-level approach to the hearts of his voters. In his New York office he established an amazing multilingual assembly line for the efficient mass processing of myriad requests. Nor was the Representative himself ever too busy to talk to the lines of constituents who flocked there for advice, for favors, and for assistance. Coupled with this were Marcantonio's steady and vocal espousal of causes favored by these submerged groups and his ability to keep the forces of Democratic and Republican opposition divided.

But the American Labor Party machinery was far broader than the Eighteenth District, even though Marcantonio was its sole congressional representative until the Isaacson victory. The New York County (Manhattan) organization had been building for many years—again on the traditional ward-service pattern. At the base of the pyramid were some thirty local precinct clubs, with at least one in each of the sixteen assembly districts. Each with its own headquarters, officers, and executive committees, these clubs formed the nucleus for a multitude of personal services. For instance, at income tax time these clubs would advertise free assistance in filling out returns. No questions were asked—no indoctrination attempted—no party affiliation checked—there was only a consistent effort to impress the voters that here was a legitimate and a friendly political group. Numerous other errands were performed—assistance to tenants in curbing unlawful landlord practices and aid in securing immigration papers for relatives or in arranging transportation for those flying in from San Juan, Puerto Rico. As Geraldine Shandross, county committee executive secretary, put it, "This assistance was placed on the basis of principle . . . and since the

Democratic Party had begun to fail in its endeavors of a similar nature, the ALP gained acceptance, if not adherents."

Within these local clubs themselves, monthly meetings were held, policy discussed, and decisions arrived at. According to ALP information, these meetings were open, and anyone desiring to pay one-dollar-per-year dues could become a full member. Policy could originate at these lower levels and pass up through the county committee to the state committee for action. For instance, the party request that President Truman intervene in the 1949–50 coal strike on behalf of the miners was said to have come from the club level.

This sense of participation on the part of the members explained, at least in part, why they proved such valuable workers in the 1948 campaign—donating their services as watchers at the polls, as drivers of cars, and as ringers of doorbells. There were problems, of course, for this minority party—the lack of patronage and favors to dispense, the lack of free-flowing funds, and the strength of the propaganda forces combined against them by both major parties. And with no scrutiny of the political beliefs of prospective members, infiltration to influence policy may have proved relatively simple. For instance, in Albany County the O'Connell Democratic machine, with different motives, sent 1,500 infiltrators to dominate the 1948 ALP primary, nominating its own local candidates, who then withdrew, leaving vacant the Row *C* spaces on the ballot. Despite all these handicaps, the ALP had, by 1948, established itself on the state political scene.

The preconvention battle in New York revolved around the questions of who would dominate, who would support the Wallace candidacy, and what would be its campaign vehicle. As noted in a preceding chapter, the Amalgamated Clothing Workers, with their claimed strength of 135,000, had withdrawn early in January from the American Labor Party, as it backed the Wallace candidacy. Three months later, Mike Quill, flamboyant president of the Transport

Workers Union, earlier in the third-party ranks on the CIO National Board, dramatically reversed his position—resigning from the ALP he had helped found, with a denunciation of "the screwballs and crackpots who will continue to carry on as if the Communist Party and the American Labor Party were the same house with two doors." These withdrawals left Vito Marcantonio clearly in command of the ALP machinery—with its ballot place already promised the Wallace-Taylor ticket as soon as its state committee could legally make the formal endorsement.

At this time there was, however, a question about whether or not the ALP would serve as the exclusive third-party vehicle in the Empire State. When O. John Rogge, New York City attorney prominent in many Liberal causes, issued the call in March for a New York State Wallace-for-President Committee that would include PCA and upstate components as well as ALP, his action was interpreted as the start of a drive to place the Progressive name on the November ballot separately. Marcantonio, however, was quoted in the *New York Herald Tribune* as saying, "There will be no fifth line on the machine!" (in addition to Republican, Democratic, ALP, and Liberal lines) Although PCA delegates outnumbered those from the ALP at the April Founding Convention of the New York Committee, a majority favored the Marcantonio position.[2] No attempt would be made to qualify under the Progressive label, and the ALP would become the exclusive vehicle for the crusade in the Empire State. As Marc had dictated, there was no fifth line on the ballot.

Events in the second state where the Progressives hoped to utilize an existing party—Minnesota—will be described

[2] The *New York Times,* April 14, 1948, reported that of 1,031 delegates the PCA had 310 from New York City and 121 from upstate, the ALP 159 city and 74 upstate, and the unions had 161, with the balance divided among youth, student, Jewish, and Negro organizations.

in greater detail in the following chapter. It suffices for the present to note that the left wing of the Democratic Farmer-Labor Party under former Governor Elmer Benson met defeat at every turn. In control of the state executive committee, but not the larger state central committee, this faction was unable to outmaneuver the rightwing Humphrey-led group. Convention arrangements were voted out of its hands, and county convention support failed to materialize. Finally, refused seats in the state convention, the left-wingers convened a rump convention, whose choice of pro-Wallace DFL electors was later invalidated by the state Supreme Court.

But what of the states where new organizations had begun to blossom during 1947? In California, as noted earlier, the third-party movement had started in a drive among left-wing Democrats to secure the Democratic presidential nomination for Henry A. Wallace. There was considerable dissatisfaction reported on the West Coast—particularly among labor leaders such as those of the International Longshoremen's and Warehousemen's Union, who condemned President Truman's earlier actions concerning the railway strike. Moreover, it seemed possible that a large segment of the Liberal wing of the party might back the Wallace movement. James Roosevelt, eldest son of the late President and state chairman of the Democratic Committee, was reported favorably disposed, as were such Liberal members of Congress as Helen Gahagan Douglas and Chet Holifield.

This hope faded however, when Roosevelt ultimately decided to join his previous opponents on the state committee, Edwin Pauley and William Malone, in an endorsement of President Truman's policies. Nevertheless, union agitation continued, and the decision was made to press for a third party. The strategy was this: If the leftists could still force the selection of pro-Wallace delegates to the Democratic National Convention, they would do so, but in the event that they should fail, the necessary machinery for a third party must be already in motion in view of the early deadline for a place on the ballot.

Accordingly, in August, 1947, a Joint Trade Union Conference for a Third Party was held in Los Angeles. Although this body discussed a new party, it took no action.[3] But the day after it had adjourned, in a building just across the street, with many of the same personnel present, the Organizing Committee of the Independent Progressive Party of California was founded by some six hundred delegates and observers.

What were their hopes of success? They lay chiefly, according to Progressive Party organizer Barney Conal, in the "fluid politics" of Southern California. Party discipline was rendered feeble by the state cross-filing system and by the absence of political machines, except in San Francisco. There were no clubs, no bosses, no precinct workers of the traditional Democratic-Tammany type. There were no ward, assembly district, or county committees with entrenched machinery. Lines of party authority ran directly from precinct committeeman to state committee to state executive committee at the higher level.

With many of the precinct leaders favorable to Wallace and no entrenched apparatus to overturn, a strong new movement seemed possible. Moreover, of the three main state political groups outside the Democratic Party, one had already committed itself to the crusade, and the others were not completely unfriendly. These three main groups—the Townsendites, the EPICS ("End Poverty in California") of Upton Sinclair, and the "Ham and Eggers"—had been linked with the Democratic Party by Franklin D. Roosevelt to turn

---

[3] There were 1,236 delegates representing 51 AFL, 116 CIO, 19 railroad, and 11 independent unions and 34 veterans', 22 youth, 205 Townsend, 45 Jewish, 13 Negro, 18 nationality, and 58 Progressive Citizens of America groups according to Jack Young, "California Started Something," *New Masses*, October 14, 1947.

California from the Republicans. They were now somewhat loosely tied to it as a Progressive, even "Radical," fringe. Dr. Francis Townsend had announced in May, 1947, his support of a third-party endeavor.

Another unusual factor in California stemmed from the state's "political fluidity." Progressive-Party strategists felt that an ideological approach would be possible. With party loyalty so weak and with a vast influx of foreign-born population, particularly into the Los Angeles area, they felt they could reach many independent and uncommitted voters—especially Mexican-Americans—on the basis of Wallace's program, as well as his Latin-American ties—his earlier tours, his link with the Good Neighbor Policy, and his ability to speak Spanish.

In this favorable climate, the Progressive Party began to build what was to become its broadest state organization. Participating in this construction were Townsendites, leftwing CIO unions—chiefly the International Longshoremen's and Warehousemen's Union and Marine Cooks and Stewards—the leftwing Democrats, and eventually the Progressive Citizens of America. Of these groups, the Townsendites were the best organized. They possessed clubs and politically minded members. Both had gone through many a campaign, many a petition drive. Dr. Townsend himself had some practical suggestions to make: "Give your public a personal stake in the outcome . . . top the opposition with a better organizer in each district . . . . Women make better organizers than men."

On the other hand, union participation proved disappointing. Although a considerable number of small locals pitched in, it soon became apparent that the International Longshoremen's and Warehousemen's Union had the only really effective organization. Nevertheless, there was already established, as Wallace announced his candidacy, an active California machine—its strength concentrated in the Los Angeles area, its success about to be measured in the petition drive for a place on the ballot.

Among the states with no third-party organization prior to 1948, Connecticut was one of twenty-five in which there had been an active Progressive Citizens of America movement during 1947. Even before that, the Nutmeg State had housed a branch of the National Citizens Political Action Committee, the group which had tried to broaden the labor-based CIO Political Action Committee. Although there had been new-party talk late in 1947, the actual tasks of organization did not get under way until the December announcement. With the decision to back Wallace, the Connecticut Political Action Committee, as happened in other state committees, lost many of its members as well as its director. Regardless of these withdrawals, the majority was still enthusiastic and proceeded to organize a provisional Wallace-for-President Committee with Professor Thomas I. Emerson, of Yale Law School, at its head.

The first problem was to secure a new director for the headless forces. From Washington's Capitol Hill came Charles B. Calkins, secretary to Senator Brien McMahon, to volunteer his services. Beginning a state-wide tour to establish contacts, in order to build a network of organizations in every one of Connecticut's 169 towns, Calkins found considerable indication of discontent in Connecticut—the two main issues of peace and labor relations being the same as elsewhere. Along with private conferences, a series of open meetings was planned to keep public opinion informal on the Progressive issues, and to keep discontent bubbling under the Truman administration. Meanwhile, the provisional committee proceeded with an interim organization. Constitutional, finance, and campaign committees were established and operations started.

This preliminary work was all designed to lead up to an

April founding convention. But the night before the convention was to open, Calkins, who had played such a leading role, fell victim to his overexertion, dying of a sudden heart attack. The unexpected loss almost disrupted the delegates, but after some confusion the convention began. Slowly a new machine—a People's Party—emerged for the Nutmeg State battle.

Organizations were planned for each of the state's five congressional districts. Each district was to have a finance and a campaign committee which would supervise the work of the existing town organizations and which would in turn report to corresponding state groups. The task of organizing down to the ward and precinct levels was delegated to the town groups. Actually, according to Professor Emerson, not too many of these groups were successful in this respect, and it was here that the party mechanism broke down.

It was hoped that the lower levels would be stimulated by two factors—personal appearances of the candidates and preparations for the drive to get on the ballot. As in most states, the link between organization and petition drive was expected to aid both these aspects of the party's work. But in Connecticut, reported Emerson, this "didn't pan out too well." While Wallace's appearance at a New Haven rally was successful from the financial viewpoint—to the tune of some $35,000 or more—it did not appreciably help the task of organizing on lower levels.

The next step in the campaign was a state nominating convention at which a platform was adopted, the Wallace-Taylor slate endorsed, and candidates for state and local offices decided upon. District organizations selected their own congressional candidates, but the convention chose the representative-at-large nominee as well as a six-man slate for state offices. The nomination for governor went to Professor Emerson on the understanding that he would withdraw later if the Democrats put up an acceptable candidate. Only Chester

Bowles seemed to fit this description, and when he later received the Democratic nomination, Emerson did in fact withdraw. In addition to these matters, the state convention selected delegates to the national convention and discussed the problems of organizing for the petition campaign.

On paper it appeared that Connecticut had set up a comprehensive state-wide establishment, but such was not the case. In this state, as in so many others, there were two main failures—the failure to convert an impressive superstructure into precinct-level reality and the failure to secure organized labor support. In Connecticut, the nonparticipation of the United Electrical Workers, powerful in the Bridgeport area particularly, was most damaging. The People's Party remained for the most part a top-level white-collar affair.

In Colorado, the failure to achieve adequate breadth stemmed from the difference of opinion between the right and left wings of the party concerning the type of structure to be built. Broad-base organization was desired by the center and right wings, led by Charles A. Graham, a Denver lawyer serving as state Wallace committee chairman; a narrow base was sought by the left wing, under Craig Vincent. Despite the fact that Wallace made a personal appearance to urge strongly the broad position, the leftists won out in a bitter all-night convention session. Having lost the decision, the moderates walked out, and Graham refused to accept the chairmanship of the newly formed Progressive Party of Colorado.

The Colorado action threw into bold relief both the contrasting opinions and the groups holding them. Those who wanted breadth cited the American Labor Party in New York as a successful example of party membership open to all. Only in this fashion, they argued, could the party build rapidly enough for the 1948 campaign. The advocates of narrowness urged a well-disciplined party core—a compact cohesive group which would be able to build for their primary goal, the 1952 campaign. The similarity of this position and that of the Communist Party was remarked at the time by at least one reporter—Howard Norton in the *Baltimore Evening Sun.* The narrow-base advocates won, despite Wallace's entreaties to make this "a broadly based party of the people."

The states examined reveal the general organizational pattern followed by the Progressives elsewhere. The preliminary organization—initiated late in 1947 or early in 1948—usually consisted of a series of local committees for Wallace, who then established a state-wide Wallace committee. The latter, having set up a provisional apparatus, would summon a state-wide convention, at which the party would be officially launched, a platform adopted, the national candidates endorsed, and local candidates decided upon. Then, employing the twin techniques of petition drives and mass meetings with name speakers, the dual task of getting on the ballot and obtaining funds was intertwined with the attempt to set up a real party machine. Although fine on paper, the over-all outcome was one of failure—the party neither gained the breadth of support, nor did it organize down to the ward and precinct levels. The sole exceptions— and qualified exceptions at that—were in New York, where the American Labor Party provided some depth, at least in the city area, and California, where a degree of breadth was attained. In no instance where the party had to start from scratch in 1948 was it able to achieve either of these goals. And within a few short years both the American Labor Party and the Independent Progressive Party would have completely vanished—following Wallace's withdrawal from the party of his creation.

Whereas the state organizational ventures of the New Party followed established political paths, their work to line up various functional groups was something of a departure from the American geographical norm. These "associated groups," including the National Labor Committee for Wallace and Taylor, Women-for-Wallace, the Progressive Youth of America, the Nationalities Division, Farm and Veteran groups, and Businessmen-for-Wallace, were designed on a functional basis to appeal to the specific voting segments suggested by their titles.

Unlike attempts made previously to garner the support and endorsement of labor leaders, the National Labor Committee for Wallace and Taylor was established to promote rank-and-file affiliation. The committee consisted of some one thousand trade unionists all across the nation. Although Albert J. Fitzgerald, United Electrical Workers president, was the chairman, the bulk of the actual work of the committee rested on the shoulders of Executive Secretary Russell Nixon. During the campaign, Nixon, on "loan" from the United Electrical Workers, was paid in part by the union and in part by the National Committee.

Early in 1948 UE strategists formulated plans for an organization that would reach "all branches of the labor movement." Nixon submitted to the Chicago Convention a "Report on Organization" in which he expected that:

Labor's support for Wallace and Taylor [would be] based in the trade unions on a grass roots rank and file basis . . . . The foundation of this support is found among the local union officers, grievance men, stewards, and active rank and filers.

Unsuccessful in their attempt to secure leadership endorsement, the Progressives would attempt to carry the campaign directly to the workers and to the locals, in the hopes of wooing them away from their chiefs' political direction. A complete hierarchy was blueprinted. On the lowest levels, shop committees were planned for plants and locals. Their task was to distribute literature, raise funds, register voters, and get out the vote. On the next level, there were to be state and area committees. These were to coordinate the work of the shop committees in their respective areas, as well as to prepare literature adapted to local conditions and arrange for mass meetings. One of their most important duties was to see that the relatively weaker areas of organized labor would be covered. For example, it was hoped that considerable Wallace support could be recruited from among the comparatively unorganized workers of the Baltimore industrial area.

Finally, on the industry level, a dual approach was planned. As Nixon explained it in his "Report . . .":

> In the industries covered by several unions, it was possible because of leadership sympathetic to Wallace for "New Party" supporters to work within the trade unions themselves . . . .
>
> Where this [was] not feasible, the organization of support for Wallace on an industrial basis [was to be] organized, not on a basis of competition with the international union leadership involved, but merely as a campaign organization of the workers supporting Wallace and Taylor in these industries.

The four main areas in which this second type of organization was attempted were the automobile, railroad, Maritime, and steel industries. Less attention was paid coal miners, textile and garment workers, and printers.

In the auto industry, a National Auto Workers for Wallace Committee was established, which proved successful in forming approximately one hundred shop committees across the nation. A similar committee was set up among railroad workers at the outset of the campaign and was reported to have distributed about one million pieces of literature. Along the water fronts of the East Coast—the territory of the National Maritime Union—an attempt was made to establish both shore and ship committees to spread propaganda and to conduct fundraising drives. And finally, among the steelworkers, a concerted effort was made in western Pennsylvania to found a steelworkers' conference. This conference called a convention, attended by several hundred delegates, and set up a national Wallace committee for the steel industry.

Within this broad framework, what were the techniques employed? The strategy stressed action on current issues. For instance, the Progressives actively aided and supported strikers in various plants and localities. They allied themselves with the Packinghouse Workers in Chicago and the Chrysler employees in Detroit. They set great store by the distribution of literature—total handouts were estimated at more than three million. The main emphasis in this literature was placed on portraying the New Party as the only true friend of labor—playing up the Taft-Hartley Act and the Truman threats to draft railroad employees as evidence of a bipartisan big business coalition. "The collection of campaign funds in small sums from large numbers of workers" was also a "basic organizational task." And finally, the labor committee placed emphasis on the task of getting the workers to register and turn out to vote.

On paper this added up to an impressive campaign among organized labor, but in reality the committee's accomplishments were limited. Even among those unions whose leaders were friendly to the Progressives, it never succeeded in working up enthusiasm among the rank and file. There were three major factors that made the labor committee's task a hopeless one: First, there were the general conditions of prosperity—high wages and full employment—that made labor unwilling to change horses. Second, there was the

Communist label that rightwing labor leaders successfully pinned on the heads of those unions supporting the Progressive Party. Finally, there was the fear of a Republican victory. Few felt that Wallace had any real chance of victory, and Truman seemed by far, from the labor viewpoint, the lesser of the two evils.

Among the unfriendly unions a fourth factor entered into the outcome. This factor was intimidation—the use of threats and even violence—to keep union members from even attending third-party meetings. One such example emerged at a western Pennsylvania Wallace rally. Here, Barney Conal, an on-the-scene organizer, reported that a steelworkers' local stationed checkers at the door to count off on union lists the names of those attending.

But what of the ladies? How did they respond to the peace banner borne by the Wallace crusaders? A major attempt to organize their endeavors came in the Women-for-Wallace group.

Prior to the declaration of the Wallace candidacy, several local women's clubs had been established in favorable localities—New York City and Southern California—under leaders such as Elinor Gimbel and Elinor Kahn, to plan a women's program that would be integrated with the national party organization. Formal organization of the national Women-for-Wallace movement, however, was deferred until the April party conference in Chicago. The emphasis was placed, by these delegates from more than twenty-seven states, on altering the traditional secondary role accorded women in the major parties. In the Progressive Party, they would achieve complete equality—filling roles as "leaders, as candidates, and as door to door campaign workers." Informing the group that their "major job was to organize the millions of women voters behind the New Party," Chairman Elinor Gimbel also promised that "for the first time in our political

history, there is going to be a new party which will have
women not only as organizers, but have them in at the very
beginning . . . to give it guidance."

The women's appeal was aimed at groups all across the
nation, but particularly in the smaller towns—with the Wallace foreign policy views expected to strike a responsive chord
in the minds of wives and mothers. Party leaders anticipated
that it would prove much more difficult to Red-bait a woman,
since the average member of a women's club in a small midwestern town seemed unlikely to be called a Communist. Mrs.
Gimbel herself embarked upon a nation-wide tour of the
"whistlestops"—East Coast, West Coast, Middle West, almost
everywhere except the Deep South. Countless luncheons and
other affairs served to raise both funds and, it was hoped,
women's support. Although the Women-for-Wallace group
was successful in obtaining a great deal of political action
from women—leg work and doorbell ringing on the house-to-
house level—and although it was quite successful in raising
funds, its successes were largely localized—in the metropolitan New York and Southern California areas where the
women's groups had the advantage of pre-existing support as
well as superior leadership. Despite their hopes, the small
towns and the "whistlestops" never seem to have responded
to the rallying cry of "Peace, Freedom and Abundance."

Was there a greater response from the potential leaders of
tomorrow—the youths and students brought together in a
third association, the Progressive Youth of America?

The organizational pattern here was not markedly different
from that of the women's groups. Active and well represented
in New York and other metropolitan areas such as Philadelphia, Baltimore, and Los Angeles, the Young Progressives
failed to gain any following across the nation as a whole.

The conservative cross section of youth that constituted college America in 1948 exhibited far less interest in the peace
and progress issues raised by Wallace than might have been

expected from nonacademicians. There was general apathy over the possibility of future war or depression and a much greater concern over immediate job prospects. The few student political groups in existence were more attracted to the pseudoliberal Harold E. Stassen, than to the allegedly radical Henry A. Wallace. Few crusaders emerged from the Halls of Ivy—particularly in the midst of increasing pressures for intellectual conformity.

Perhaps the most interesting and unique contribution of the Young Progressives was their July National Youth Convention at Philadelphia immediately following the Progressive Party Convention. Modeled on much the same pattern as traditional party affairs, but with the platform rather than the candidates holding the center of the stage, the young convention was almost equally big, noisy, and frustrating. While it served to drum up enthusiasm among the already convinced delegates, it boomeranged as a means of attracting converts to the cause. The success of newspaper columnists in labeling this organization "Communist-dominated" undoubtedly served to completely alienate any persons who were still politically undecided.

Moreover, the inability of the youth organization to plan its agenda sufficiently well to complete a platform left an impression far from inspiring. The prolonged wrangling—late into Saturday night and all day Sunday—over trivial details and bits of minutiae was maddening. In two days the Philadelphia youth convention failed to act on a single matter of importance. It wound up ignominiously in the dark of Convention Hall—the lights turned out on its windmill battle of semantics.

Another of the associated groups—the Nationalities Division of the National Committee—was pitched on the level of recent immigrant groups. Organized at the Chicago conference by some eighty representatives of twenty-four different nationalities, headed by Zlatko Balokovic of the American

Slav Congress, its announced purpose was to "devote itself to the political and cultural problems peculiar to each group." Accordingly, some eighteen subcommittees were formed representing major nationality groupings—Yugoslav-Americans, Italian-Americans, and even Irish-Americans, as well as Poles, Rumanians, Russians, and Greeks.

But once it had been formed, the Nationalities Division dropped almost completely from sight. Only in the small financial contributions traceable to it, did it emerge again— evidence that this too was just another paper organization.

A similar outcome was the fate of the Farm and Veterans groups. Although preliminary committees were formed in each of these fields, their activities proved untraceable either in the press or through financial statements. Farmers, particularly those of Progressive tradition, were in evidence at Philadelphia and throughout the campaign, but their numbers were not impressive. Similarly, the only liberal veterans group—the American Veterans Committee—failed to respond to the Wallace crusade, although some of its members undoubtedly donned the battle garb.

The National Businessmen's Committee for Wallace constituted another associated group, somewhat more successful than the foregoing—particularly in the New York City area, where it had support in import-export circles. A carry-over of sorts from the earlier Businessmen for Roosevelt groups in the 1940 and 1944 campaigns, it included a core of Wallace's personal followers, gained through speeches for the Democratic Party, his tariff stand during the 1930's, and his support of small business assistance while Secretary of Commerce. Additionally, a bloc of Jewish businessmen in New York City had recently been attracted to Wallace by his position on the Palestine issue.

Although the contribution of the National Businessmen's Committee to the Progressives in the realm of organization was relatively insignificant, their financial support from various "businessmen's lunches and dinners" proved substantial.

The last of the major associated organizations was the National Council of Arts, Sciences and Professions. At an earlier date, the Independent Citizens Committee for the ASP had been merged with the National Citizens Political Action Committee to form the Progressive Citizens of America. A second group, the National Council of the ASP, was formed in June, 1948 as an independent organization—primarily to accommodate those who did not wish to identify themselves completely with the third party. In their own words:

> We, of the arts, sciences and professions, while basically nonpartisan, have always supported candidates, of whatever political affiliation, best qualified to carry forward a genuine program in the best interests of humanity and progress . . . . Today [1948] these hopes and achievements are embodied in the program and candidacy of Henry A. Wallace.

The NC-ASP never affiliated with the Progressive Party. Nor did its twenty thousand members in some nineteen local councils enter into the organizational operation on the ward-precinct level. They were not interested in doorbell ringing, house-to-house canvassing, and the other details of political work. But they did contribute in their own respective spheres. For example, Lillian Hellman and Norman Corwin brought their talent to the preparation of radio scripts, while others were responsible for stage techniques, lighting, and dramatization of the party's rallies.

But what of the three tasks the party had set for itself in its organizational drive? From the outset, the Wallace crusade had seemed quixotic to many, inasmuch as it had been launched without the broad base of support or of popular discontent so essential to success for any American third party. In its organizational work of building a new party, these deficiencies were brought home clearly. Starting from an already restricted base, the party soon found itself divided along broad versus narrow lines. Despite Wallace's support of the former position, he failed to inject himself into organizational matters with enough vigor or sustained interest to impose his views. Coupled with this, the presence of the "Peekskill Boys" tended to exclude the moderates who might have supplied the necessary breadth. Yet only these leftists seemed prepared to turn out, to work zealously—eventually to attain through default a position of prominence in a narrowly defined organization.

Nor was the second task, of building in depth, any more successfully accomplished. Starting from the top and building downward would have been difficult even under the most favorable circumstances. In the face of public apathy to the issues of "Peace, Freedom and Abundance," the task of organizing support on ward and precinct levels proved almost impossible. But the climate of opinion became worse than neutral as anti-Red hostility served increasingly even to prevent public discussion of the serious issues raised, let alone promote the building of a party machine. Only in New York City was there much success along these lines. And here the American Labor Party had enjoyed a twelve-year period in which to fashion an effective organization.

Even here, time, world events, the insistence of Marcantonio on a narrower and narrower party, and the final departure of Wallace himself were ultimately to shatter the only effective organization of the Progressives in their "fight for peace." Elsewhere across the nation, the factor of personal allegiance to and support of one man—the former Vice President—was even more rapidly to prove fatal to party longevity. The organizational foundations laid down by those intent on building a new party proved to have been built on sand.

Neither breadth, nor depth, nor permanence was attained in the course of organizing the Progressive Party of 1948.

In 1947, Fiorello H. LaGuardia had predicted in a *PM* article, "The new progressive movement, when it comes, will come from the Main Street of thousands of Prairie Junctions, and not from Union Square in Manhattan." Unfortunately for the Wallace Progressive Party, Main Street had not responded to its call to organize. Union Square had.

# CHAPTER 6

# "The People

# Must Have a Choice"

THE THEME running through all of Henry Wallace's speeches early in 1948 was that the people must have a choice; they must be able to express their approval or disapproval of the conduct of the government. With a bipartisan foreign policy accepted by both major parties, it became the self-appointed task of the new party to present an alternative to the people for their decision. Moreover, claimed Wallace, in their *domestic* policies the major parties were as Tweedledum and Tweedledee, both representing identical militaristic–Wall Street interests. They no longer offered the sharp contrast of early New Deal days. Here too the third party would present the people with a clearly defined alternative.

For the voters to make their choice, it was necessary not only to build a new party but to make sure that the party's candidates would have places on the ballots in every state of the Union. Experts claimed this was virtually impossible in view of the increasing restrictions placed on third parties by many states, particularly within recent years. They noted that in 1924 Robert W. La Follette had been able to put his Progressive slate before the voters in each of the forty-eight states, but that in 1936 the Union Party of William Lemke had been successful in only thirty-four.

This point of view had been well expressed by L. D. Wheildon during the previous year in *Editorial Research Reports:*

> Even if a third party overcomes the forces of habit and tradition and succeeds in winning a large popular following, it still faces formidable obstacles in state election laws, which have been written for the most part by representatives of the established parties with an eye to discouraging newcomers. Although minor parties are not *forbidden* as such in any state, it is becoming increasingly difficult in most states for them to qualify for a place on the ballot.

The problem faced was a dual one, for in addition to the legal requirements imposed by state election laws, there were also the political implications involved in interpreting and enforcing these laws.

The Constitution of the United States has left to individual state legislatures the power to determine the manner of choosing presidential electors (Art. 2, Sec. 1, Par. 2), and in 1948 the forty-eight states had established forty-eight different methods by which electoral candidates might secure their places on the ballot. Generally speaking, however, there were two broad methods for both existing and new parties.

Several states had established definitions and requirements for a "legal" party and then accorded such parties the virtually automatic privilege of placing nominees on the ballot. For example, the American Labor Party constituted a "legal" party in New York State since it had received more than the requisite 50,000 votes in the last gubernatorial election. The Wallace slate was thus already assured of the ALP's Row *C* on the Empire State ballot. In Illinois a Cook County Progressive Party had organized prior to the 1947 election and entered a slate of candidates in the generally uncontested nonpartisan judicial elections. Since its top candidate had amassed a total of 313,000 votes, just short of a majority but well over the 5 per cent legal requirement, the third party seemed assured of a place there.

On the other hand, a completely new party or an existing one that had not achieved "legal" status had to employ other methods. The most widely utilized procedure was that requiring nominating petitions, with either a fixed number of signatures or a percentage of the total vote for some designated office in a prior election. Several states required nomination by convention, and there were still others with less formal stipulations.[1]

Those states requiring petition signatures by a percentage of voters ranged from South Dakota which demanded 20 per cent through Ohio at 15 per cent and California at 10 per cent to Indiana which required only ½ of 1 per cent. Georgia, Nevada, and Oregon required 5 per cent; Arizona, 2 per cent; Connecticut, Vermont, and West Virginia, 1 per cent. The set of election returns on which these percentages was based also varied—the last congressional election being used in Nevada and Oregon, last presidential election in Connecticut, last gubernatorial election in Arizona, California, and Vermont, while Indiana and Michigan used the vote for Secretary of State, and Pennsylvania the highest vote for a state office.

In the states specifying a fixed number of signatures, the requirements again varied—from 50 in Mississippi to 25,000 (with at least 200 from each of 50 of the 102 counties) in Illinois and 50,000 in Massachusetts. But even the most stringent of these states, Illinois and Massachusetts, were generally more lenient than those requiring percentages.

The nine states employing the convention method had rules ranging in stringency from Nebraska, where 750 dele-

---

[1] See Appendix, Table 1, for a detailed listing of the requirements.

gates had to attend, on down to neighboring Iowa, where only 2 (1 to sign the required certificate as chairman, the other as secretary) were sufficient to constitute a legal convention.

In three states, Mississippi, New Mexico and Texas, the only requirements were formal organization and filing of a slate of electors. In South Carolina the only compulsion was to print and distribute ballots at the polling places, since at this time the Palmetto State still employed the outmoded party ballot system, instead of an officially printed, or Australian, ballot.

Some of the states provided alternate methods of nominating electoral candidates. For instance, in California the 10 per cent petition requirement might be replaced by inducing 1 per cent of the registered voters to change their affiliation to a new party.

With the exception of a few states, such as California, Georgia, Illinois, Massachusetts, Nebraska, New York, Oklahoma, Oregon, and South Dakota, the *legal* aspects of the task of securing a requisite number of signatures or delegates might not have proven as difficult as commonly believed (the *political* obstacles being more nearly insurmountable). But the matter of *numbers* was not the only statutory consideration involved. There still remained such details as deadlines and filing fees.

Filing deadlines in many instances presented the stiffest legal barrier for a new party, *unless* it had been organized at least one year prior to the election. As described earlier, the California requirement—a March deadline eight months prior to the November balloting—helped force Wallace's hand in making a decision as early as December of 1947. Elsewhere the dates varied—March in New Jersey; April in Pennsylvania, Maryland, and Oklahoma; May in Michigan, West Virginia, Florida, and Alabama; June in Kentucky. A total of fourteen states required that filing be completed prior to the first of July. Aimed at any group splitting off from a major party at or after a national convention, these deadlines effectively eliminated in nearly one third of the states any recurrence of a 1912 Bull Moose style split.

While some states provided write-in voting for those parties missing the deadlines, the disadvantages were evident. To cite one example, the States' Rights Party received only 2,476 write-in votes in Maryland, since they had been excluded from a place on the ballot by their inability to meet the April 17, 1948 deadline.

The provision for filing fees proved much less important, even in states with a relatively high assessment, such as Maryland's $270. While this sum might have deterred individuals from seeking a ballot position, it was relatively insignificant in light of the other multitudinous expenditures for a nation-wide third party.

Political considerations proved far more important. A major party, in control of state election machinery and determined to block a minor contender, may employ seemingly innocuous statutory provisions to raise insuperable obstacles. Challenges to signatures, court actions at every step, prolonged litigation, and other devices may serve in practice to nullify legal rights. For instance, prior to the April primary in Cook County, Illinois, where they were seemingly entitled to a place on the ballot by their performance in the 1947 judiciary elections, the Progressives found this right challenged by the major parties. Despite a favorable court decision (*Progressive Party* v. *Flynn,* 79 N.E. 2d 516), they never received this place because the election officials then ruled that the decision had been made too late to print new ballots with the Progressive candidates included.

By the same token, techniques are available by which a major party favorably disposed to a third entrant can assist its efforts to secure a place on the ballot. In the 1948 campaign, according to reports from Progressive Party field organizer Barney Conal, there was little doubt that had it not been for Republican assistance the Wallace slate would not have been listed in the state of Kansas.

Thus the task facing the New Party in its drive to get on the ballot in 1948 appeared highly formidable, but not completely impossible. Given an early start, which they already possessed, the breadth of representation they were claiming, a sufficient number of patient workers they were soon to acquire, and an organization adequate to plan and guide their energies, chances of success seemed reasonably good.

Moreover, it appeared that political circumstances would operate at least partly in their favor. While it was to be expected that the Democrats would oppose the appearance of Wallace electors in the states whose election machinery they controlled, it also seemed logical to assume that the Republican party would aid the Progressives, at least behind the scenes. This appeared to be no more than sound political strategy in view of the expectation that 90 per cent of the Wallace votes would be drawn from voters otherwise casting Democratic ballots.

The pattern, however, was not to unfold as anticipated. The Republicans—either lulled into a sense of false security by the polls predicting a GOP sweep, unwilling to admit the Wallace-ites as allies under any circumstances, or led by men who failed to assess the situation correctly until too late— failed in many instances to lend a hand in getting the Progressive slates on the ballot. On the other hand, the Democratic Party found itself split into Fair Deal and Dixiecrat wings before the end of the summer. While the Truman wing continued to oppose the third party, the States' Rights group, as a *fourth* party, took an immediate hand in efforts to ease the task of qualifying a new party in several states. Unable to devise laws that would admit themselves, yet exclude the Progressives, the States' Righters wound up in inadvertent support of the Wallace drive for a place on the ballot.

With both the legal and political circumstances in view, what were the Progressives' strategy and techniques, the court battles in which they became involved, and the political maneuvering in the more crucial states?

Over-all strategy, techniques, and timing of the ballot campaign were planned from national headquarters in New York City. As noted in the preceding chapter, this had a significant impact on the New York State decision not to initiate a petition drive to list the Wallace-Taylor slate under the Progressive name. Elsewhere, however, the Progressives were faced with the necessity of immediate positive action. With top-level planning of the petition drives taking place in headquarters, field organizers were dispatched to those states where success hung in the balance. As noted in the preceding chapter, over-all strategy was to link the petition drives to the organizational activity in the various states, and to the campaign for funds as well. Timing to meet the deadlines as they came due was an essential part of this strategic battle waged from New York.

Within the states the field organizers analyzed the areas in which to concentrate and then devised appropriate coverage. Based on socioeconomic data, these analyses were aimed at predicting the locations, such as Former Populist centers, in which Progressive support might best be uncovered. For example, in Oklahoma, according to Barney Conal, this preliminary planning was so successful that the party was able to acquire more than the necessary five thousand signatures in only two days of actual collecting. Surprisingly enough, in such states as Kansas, Oklahoma, and West Virginia efforts were concentrated not in the cities and towns but in outlying rural areas.

Before the strategy planning had begun, even before Wallace had formally announced his candidacy, the first political shot in the battle of the ballots had been fired by the opposition in Congress. This had taken the form of a measure introduced on November 17, 1947 by Representative Cole (Republican, Missouri) and designed to bar "un-American parties from the election ballot." (H.R. 4482, 80th Cong., 1st sess.) It provided that no party would be allowed to participate in an election if it was "directly or indirectly affiliated . . . with the Communist Party . . . the Communist international, or any other foreign agency, political party, organization or government."

Hearings were held in January by a subcommittee of the Committee on House Administration at which testimony was offered to indicate that the measure would bar the Wallace party because it had not repudiated Communist support. The Attorney General was asked for a ruling on the constitutionality of the proposed measure and on additional hearings which were held, but it was never reported out by the committee. The possible role of the Republican House leadership in halting the bill is virtually impossible to determine, but, in view of the fact that party strategists were relying on the Progressive candidacy to cut into the Democratic vote, this is a possibility that must be borne in mind.

This preliminary "sniping," however, was far less important than the task of securing the necessary petition signatures in the states across the nation as the respective filing deadlines came up.

In California, work was already under way before Wallace's decision had been announced. The Independent Progressive Party had begun the tremendous task of obtaining 275,970 petition signatures—10 per cent of the 2,759,700 votes cast in the last (1946) gubernatorial election. The burden was being carried by the leftwing unions of the CIO and the Townsendites. Sentiment among the Progressive Citizens of America was divided on the advisability of the petition drive. Since Robert Kenny, PCA chairman, felt it would be impossible to obtain the requisite number of signers, he was still urging a fight within the Democratic Party, retaining the registration transfer procedure as a last-minute weapon to put the Progressive Party on the ballot if necessary. Accordingly, the PCA chapters, of considerable strength in the Los Angeles area, did not join in the petition drive until after the announcement of the Wallace candidacy. But when they did, they turned the tide.

With unions, Townsendites, and PCA cooperating, volunteer crews inundated the Southern California area, in which the campaign was concentrated. There were housewives and student groups from the universities for house-to-house canvassing in all the suburbs and permanent crews for downtown Los Angeles corners. The net result was an overwhelming success, even though toward the end of the campaign the party found it necessary to pay its canvassers from 5¢ to 10¢ for each name obtained and even though in San Francisco it was necessary to hire a professional firm whose business it was to obtain petition signatures for various causes on a regular fee basis.

Aided by these deviations from amateur status, the assorted groups amassed a total of some 464,000 signatures a full month prior to the March 18 deadline. Fifty-seven of the state's fifty-eight counties were represented—giving some indication of the campaign's breadth. Hugh Bryson, chairman of the Independent Progressive Party Organizing Committee, assigned the credit in a wire to Wallace that was quoted in the *Daily Worker:*

> . . . The third party drive in California succeeded only because of the active support of thousands of working people, including a large number from trade unions and other organizations, and the active daily work of thousands of volunteers.

The final total of 482,781 signatures was later certified by the Secretary of State as including some 295,000 valid endorsements—15,000 more than the required minimum. The Wallace campaign was off to a flying start in this first and most severe test of its ability to get on the ballot.

From this triumph to a series of victories in Maryland, New Jersey, and Pennsylvania, the Progressive Party moved almost without untoward incident, except in the Keystone State.

In the midst of a drive to obtain the 7,974 signatures necessary in the Commonwealth of Pennsylvania, the Scripps-Howard *Pittsburgh Press* undertook an unconventional contribution to public information: front-page publication of lists giving the names, addresses, and occupations of those who had signed Wallace nominating petitions. At the same time the *Press* magnanimously announced that those "claiming they signed under misapprehension or through misunderstanding will have their statements printed the same day their names are used." [2]

Although newspapers had been generally hostile to the Wallace candidacy, this policy marked an extreme in attempted broad-scale intimidation. The result, however, was hardly that anticipated by the *Press*. Of the first one thousand signers whose names were published, only ten retracted, although there were reports that some twenty others had been summoned by their employers and told to "repudiate or else." On the other hand, the *Press* was flooded with letters from both signers and sympathizers, the majority of whom opposed its action, as the *Press* admitted near the conclusion of the presentation of this "matter of news." The American Civil Liberties Union took a dim view of the proceedings, commenting in a letter to the editor that

. . . Publication of the Progressive Party lists, and those only, must have the effect of intimidating [free] discussion and inviting discrimination and retaliation against the persons listed.

According to Professor Thomas I. Emerson, the *New Haven Register* used a variation of this technique, employing

[2] See *Pittsburgh Press,* April 11–April 30, 1948. The direct quotation was printed April 13, 1948.

previous Communist petition signatures in an attempt to discourage voters from signing People's Party blanks. Party publicist Ralph Shikes reported that several other Scripps-Howard papers, the *Milwaukee Journal,* and one Boston and one Cleveland paper used variations of the Pittsburgh formula, though less persistently. Although these incidents went unreported in most journals across the nation, few of them saw fit to attempt repetitions in their own communities.

Other forms of intimidation were employed in West Virginia, and this state became one of the bitterest battlegrounds in the petition fight. Despite the fact that the ballot drive there received little or no publicity—perhaps because the requirements *seemed* to demand so little effort—the campaign was one of the most difficult and perhaps came the closest to failure of any that the Progressives finally won.

In 1941 the Legislature of West Virginia had passed a law clearly aimed at keeping third parties off the ballot. It provided that signing a nominating petition should be construed as legally binding the voter to the party assisted. The statute established as the deadline for filing petitions the day immediately preceding the primary election. Wallace petition signers would thus be barred from participating in the highly important West Virginia primary. Competition for such posts as sheriff and constable has generally been bitter in West Virginia, because of the fees and privileges that accompany these positions. Reports had it that fifteen dollars per vote was not an uncommon offer. Consequently, local politicians were strongly opposed to the circulation of third-party petitions which might disqualify any of their hoped-for primary supporters.

Moreover, in West Virginia it was necessary to purchase petition certificates on which the nominating signatures must be obtained, and only certified gatherers were allowed to seek names. In addition, these workers could operate only in the specific district assigned them.

In addition to these restrictive circumstances, there was a virtually complete lack of existing organization within the state to spearhead a petition drive. It was necessary to build from the ground up. Party headquarters scanned the various letters of endorsement sent to Wallace and chose from them persons who seemed interested and willing to do actual organizational work. Field organizers, headed by Barney Conal, were then sent to canvass these prospects and build a machine. It proved impossible to recruit a sufficient number of workers within the two weeks allotted for the task, and crews had to be brought from New York and other metropolitan areas to aid in the work. Eventually, the number of workers totaled between two hundred and three hundred.

A Committee for Wallace was established and a socio-economic analysis of the state completed. The conclusion reached from this analysis was that the Progressives should concentrate their endeavors in the small mining communities, particularly those within twelve counties—five in the south, two in the central area, three in the Fairmount and two in the Wheeling areas. The fact that the United Mine Workers had recently been fined one and one half million dollars for contempt of court enabled the Progressives to employ a rather deceptive, if ingenious, technique in their attempt to gather signatures. A petition to President Truman protesting against the UMW fine was prepared and circulated by the Progressive workers. Appended to this were petitions for nominating third-party electors. It was easy to convince miners to sign the antifine petition, and, according to party accounts, this document furnished an opening wedge for a sales talk on Wallace and Taylor. Obviously such a device may have easily lent itself to abuse, with many a miner signing both petitions rapidly, without ascertaining their individual contents.

Another propaganda weapon employed in the West Virginia campaign was a speech of the late President Roosevelt to a Union for Democratic Action meeting in which he had praised Wallace highly as a friend of labor generally and miners specifically. All other pamphlets and mimeographs were discarded and only this one employed.

As the campaign progressed, feelings ran high, and violence was near on numerous occasions. In Logan County, the sheriff had made blunt statements to the press, threatening violators of the primary law with prosecution and implying that extra-legal means might be employed to halt the Wallace petition drive. Picking up the challenge, party strategists planned a meeting for the center of this section. Acting on the theory that a good offense may be the best defense, they advertised that they were coming in after signatures. The counterattack obtained results, but it also led to car chases, threats, and near-shootings. One of the third-party workers, after several warnings that he was endangering his health by obtaining signatures, finally set himself up in business on his front porch. There he sat, gun in hand, with a microphone and loud-speaker hooked up, challenging all visitors, "Anyone coming up here for anything but signing a petition is going to get it," and pointing meaningfully at the gun.

Not all the questionable tactics were on the side of the Progressives, however. In fact, they seem to have been on the defensive most of the time, for West Virginia was crucial to the Democrats nationally, as well as to their local cohorts. There were a few, such as U.S. Senator Matthew Neely, who felt that the Progressives would help rather than hinder state Democrats by encouraging a larger turnout of citizens likely to vote Democratic in local contests. But for the most part the Democratic opposition failed to accept this view and remained bitterly hostile to the Wallace-ites. Allegedly they were at the bottom of much of the intimidation attempted—threats of job loss, landlord "hints" of eviction for tenants working or voting for the third party, and threats of retaliation against Negroes who might aid, as well as against ministers and university professors. All of these tactics combined to make the task of the party highly difficult, even though Wallace received the endorsement of approximately fifty-four mine locals.

The Progressives were never certain of ballot success until the day the petitions were filed. It was a last-minute, touch-and-go proposition with workers driving all night to bring in their completed blanks before the deadline. Last-second compilation of the totals was difficult, but when the smoke had cleared, the Progressives found they had submitted some 10,189 names, including, as it proved, enough valid signatures to meet the requirement of 7,155.

Although a later court ruling deprived them of their gubernatorial candidate, the Progressives had come out victorious in this, the "bitterest of any fight." [3]

Other petition states presented a variety of problems, but none of them so fierce a battle. In North Carolina the Progressives claimed success in stimulating Negroes to political self-organization in that state for the first time since the Populists. Negro students were organized into crews, and mixed racial groups were also employed in the drive to secure petition signatures. This technique was reported by Barney Conal to have been so successful that in the Eleventh Ward of Charlotte, not a single qualified Negro turned down the party workers' requests.

As the continuing drive to obtain signatures in the petition states went on through the summer, the party soon found its filings challenged in the courts of two states—Oklahoma and Illinois.

In Oklahoma, the Democratic Secretary of State had accepted the Wallace petitions, with some eight thousand signatures, as satisfying the requirements of the state election

---

[3] The state Supreme Court refused to accept the petitions of Henry H. Harvey on the grounds that "a candidate of other than a previously recognized party is not eligible unless nominated by petition prior to the date of the primary election." *New York Times,* October 13, 1948.

laws. Not only had they exceeded the legal requirements by some three thousand—enough to compensate for challenged signatures—but they had also beaten the April 30 deadline by several weeks.

Suits questioning the validity of the Secretary of State's action were immediately filed. One of these was brought by the neo-Fascist Gerald L. K. Smith, intent on saving Oklahoma from this Progressive evil. In the *Oklahoma Daily* (Norman), student newspaper at the University of Oklahoma, Smith charged:

> Stalin is in Oklahoma under the guise of the Progressive Party . . . . And the Communist party would have gone on the ballot if the Christian National Crusade had not heard of it and through the anti-communist league challenged the petitions of the Wallace party.

The state election board refused to accept the Wallace electors for a place on the ballot, claiming that the Progressives did not constitute a political party, since the Secretary of State had not approved the party's non-Communist affidavit prior to the final date for filing declarations of candidacy. According to statute, the Secretary of State *could not* accept the non-Communist affidavit until May 2, 1948, and the deadline for filing was April 30, 1948. The Progressives contended that they had come into existence as a party as soon as their nominating petitions had been certified and that the non-Communist affidavit was a requirement for appearance on the ballot, not for forming a party. They claimed in their brief that the language of both law and affidavit supported their contention.

Refusing to accept this position, the Oklahoma State Supreme Court denied the party's petition for a writ of mandamus to compel the election board to accept and file the declarations of intention (*Cooper* v. *Cartwright*, 195 P. 2d

290). By a five to two vote, the Court accepted the contention of the board that the Progressives had not actually constituted a party when they sought to file their declarations.
Thus the party was barred from the ballot in Oklahoma.

An appeal to the United States Supreme Court was contem-
plated, but party counsel John Abt abandoned the plan because of the "difficulty of getting grounds for a Federal suit."
The decision stood, and the party had met its first defeat.
Even the fact that Oklahoma possessed only ten electoral
votes could not fully temper the blow, since this meant that
in Oklahoma, at least, the people would *not* have a choice.

The second series of court decisions against the Progressives came in Illinois—where the party had anticipated substantial support on the basis of their 1947 judicial election
turnout of some 313,000 votes in Cook County (Chicago).
After a series of court battles, the Cook County Progressive
Party had finally obtained places for its local candidates on
the fall ballot. But in order to secure places for the national
candidates on the state-wide ballot it was necessary for the
party to meet the requirement of obtaining 25,000 signatures,
with at least 200 from each of 50 of the 102 counties. Although more stringent than requirements in most of the
states, this demand seemed far from insuperable, and the
party set out to amass and file its petitions. There appears to
have been a tacit understanding that the Republicans in the
state administration would look with favor upon the Progressive drive. Accordingly, third-party officials underestimated
the number of signatures likely to be invalidated in the downstate counties.

At any rate, the party filed petitions bearing some 75,268
signatures and claimed that they possessed the requisite 200
in each of *sixty-two* counties. At this stage, the politics of
the Republican Party entered the scene. Administration forces
of the view that the Progressives would help defeat the Democrats in the coming election controlled the State Certifying

Board, but not the State Officers Electoral Board.[4] This latter group was composed primarily of downstate Republicans violently opposed to the entrance of a third party. Confident of Republican prospects for November, 1948, they felt the party could win without splintering the Democratic vote.

The State Officers Electoral Board held that those persons who had voted in the April primaries of either major party could not validly sign third-party petitions. It ruled that the petitions lacked a few valid signatures (in the downstate counties) of the required total. (Unofficial reports placed the figure at eight.) The Progressives objected, claiming that since no presidential electors had been chosen in April, their signatories had a right to sign third-party petitions for those offices. Moreover, they claimed that the state law itself was invalid. An appeal was taken to the Illinois State Supreme Court, which ruled that it had no power to review the facts before the board.

The next move was to prepare a new case for submission to a special three-member Federal District Court, where an injunction was sought on the grounds that action in ruling the Progressives off the ballot was being taken under statutory provisions repugnant to the Federal Constitution. The third party claimed that the law deprived large numbers of Illinois citizens of their political rights as guaranteed by the Fourteenth Amendment, since it allegedly discriminated against voters living in Cook County (Chicago) and the remaining forty-eight most populous counties, which contained some 87 per cent of the state's voters. The Progressives argued that it

[4] Under Illinois law, the State Certifying Board, composed of the Governor, the Auditor of Public Accounts, and the Secretary of State, merely received the petitions. In the event of objections, the State Officers Electoral Board examined the petitions and objections and informed the State Certifying Board of its ruling. The latter was obligated to comply with the findings.

unjustly gave the power to rural areas, particularly the remaining fifty-three counties, containing only 13 per cent of the voters, to prevent freedom of choice by the rest of the state.

The District Court refused to grant the injunction asked for (*MacDougall* v. *Green,* 80 F. Supp. 725), and an appeal was taken directly to the United States Supreme Court on October 11, 1948. Acting with the speed required by the approaching election day deadline, the Court heard the case on October 18 and handed down its ruling only three days later. It sustained the action of the District Court by a six-to-three vote, thus keeping the Progressives off the Illinois ballot (335 U.S. 281).

In a brief unsigned decision, Chief Justice Fred Vinson declared for himself and four others that

> It is clear that the requirement of 200 signatures from at least fifty counties gives to the voters of the less populous counties of Illinois the power to block the nomination of candidates whose support is confined to geographically limited areas. But the state is entitled to deem this power not disproportionate.
>
> To assume that political power is a function exclusively of numbers is to disregard the practicalities of government. Thus the Constitution protects the interests of the smaller against the greater by giving in the Senate entirely unequal representation of populations.
>
> It would be strange indeed . . . to deny a state the power to assure a proper diffusion of political initiative as between its thinly populated counties and those having concentrated masses, in view of the fact that the latter have practical opportunities for exerting their political weight at the polls not available to the former. The Constitution—a practical instrument of government—makes no such demands on the states.

Associate Justice Wiley Rutledge wrote a separate concurring opinion in which he ignored the constitutional problem, because he felt that to order the party placed on the ballot at this late date might disrupt the Illinois electoral procedure.

However, in a vigorous dissent on behalf of himself and Justices Hugo L. Black and Frank Murphy, Associate Justice William O. Douglas wrote:

> None would deny that a state law giving some citizens twice the vote of other citizens in either the primary or general election would lack that equality which the Fourteenth Amendment guarantees. The dilution of political rights may be as complete and effective if the same discrimination appears in the procedure prescribed for nominating petitions. The fact that the Constitution itself sanctions inequalities in some phases of our political system does not justify us in allowing a state to create additional ones. The theme of the Constitution is equality among citizens in the exercise of their political rights. The notion that one group can be granted greater voting strength than another is hostile to our standards for popular representative government.

Political considerations also played an important role in this appeal to the Supreme Court, for the Progressive-Party position in the case was supported by the Republican Attorney General of the state, a member of the pro–third party Cook County faction. He and the Governor joined in urging that the Illinois statute be set aside as unconstitutional. As Arthur Krock pointed out in the *New York Times,* it was highly unusual for two state officials to be appealing to the United States Supreme Court for invalidation of their own state's law, particularly in view of the fact that the Republican platform was at this same time appealing for a restoration of States rights.

It is difficult to account for this Republican failure to agree on a program of concealed aid to the Wallace party, for the absence of the third-party slate was to cause the GOP to lose the state of Illinois to the Democrats in the November election. The latter received a margin of only 33,612 out of nearly 4,000,000 votes cast. The fact that the Progressive candidates had garnered some 313,000 votes in 1947 seems conclusive evidence that Henry Wallace would have siphoned off—even with a weak showing—enough Democratic votes to swing the state's electoral total of twenty-eight to Dewey and Warren.

Regardless of the factors involved, the Progressives had suffered their second and most damaging loss. Their hopes had been high in Illinois, and defeat came as a stunning blow.

Republican politics were also prominent in the Ohio court battle, in which legal questions were markedly different. According to Helen Fuller in *New Republic,* Ohio was "the worst legal headache of all," because the wording of a new election law left doubt about whether or not a new party would be able to qualify under any circumstances for a place on the ballot.

Initial action to bar the party in Ohio, however, was taken singlehandedly by Secretary of State Edward J. Hummel. Ostensibly a Republican, Hummel had obtained his state post through the unexpected and untimely demise of his administration-backed primary opponent and was regarded in Ohio Republican circles as "something of an accidental maverick." His motives, other than personal predilections, were difficult to discern. At any rate, he announced on June 4 that the New Party had been denied a place on the ballot by virtue of a 1941 statute barring "parties or groups engaged in un-American activities." The Secretary of State announced that an "investigation" had shown that the party was not entitled to a place on the ballot. At no time had he held a hearing, however, nor would he specify exact testimony or evidence that led to his decision. When the case was later appealed to the Ohio State Supreme Court, Hummel informed the court that "three of Henry A. Wallace's principal campaigners in Ohio were Communists."

A storm of protest was stirred up by Hummel's one-man verdict. The *Toledo Blade,* a Paul Block paper opposed to the Wallace party, remarked editorially:

> Things have come to a pretty pass, indeed, when Ed Hummel starts saying who can run for the Presidency here in Ohio . . . . Apparently our democratic processes have been subverted more than we realize.

The Wallace backers carried the case to the Ohio State Supreme Court, and Hummel's ruling was reversed.[5] But this was not the only aspect of the court battle in Ohio. Two methods of qualifying for a place on the ballot were specified in the Ohio election laws. First, it was *possible,* though barely so, to organize a new party by employing a highly technical and complicated procedure which entailed, among other things, obtaining some 500,000 petition signatures. A second method of qualifying independent candidates which necessitated far fewer signatures was also provided. However, a 1947 law, aimed at third parties, had so amended this provision that it was now believed impossible for a presidential candidate to run as an independent. Despite this belief, the Progressives had chosen the second method, that of qualifying independent electors, as the only feasible approach. Secretary of State Hummel, however, refused to certify the party's nominee, claiming that the 1947 amendment made no provision for independent candidates.

[5] *State* v. *Hummel,* 80 N.E. 2d 899. The Ohio State Supreme Court linked into this one case and decision two separate actions before it: *State ex rel. Beck et al.* v. *Hummel,* No. 31496 and *Zahm* v. *Hummel,* No. 31498. The court ruled in this first part of the case that the presence of 3 Communist Party members among a total of 46,000 petition signers did not disqualify the Progressives under the statute.

Progressive Party lawyers had uncovered a technical defect. The state legislature had neglected to amend the second of two provisions in the original statute pertaining to the matter. The party contended, and the court agreed (*State* v. *Hummel,* 80 N.E. 2d 899, Part 2), that the only possible consistent interpretation of the statute as amended was that it permitted the nomination of independent presidential electors, although the name of the presidential candidate might not appear. Thus twenty-five independent electors for Wallace eventually found their names on the ballot, but with no party or candidate designation and with no provision whereby a straight vote might be cast for the entire slate.

It was, of course, possible to vote straight for the Democratic and Republican electoral tickets. The inherent confusion in this situation led to an election ruling that favored the Progressives. Made by an administration Republican, Attorney General Hugh S. Jenkins, the decision may well have been politically motivated, since it ruled that all ballots found to contain a straight vote for the Republican or Democratic slate as well as marks for one or more Progressive (Independent) electors should be counted for the Wallace candidate, rather than being voided or counted as a major-party vote. Presumably, the Republicans expected that the Democrats would lose more from this system than they would, and that the votes thus acquired by one or two Wallace electors would prove insignificant.

With this one slim concession, the final outcome in Ohio was far from favorable to the third party. The Progressive electors were on the ballot without party designation, and a citizen wishing to cast his vote for Henry A. Wallace was faced with the necessity of making twenty-five separate *X*'s—one before each name. Thus, in two of the largest states—states whose industrial populations had been counted on to turn out a heavy Wallace vote—the ballot barriers had proved too steep for the third party to hurdle.

But what of the states where means other than petitions

were employed to get on the ballot? First, there was the failure—the third and final complete one—in Nebraska. Here
the party met the only defeat attributable to its own shortcomings. Nebraska law required an organizing convention at
which 750 delegates must sign a new party's filing petition.
Accordingly, the Progressives scheduled a convention for
September 10, 1948 in Omaha. But instead of the large
assemblage anticipated, exactly 283 delegates turned out. The
Nebraska ballot position went by default, as the Secretary of
State later ruled that presidential electors could not be nominated by the alternative petition means provided for *state*
candidates. The Nebraska State Supreme Court adopted this
view, refusing to issue a writ of mandamus to compel the
Secretary of State to accept subsequent Progressive petitions.

At about the same time a more successful convention was
held in the state of Mississippi, where there were no requirements concerning the number of attending delegates. Here a
small group of Negroes and whites utilized the occasion of a
Wallace visit to their state, in the course of a southern tour, to
hold their convention.

It was a highly informal affair—actually no more than a
luncheon—in Edwards, home of a Negro college where Wallace spoke. Following this, the presidential candidate himself
motored to the state capital to present his slate of nine
electors. Secretary of State Heber Ladner received them just
as informally, advising Wallace that he would request a
ruling from the Attorney General about whether or not the
legal requirements had been met, inasmuch as the state convention had not been preceded by the customary precinct or
county conventions. But, in friendly fashion, he went on to
inform Wallace that, if the ruling should prove unfavorable,
there would still be time to use an alternative procedure—
filing petitions of fifty signatures each by October 15. Ladner,
who was, coincidentally, a Dixiecrat, summarized the state
procedure succinctly, according to the *New York Times:* "It's
very easy to get on the ballot in Mississippi."

A similarly informal procedure was followed the next day in neighboring Arkansas, with Wallace again presenting personally to the secretary of state, C. C. Hall, his slate of seven electors. The comment of this gentleman, a *regular* Democrat, was in a somewhat different vein—a suggestion that Wallace, in accordance with state laws, file an affidavit stating that he was not a Communist. And although no further objections were raised by the States' Rights administration in Mississippi, the regular Democratic machine in Arkansas insisted upon barring the Wallace slate until the Progressive Party candidates signed the required affidavits. Far from conclusive, these two incidents provided an indication of the relative receptivity of the Dixiecrats and Truman Democrats from whose ranks Wallace votes were likely to come.

But what of the sole attempt made by the Progressives to capture an existing major-party mechanism—that of the Democratic Farmer-Labor Party in Minnesota? There had been indications at the time of the Wallace announcement in December, 1947, that the dissident DFL elements in Minnesota, led by former Governor Elmer Benson, might, by capturing the state DFL organization, force President Truman to run as an independent. This actually happened the same year in Alabama, where the Dixiecrats gained control, and it almost happened in Minnesota with the Progressives. Wallace backers were actually in control of the State Executive Committee of thirty-five, and, normally, arrangements for the state convention would have been left to this group. But in February their opponents, led by Mayor Hubert Humphrey of Minneapolis, accurately appraising the Wallace tactics, forced an unscheduled meeting of the 217-member State Central Committee in which they possessed a three-to-one supremacy. At this meeting the Humphrey rightists were able to set all conditions and name all committees for the state convention, including all seven members of the highly important credentials committee.

The Benson group was unable to make substantial headway in the series of county conventions that followed, although nineteen of these assemblages (out of eighty-five) selected leftist delegations for the June state convention at Brainerd. The Credentials Committee, however, refused to seat a single one of these nineteen delegations, and the Benson group "took a walk" to an already prepared rump convention at Minneapolis. Meeting the same day, they named a ticket of pro-Wallace electors as "official DFL designees" and presented this slate to Republican Secretary of State Mike Holm. On the advice of the Attorney General, also a Republican, Holm certified this leftist slate and refused later to accept the pro-Truman slate that was put up by the Brainerd convention.

Another court battle ensued, with the Minnesota State Supreme Court overruling the Secretary of State on the grounds that the Brainerd convention had been legally called and organized. (*Democratic Farmer-Labor State Central Committee* v. *Holm,* 33 N.W. 2d 831). Stating that intraparty matters were not open to court interpretation, it ordered the eleven electors pledged to President Truman placed on the ballot and those pledged to the former Vice President withdrawn.

Having failed in their capture attempt, the Wallace organization now needed two thousand nominating petition signatures for a place on the ballot. With an October 2 deadline allowing adequate time, they had little difficulty, but the fact that they were now the independent rather than the party designees weighed heavily against them. While the DFL ticket with Wallace at its head would not in all likelihood have carried the state on November 2, as it did under Truman, the third-party candidate undoubtedly would have received a far greater number of presidential votes than he did as an independent.

The possibility of a state Republican victory arising from this situation lent considerable support to conjectures that the Secretary of State and the Attorney General, both Republicans, were guided primarily by political considerations in accepting the Wallace rather than the Truman designees in view of the obvious invalidity of actions taken by the rump convention. Despite the assist, however, the Progressives failed in this, their only hope of getting on a state ballot under major-party listing.

Political considerations played a pre-eminent role in several other states—Florida, Georgia, and Missouri. In Florida, early in the campaign, the Progressives had little real hope of securing a place on the ballot. The state law posed a virtually impossible requirement—that of persuading 5 per cent of the registered voters to change their affiliations and enroll in the New Party prior to the May primary. With the books closing in March and April, the Progressives wound up with only some 7,000 or 8,000 instead of the 35,000 required. Campaign manager C. B. Baldwin conceded that the party had been defeated and would not appear on the Florida ballot.

But, following the split of the States' Rights Democrats at the Philadelphia Convention in July, 1948, the Florida Legislature found itself under pressure to amend the statutes for qualifying new presidential slates. An amendment was passed allowing electoral nominees to file without formality. With the legislature unable to write a law that would exclude the Progressives while including the Dixiecrats, the Wallace-Taylor slate was suddenly handed a place on the ballot in the state of Florida.

Similar politics were involved in Georgia. Here the law required petition signatures from 5 per cent of all registered voters, an estimated sixty thousand signatures. Registration books were reportedly in a condition making it impossible for a party to assume the burden of proving that all its signers were qualified. Yet this was precisely the ruling made by the Secretary of State—that the Progressive Party must prove all its endorsements had been made by enrolled voters.

Under the same Dixiecrat pressure found in Florida, the

Georgia Legislature amended its statute to permit merely certifying the names of presidential electoral candidates for the ballot. There still remained a non-Communist affidavit requirement, however, and it eventually became necessary for the Progressive Party to replace seven of its electors who refused to take such an oath. On the night of the deadline, it substituted electors willing to sign and thus qualified for a place on the Georgia ballot.

The question of qualifying *state* candidates was still pending, however, inasmuch as the pro-Dixiecrat amendment had affected only presidential electoral candidates. An appeal was taken from the ruling of the Secretary of State to another three-judge Federal District Court, on the grounds that the law, as interpreted, was unconstitutional. The special court, however, refused to accept the Progressives' contention, and there was no time to carry an appeal to the Supreme Court. Their presidential electors were on, but their state candidates remained off the Georgia ballot.

Finally, in the ballot battle political considerations were involved in Missouri. In this court test, there were factors dating back to the first Progressive presidential campaign—that of Teddy Roosevelt in 1912. At that time a pro-Roosevelt Missouri State Supreme Court had ruled that a group desiring to nominate presidential electoral candidates merely had to hold a meeting, call itself a party, and thus be entitled to place its names on the ballot. The Wallace Progressives called upon a lower State Court in Missouri to follow this 36-year-old case law and grant them places without petition signatures. Finding a distinction between the 1912 and 1948 cases, the court refused to certify the party's nominees. No appeal was carried to the state Supreme Court,[6] since in the meantime the Progressives had qualified, much to their own surprise, by the petition method. Despite objections lodged by the Pendergast

---

[6] Later, the Socialist Party appealed a similar case to the Missouri State Supreme Court, where its position was upheld.

machine in Kansas City, the pro-Pendergast Secretary of State certified that the Progressives had filed well over the minimum number of signatures required.

In this instance at least, the Progressives seemingly received honest and impartial treatment from a state election official who might have obstructed their petition filing. Some of Wallace's followers remained skeptical, suggesting that President Truman may have brought pressure to bear, assured that the state was safely his. Regardless of the motivation involved, the Progressive Party had achieved a place on the ballot in the President's home state.

Thus the Progressives wound up the 1948 battle to give the voters a choice with their candidates, under one party label or another, on the ballots of forty-five states.[7] Three significant conclusions emerge from this phase of the crusade. Once again politics had indeed produced strange bedfellows, for here were the parties of the campaign which were at opposite poles—Dixiecrats and Progressives—finding accommodation through their mutual necessity for a place on the ballot and their similar expectation of taking votes away from the common Democratic enemy. On the other hand, some state segments of the Republican Party emerged as less than politically astute or farsighted. Not only did they grossly overestimate their own political appeal, they also failed to take all possible steps to weaken the enemy by a thorough, if *sub rosa,* support of the Wallace petition drives that might ultimately have given them the electoral support of Illinois. Only the Democrats reacted as generally anticipated—opposing the ballot appearance of the Progressives with all the strength lent by

[7] *Statistics of the Presidential and Congressional Elections of November 2, 1948,* comp. from official sources by William Graf under the direction of Ralph R. Roberts, Clerk of the U.S. House of Representatives (Washington, D.C., 1949), lists only forty-four states, but the Progressives also appeared on the ballot in New Mexico as the New Party.

the conviction that theirs would be the ranks decimated by defections to the New Party.

Although the Progressives' few failures cannot be easily written off—those in Illinois and Ohio being particularly costly—they had been successful beyond all expectations in getting their candidates on the ballots of forty-five states. With an opportunity to cast their votes for Wallace-Taylor electoral slates all across the United States, the people would, in November of 1948, have a choice.

# CHAPTER 7

# Costliest Campaign

FOR A third party that has successfully hurdled the bars of organizing its machinery and of getting its name on the ballot, there remains perhaps the most difficult barrier of all—securing adequate finances. The task of conducting a nationwide campaign in a land as vast as the United States has always been difficult and expensive, and in 1948 costs were higher than ever before. Since 1944, there had been a marked inflation, and there were new and costly campaign media to be employed. While television had not yet come into its own, a single half-hour of radio time on a national network cost some $17,000, air travel by chartered plane between $1 and $2 a mile. For all parties involved this campaign was clearly the "costliest in the history of the nation," as Clayton Knowles observed in the *New York Times*.

What were the implications of this high cost of politics for the Wallace party? In the past, with only normal expenditure heights to hurdle, many a third party had come to grief. In 1924, according to party historian Kenneth MacKay, "The financial efforts of the Progressives had been such a dismal failure that there were insufficient funds to carry the candidate's train beyond St. Louis." In the light of 1948's even higher costs, would the new party encounter tremendous difficulty in securing sufficient funds or find it necessary to curtail expenditures drastically? What were the Progressives' goals? Where did they expect the money would come from?

Early in 1948, party strategists concluded that it would cost about $3,000,000 to finance Wallace's candidacy. They expected that the leftwing unions—chiefly CIO—and the Progressive Citizens of America would bear the brunt of their fundraising efforts. They anticipated that a program of paid admissions for Wallace rallies and speeches would raise about $1,000,000, with another $1,000,000 expected from individual members of leftwing unions, as well as substantial individual contributions from theatrical and other sources.

In the light of these expectations, what was the actual performance of the Wallace forces? To what extent were these contribution goals achieved? What techniques were utilized for gathering the funds? And how was the money ultimately spent?

The highways and byways of party finance are dark and devious for all American parties—major as well as minor. Following them is no task for the uninitiated. Yet the exploration must be made if the above and other questions are to be answered. Although federal statutes—the Hatch and Corrupt Practices acts—purportedly set limits on campaign contributions and spending and although they require the reporting of all such monies, they have proved less than effective in practice. In the first place, they exempt all political groups operating in a single state unless such an organization is a "branch or subsidiary of a national committee, association or organization." While they limit national group expenditures to $3,000,000 and individual contributions to $5,000, they fail to spell out any prohibition against multiple organization or multiple donation. Thus it has been customary for the major parties to organize as many separate groups as necessary to encompass the anticipated funds. And individual donors have found no restrictions on the size of their gifts to state organizations or the number of their grants to separate national groups.

With respect to the reporting provisions of the law, there has been ignorance, doubt, and even outright evasion, with little or no attempt to punish violators. The resultant impossibility of formulating any exact picture of the amount contributed to or spent by any party—whether major or minor, Republican, Democratic, or Progressive—has led informed observers to a double-the-visible rule of thumb as a minimal estimate of actual contributions or expenditures.

Consequently, the reported contributions of the two national groups of the 1948 crusade—the Progressive Party and the National Wallace-for-President Committee—have been measured against newspaper reports and party officials' estimates in an attempt to arrive at an answer to the question, "How much did the third party actually receive in contributions?" Party leaders' comments were particularly important in view of the accounting system adopted for the reports filed with the Clerk of the U.S. House of Representatives—a system that caused such an experienced reporter as Clayton Knowles of the *New York Times* to report a deficit for the party groups at a time they were actually enjoying a surplus.[1]

Having carefully negotiated the intricate report paths and made the necessary adjustments along lines pointed out by party leaders C. B. "Beanie" Baldwin and Ralph Shikes, it may be reasonably concluded that the two national groups of the Wallace campaign reported net contributions of approximately one and one quarter million dollars ($1,280,279.49). Campaign manager Baldwin himself apparently applied the double-the-visible rule in setting his estimate of over-all con-

[1] See reports of "$320,000 deficit" in *New York Times,* October 22, 1948, and correction by Ralph Shikes to "$7,525 surplus" in the *Times,* October 23, 1948. (These reports covered the period ending October 16, 1948.)

tributions at $2,500,000, although he admitted that his figure might be off by 25 or 30 per cent.


But where did the money come from? To what extent was the financing left to the people, as anticipated by Henry A. Wallace? In announcing his candidacy, the former Vice President had indicated his expectation that the common man—workers, housewives, and professional people all across America—would bear the financial burden. He had remarked wryly, "I certainly don't know any other way. I don't think the corporations will finance it."

On the basis of the reports filed, it is possible to reach a threefold classification of Progressive Party contributions: (1) individual contributions, both under and over $100; (2) paid admissions under $100; and (3) organizational contributions, including direct and indirect through the purchase of campaign material at cost. Although it is obviously impossible to determine whether the organizational contributions originated with large or with small donors, an over-all pattern in total giving can be discerned.

If the known national pattern is assumed to hold true for the organizations, slightly more than one half—57 per cent— of the Wallace contributions came from those donating less than $100 each. The figures for each grouping are shown in the table which appears on the opposite page.

By way of contrast, the reported figures for both major parties from 1920 through 1940 indicate that their contributions came far more heavily from large-scale contributors. For the six presidential years involved, the Democrats reported only 18.4 per cent of their funds came from donors of less than $100, the Republicans only 11.8 per cent. In this area at least, the 1948 Progressive candidate's expectations were fairly well realized. Far more than the major parties of his competitors, his Progressive following was, in

## TABLE A
SOURCES OF CONTRIBUTIONS TO THE PROGRESSIVE PARTY
AND THE NATIONAL WALLACE-FOR-PRESIDENT COMMIT-
TEE

| | | | |
|---|---|---|---|
| 1. Individual Contributions | 41.1% | | |
|   a. Under $100.00 | | 19.3% | $247,717.99 |
|   b. Over $100.00 | | 21.8 | 278,494.73 |
| 2. Admissions under $100.00 | 9.4 | | 120,883.27 |
| 3. Organizational Contribu-<br>    tions from State, Local,<br>    and Associated Groups | 49.5 | | |
|   a. Direct Contributions | | 34.0 | 434,982.87 |
|   b. Purchase of Campaign<br>    Material at Cost | | 15.5 | 198,200.63 |
| | 100.0% | | $1,280,279.49 |

terms of financial contributions, a "party of the people."

Topping the list of those who presented large-scale gifts to the Wallace venture was the late Mrs. Anita McCormick Blaine of Chicago, heiress to the International Harvester fortune. Available reports disclose contributions of at least $28,500 to one third-party group or another—$20,000 donated to the Maryland Progressive Party, $6,000 to the Montana Party, and $2,500 to the National Wallace-for-President Committee. Wallace, however, has estimated that Mrs. Blaine's contributions ultimately reached a total of more than $100,000. Two other women were represented by substantial sums—Mrs. Elinor S. Gimbel, one of the party's vice-chairmen and organizer of the Women-for-Wallace group, and Mrs. Luke Wilson, mother of the Washington, D.C., Progressive Citizens of America leader. Both were listed as having donated the legal maximum of $5,000 to both the Progressive Party and the National Committee.

The theatrical profession was well represented among the major donors, with such names as Paul Draper (listed together with his wife for a contribution of $100 to the Wallace Committee), Libby Holman Reynolds ($500 to the same committee), Lillian Hellman (two contributions of $500 each), and E. Y. Harburg ($1,000). Names with social connotations were also to be found—Margaret and Corliss Lamont, Mrs. Marjorie Sloan, Mr. and Mrs. J. B. Sloan, as well as Lady Pascoe Rutter.

From the left wing were millionaire Frederick Vanderbilt Field and Miles Sherover, who in 1938, according to the House Committee on un-American Activities, had been in charge of the Soviet-American Securities Corporation, an organization engaged in selling Soviet bonds to the American public. Another repeat donor was Dan S. Gillmor, of New York, who gave at least $3,500—two $1,000 contributions and one of $1,500—to the National Wallace Committee.

Although most of the party officials—C. B. Baldwin, Ralph Shikes, and Clark Foreman—were listed as having contributed on several occasions, Wallace himself was listed only once—for a $1,000 sum—despite his personal wealth. This substantiated the earlier prediction in the *New York Times* that "Mr. Wallace is noted for his careful personal spending . . . [he is] not expected to contribute himself." In all fairness, however, it should be remarked that the physical contribution involved in a campaign such as Wallace was to wage transcended any monetary donation he could have made.

Senator Glen Taylor, frank to admit that his congressional post was the best job he ever had, was not among the contributors, but, again, his share was in the strenuous labor of a national campaign rather than in its financing. His earlier remark, "If I do accept the offer [to run], it will be the first time in my life that I have had any money with which to campaign," was significant.

What motivated these individuals to contribute such large

sums? Certainly they had few expectations of any *quid pro quo* in a party whose chances were as slender as those of the Progressives. In fact, for many, mere listing as Progressive Party contributors led to immediate investigation by the House Committee on un-American Activities and to publication of the results of previous digging into their records by that august body.

In an interesting partnership, the Americans for Democratic Action compiled and Representative (later Senator) Karl Mundt of South Dakota inserted in the *Congressional Record* a list of contributors of amounts greater than $1,000 to Wallace groups together with their House Committee on un-American Activities dossiers. Although the committee's evidence may have indicated that Frederick V. Field, donor of $5,000 to the National Wallace-for-President Committee, had Communist leanings, most of the information was as nebulous as that about Mrs. Blaine. Of her, the Committee reported, "The *Daily Worker* of *January 11, 1938,* p. 2, listed Mrs. Anita McCormich [sic] Blaine as a signer of the Union of Concerted Peace Efforts, cited as a Communist-front organization by the Committee . . . *March 29, 1944.*" [2]

What, then, were the reasons that persuaded them, despite the likelihood of attempted intimidation, to support the crusade? Wallace himself had several suggestions to offer. First, he felt, many in the export-import trade contributed because party international policies would aid their business and because they had agreed with Wallace's position during the 1920's for expanding the United States's imports as a creditor nation. Second, he conjectured that large numbers of Jewish families contributed to the party because of their general "awareness of the international position and of world politics." To which might be added parenthetically, and because

[2] U.S. *Congressional Record,* May 5, 1948, p. A2887. Italics supplied for the significant dates.

of his party's position on the Palestine issue. The final factor, Wallace suggested, was personal friendship for himself or agreement with his over-all views. There were businessmen attracted by his work as Secretary of Commerce and a liberal group in a general agreement with his expressed foreign and domestic policies. Mrs. Blaine's contributions, said Wallace, came "absolutely out of the blue." She had read his book *Statemanship and Religion,* which had so impressed her that she wanted to give directly to its author. Wallace advised a party contribution as the best way of promoting his ideas.

Factors other than those suggested by the candidate may also have been involved. For instance, the well-to-do amateurs wanting to get into politics—such as the theatrical people—could do so easily by contributing financially. More difficult to explain was the mass phenomenon of the voluntary contributions from the more humble. The fervor leading workers in New York City's garment industry to shower the Wallace caravan with dollar bills from their windows, in the course of a district street rally, was typical. It may have been the desire to belong—the desire to merit membership in a crusade—that moved them, as it moved so many others, to dig down into slim pockets for a last handful of change to place in the collection box at a rally. In short there was something akin to "getting religion" on a political level.


Although there are relatively satisfactory sources for measuring individual contributions to the Wallace crusade, the material available on the associated groups is much less revealing.

For example, it is clear that the goal of $1,000,000 adopted by the National Labor Committee for Wallace and Taylor was never attained. Although individual union-member contributions were not taken into account, the reported organizational labor contributions of only $9,025 demonstrated conclusively the failure of the Progressive Party to achieve financial support from union sources.

The only definitely identifiable labor contribution of size was that of the Fur and Leather Workers Committee for Wallace, Taylor, and Progressive Candidates. This group, under the admittedly Communist leadership of Ben Gold, reported total donations of $21,230.99—"voluntary contributions of less than $100 each from members of affiliated locals." The word "voluntary" was disputed by fur manufacturers who testified before a subcommittee of the House that coercion had been employed to secure contributions. The union committee reported expenditures of some $19,-822.44 including a lump sum donation of $5,000 to the Progressive Party.

The Independent Political Committee of the Greater New York Council, relied upon to produce large sums from the metropolitan New York area, contributed only $1,425 to the national groups, although its direct expenditures were undoubtedly more substantial. The best party estimate available, that of campaign manager C. B. Baldwin, indicated that organized labor barely approached the halfway mark toward its million-dollar goal.

Contrast with this the estimated labor contribution of $1,-500,000 to the Truman campaign chest. Of this sum about $600,000 came from the AFL Labor League for Political Education, while another $500,000 came from the CIO Political Action Committee groups at one time expected to carry the Wallace banners. In New York the American Labor Party split proved costly, as David Dubinsky gathered more than $250,000 from his International Ladies' Garment Workers Union and its affiliates, which also went to President Truman and the Democrats.

Since much less was expected of it, the Nationalities Division turned in a relatively better, though hardly substantial, performance, primarily from East European sources—

Greeks, Lithuanians, Romanians, Russians, Serbians, Slovenians and Yugoslavs (all "hyphenated Americans")—but
also including Armenian, Italian-American, and Irish-Ameri-
can Committees. The Armenians and Slovenians were the
most successful groups, contributing some $3,500 of the
$5,407.20 total reported under the Nationalities banner.

Women-for-Wallace was credited with identifiable contributions totaling only $782.85. Yet a cursory glance at
newspaper accounts of their dinners reveals that New York
City branches of this group, led by the indefatigable Mrs.
Elinor S. Gimbel, secured at least $27,000 (net) from only
three such affairs. The figures for the national groups also
reveal a rather high proportion of women donating sums over
$100—31.2 per cent of those giving to the National Com-
mittee, for instance. It is virtually impossible to evaluate the
part that the women's organization played in producing this
result. Mrs. Gimbel, however, ascribed feminine support to
two main factors. First, she said, women were vitally interested in the "peace and home issues" that the Wallace party
espoused, and second, it was possible for a woman to contribute without fear of Red-baiting or of causing economic
losses that might have accrued to her husband's business, had
his name been listed as a donor.

The contributions of the Young Progressives of America
were negative. Theirs was the only subsidiary organization
that had to be supported by monetary transfusions from
various state organizations. Of their $18,993.66 total in-
come, about $12,000 came to the YPA from state bodies,
less than $7,000 from individual contributors. The National
Council of the Arts, Sciences and Professions was strong only
in New York and in California, where it expended directly
a total of some $38,000 ($1,500 more than it took in) on
behalf of the Wallace-Taylor candidacy.

The role of the Progressive Citizens of America is difficult
to determine, for midway in the campaign they merged into

the National Wallace-for-President Committee. Prior to that, their financial support had likewise been concentrated in New York and California, with only scattered strength elsewhere. The PCA spent approximately $82,000 and contributed identifiable amounts totaling $4,104.90 to the national groups.

On the basis of available information, it is impossible to discover either any direct contribution by the Communists to the Progressive Party or, more importantly, any possible diversion through individual contributions. The Communist Party reported a fund of some $20,000, made up of contributions from ten state parties, for its 1948 National Election Campaign Committee. Committee expenditures were only $11,982.02, with the balance of the $20,000 being turned back into the parent organization. Judging by this total, the Communists may not have been as well-heeled as they had been in earlier campaigns—or else their supporters gave directly to the Wallace party. The Communist Party in the United States had spent $162,040.45—for its own candidates—in 1936 and $89,548.26 in 1940. But, in view of the magnitude of Wallace financing in 1948 and the relatively modest Communist spending of previous years, it is evident that the party, while working actively for the Wallace candidacy, could have played no more than an exceedingly minor financial role.

Were there any significant geographical patterns of financial support revealed in the contributions of state and local groups to the two national organizations? Although donations were reported from groups in twenty-eight states as well as Puerto Rico and the District of Columbia, it is clear that four states—New York, Pennsylvania, Illinois, and California, in that order—constituted the major financial strength of the party. Not unexpectedly, these four contributed well over one half of the total organizational gifts that the national groups received. This pattern was in keeping with both early expectations and ultimate ballot strength, except in the case of Pennsylvania, where springtime dollars ran well ahead of November votes. It is impossible, however, to determine whether this situation in Pennsylvania was the result of high average contributions or last-minute allegiance shifts by Pennsylvanians who had donated to the Progressives and then voted for the Democrats—or had perhaps supported the Republicans.

A few other states ranked unexpectedly high in financial strength in view of the Progressives' platform—Texas in sixth place—and in view of the relatively small populations of these states—Colorado in eleventh. On the other hand, the weakness of financial support from Wisconsin spotlighted the Wallace failure to capture the public allegiance earlier given the La Follette Progressive Party. Ironically, in both Texas and Missouri, supporters gave the Progressive Party almost four times as many dollars as they ultimately gave votes.

But what of the means whereby the Progressive Party was able to obtain such sizable contributions? What were its strategy and techniques of fundraising—both national and local?

Few of the various techniques employed on national and local levels sprang into being during the 1948 campaign itself. Their origins were in the devices employed by the CIO Political Action Committee as early as 1944, when a one and one-half million-dollar fund had been raised to support the Roosevelt-Truman ticket. The Political Action Committee voluntary-contribution methods, including the paid-admission political rally, had been taken over and perfected by the Progressive Citizens of America during the preceding year. A test-run series of speaking tours undertaken by Wallace in

1947, utilizing both paid admissions and voluntary contributions, had netted some $265,000, according to Howard Norton in the *Baltimore Sun*. The PCA had also employed direct mail appeals, social functions such as dinners and breakfasts, and small house parties—always with the inevitable moment for passing the hat.

In 1948 the nation-wide tours of both presidential and vice-presidential candidates employed two PCA stand-bys—both the paid-admission rallies and the multiple-dollar-per-plate dinners. Two sources reveal the magnitude of the amounts realized by these methods: first, a "consolidated surplus statement" prepared for party headquarters; and, second, scattered newspaper reports during the course of the campaign, primarily in the *New York Times* and *Baltimore Sun*.

Party reports indicated that gross national cash income from "Tours (Wallace, Robeson, Taylor)" and "Fundraising Events" was $561,591.70—more than one half of one million. National expenditures were reported for the same items totaling $269,324.77, leaving a *net* income for the national groups of $292,266.93. With national and local groups sharing a fifty-fifty split, the combined over-all totals were approximately $1,120,000 gross and about $580,000 net income. Admittedly incomplete newspaper sources revealed a total of some three quarters of one million dollars from rallies and dinners, thus suggesting the accuracy of this million-plus figure.

While $100-per-plate dinners had been common to both Republican and Democratic fundraising in the past, the idea of charging admission to a political rally had been generally held to be out of the question. The Progressives were the first to try it on such a wide scale. The sums received demonstrated that it was as successful as it was unique. Instead of keeping audiences away, exacting an admission price had the opposite effect, according to party officials, leading to a much greater turnout than might otherwise have resulted.

Party workers entered enthusiastically into ticket-selling drives, and purchasers who had invested $2.40 in a ticket to hear Wallace had a financial stake to insure their attendance.

What were the details of this rally technique worked out by the Progressives in the 1948 campaign? All across the nation—from New York to California—the series of name meetings, campus assemblies, and ball-park rallies employed the same general scheme to swell third-party coffers. Admission prices ranged from a low of 10¢ at student gatherings to a high of $3.60 for choice seats at Yankee Stadium in September. For most events the range was from 60¢ to $2.40.

What was the audience's reward in return for the admission contribution exacted from it on the basis of the drawing power of the national candidates—Henry A. Wallace and Senator Glen H. Taylor? The Progressives acted on the theory, simple but previously untested, that a political rally can be just as well staged, well lighted, well timed, dramatic, and entertaining as a Broadway hit. While the exact role of the various playwrights, theatrical directors, song writers and others from the legitimate stage was difficult to assess, the end product of their cooperation exhibited all the finish and skill of a professional presentation. By comparison, the traditional Republican and Democratic meetings seemed dull, long-winded, and amateurish. And, above all, this new staging brought results—at least financial results.

At a typical rally, the festivities would start with a community sing as the audience was gradually finding its way to its seats. Then followed an invocation—often by a Negro minister—and introductory remarks by some local figure— maybe the party's candidate for state or local office. The script kept these remarks brief and pointed, just enough to set a pattern of urgency in relating the national campaign to locally important issues—Palestine partition for a Jewish audience, segregation and discrimination for mixed racial gatherings, peace and home issues for a predominantly feminine audience. Many times the local speaker would be a professor from a near-by university, perhaps a scientist portraying the immediate need for carrying out Progressive Party foreign policy to avert a new and overwhelming atomic world war. These preliminary remarks were all designed as warmup for the audience.

Once the party's ties to the community—its interest in and proposed solutions for local issues—had been exhibited, the scene was shifted gradually to national levels. A well-known actor or artist usually played the preliminary part in this transformation. Paul Robeson and Canada Lee were two who filled the spot frequently. With their professional training, histrionic and vocal talent, and, above all, their sense of timing, these seasoned performers would skillfully dramatize an important current issue, something out of the day's headlines, perhaps, to prepare their listeners for the actual fund drive.

The stage was now set for what came to be known as the pitch. This phrase, borrowed from carnival lingo, admirably described the performance of William Gailmor, who always occupied a spot on the bill. During the 1947 Progressive Citizens of America tour, Raymond Walsh had been the performer, but he had parted from the troupe when it took to the third-party road. Gailmor, a former radio newscaster, proved a natural for the role—a born pitchman.

At first, the rather stocky, almost completely bald, too nattily attired Gailmor would let the audience down from its previous peak, even arousing latent antagonism, especially in rural areas, with his New York attitude and manner of speaking. This first unfavorable impression, however, would soon be counteracted—dispelled by sheer oratorical ability. Linking personal anecdote to world problems, Gailmor had the knack of bringing remote affairs right into the room and of surrounding them with an air of urgency, a feeling of need for immediate action that only a third party—the Progressive Party—could successfully undertake.

By this time, generally a matter of some fifteen minutes, the audience would be well charmed—completely in hand. Then would come the climax:

> America needs a people's party. The Progressive Party is that people's party. Each of you needs a people's party —the Progressive Party—to carry the story of the people's needs all across this broad land of ours. But . . . that takes money, money to buy radio time to refute the lies being spread about the people's party, money to buy advertising space in the hostile press, money to let people all across the country see and hear Henry Wallace and Glen Taylor just as you are seeing them tonight. The Progressive Party lacks, and is proud that it lacks, the wealth of Wall Street and the gold of the industrialists. This party is not backed by the power of the militarists, the vested interests of both old parties. This people's party depends upon each and every one of you. Isn't it worth your while to help such a people's party?—a party that represents no cliques, no organizations of wealth, no combines of monopolists and cartels, but does represent you—the little people, the real people, of America.

"It ought to be worth"—then a planned pause, an overlong pause for "reflection" or receipt by mental transmission of an amount already carefully determined in advance—"it ought to be worth $1000 to someone here in this room to help carry the words of Henry Wallace the length and breadth of America, to print his speeches, to buy radio time . . . ." And with the request carefully tailored to fit the audience, there would be an almost immediate response. The drive was off to a fine start.

As the amounts asked for were progressively lowered—

"Who will give $50 to buy radio time, to print pamphlets . . . ?"—a new segment would be encouraged to dig down into its pockets for the party, for *its* party, for the people's party that depended upon it for financing. And finally, when the last ten- and five-dollar contribution had been milked out, there would come the exhortation for everyone in the audience to take a dollar bill out of his pocket. "Even if you can't give a dollar, take one out and hold it up in the air for the cameraman. Now wave them around, let Henry Wallace, who's waiting in the wings to talk to you, see that you're with him 100 per cent. Hold them up and wave them high! Higher still! Wave them around!" Then would come the payoff: "All right, ushers, take the bills away before they have time to put them back in their pockets."

About to leave the stage, Gailmor would dash back to the microphone to add, "A people's party depends on the dimes and nickels as well as on the dollar bills of the little people. Just reach down into your pocket and bring out the loose change you have there. Wouldn't you rather have it go toward your very own party—your people's party—instead of for beer on the way home tonight? Well then, put it in the containers that the ushers will pass among you."

The audience that had by these rites proved its worth and been accepted as partner in the "people's party" was now allowed its long-awaited glimpse of the candidate. The house lights would darken and a single spotlight pick out the figure of Henry A. Wallace making his way to the center of the stage, or down the aisle to the speaker's platform. With a sudden burst of vitality he would stride out, greeting them with the familiar Wallace smile and waving recognition while waiting for the tumultuous reception to subside. Finally, with the audience restored to order, the speech of the night for which they had paid so handsomely would commence.

The success of the pitch can be judged from the incomplete figures—the only ones available—indicating voluntary contributions at the rallies. The identifiable total—approximately $116,000—was probably less than one half of the amount actually realized, since the total take was shared with local sponsoring groups. No wonder that hardened political writers remarked that the Wallace tours had something of the air of a Billy Sunday revival meeting about them, with so many "converts" ready to part with dollars to promote their "new religion." As Milburn P. Akers, commenting on the success of a Minnesota tour in the midst of the winter's worst weather, wrote in the *Chicago Sun-Times,* "It's one way of financing a political campaign. But few politicians other than Henry could get away with it."

Although the rallies, with their inevitable pitch, held the center of the fundraising stage, the secondary feature of all Wallace campaign tours was the series of dinners at which the presidential candidate spoke. Here the technique was copied after the traditional major-party affairs, with the tariff varied according to the local situation. In April, 1,400 attended a $100-a-plate dinner in New York, while 425 paid $25 each at a Philadelphia banquet in October, and several hundred had contributed $12.50 each to a Hollywood session earlier the same month.

At these dinners, the touch for additional contributions was the main Progressive Party variation. Early in the campaign a "bed-sheet" technique was briefly employed in which four pretty girl volunteers carried the corners of a sheet into which cash, pledges, and checks were tossed. This approach enjoyed marked success in Chicago, where it netted some $35,000 at two meetings. However, it was later abandoned in favor of tactics similar to those employed at the rallies. Combining all these techniques, the series of luncheons and dinners brought to the party tills at least $202,000, and probably well over the quarter-million-dollar mark.

Party reports, newspaper accounts, and personal attendance—all substantiated the conclusion that in their rallies and meetings the Progressives had been highly successful, going well over their $1,000,000 goal set early in the campaign. While the future applicability of such techniques to other campaigns and other parties was doubtful, their value to the Wallace-inspired groups in 1948 was tremendous.

While the pitch and the multiple-dollar-per-plate dinner were the mainstays of the parent bodies, with a percentage of the receipts diverted to state and local groups, there was a wide variety of devices employed by the latter directly. The range was almost as broad as the groups employing them, and their success almost as hidden as some of the localities in which they were used.

There were lunches and dinners similar to those noted above, but with less prominent guest speakers and smaller levies exacted. There were house parties—in the homes of local backers—on the precinct level, for which a canned version of the Gailmor pitch was available on phonograph records, as were speeches by Wallace and Taylor. A series of twenty-five home movies with sound was also produced for use at these smaller gatherings. The latter device was sufficiently unusual to merit discussion by the theatrical editor of the Sunday *New York Times.*

All of these media, in addition to presenting the program of the party, emphasized the need for funds. Form letters for direct mailing to selected lists were employed. One of these urged contributions to the Progressive Party on the occasion of Wallace's sixtieth birthday, October 7, 1948, "to buy *more* radio time, print *more* leaflets, hold *more* meetings, mail the truth to *more* voters."

There was also an attempt to imitate the remunerative Christmas and Easter seal drives of health organizations by utilizing "Wallace seals." Like the letters, these were mailed to select lists in the expectation that 90 per cent would return the expected donation ($1 for a sheet), 8 per cent would return the seals, and only 2 per cent would fail to do either.

There is no evidence concerning whether or not these optimistic goals were attained.

A four-page pamphlet was prepared to set everyone up for a contribution at the parties and meetings. Titled *Not a R— Cent,* this was, according to Publicity Director Ralph Shikes, "slanted to show that while General Motors, the DuPonts, Wall Street and Standard Oil don't give a cent to the Wallace-Taylor campaign fund, housewives, veterans, clergymen, steelworkers, farmers give their hard-earned dollars . . . because it's *their* Progressive Party." These pamphlets, like all the other printed materials, were made available to the local groups at cost. After June 1, 1948, the provision was added that "all orders from local groups will be for cash only." Some of the groups had been slow in paying the national committee for the literature supplied, and the national did not intend to carry any local groups, even to the extent of supplying them with gratis publicity material.

Other devices, such as auctions, raffles, and theater benefits, were also employed by local groups, particularly in the metropolitan New York area. Again, however, data for evaluating their success are lacking. On the whole, the techniques applied on the local levels were remarkable only for their diversity. For the most part they were evolved at headquarters level and transmitted to local groups for execution. While the total funds thus obtained may have been substantial, they were small in comparison with those from the national techniques that had proven so effective.

But what was the total cost of the Wallace campaign, and what was the pattern of expenditure? With funds coming in strongly and regularly, how were they employed? How did the national and state organizations share the burden?

On the basis of known expenditures in those states where such reports are available and known contributions from such groups to the national committee and party, it is possible to arrive at an estimate of the total amount expended on the state level for the Wallace-Taylor candidacy—an amount between one million and one and one-half million dollars. To this sum must be added a less firmly based estimate for the associated groups, derived from the few known figures and from a sense of expenditures resulting from long work with the party's finances. Bringing in Campaign Manager Beanie Baldwin's estimate of $500,000 spent by the leftwing unions, an estimated $50,000 by the women's groups, and $30,000 by the Progressive Youth of America, farm, and business groups, it is possible to arrive at an over-all expenditure total of some three and one-third million dollars—the best practicable

### TABLE B
OVER-ALL ESTIMATE OF TOTAL EXPENDITURES OF THE 1948
WALLACE-TAYLOR CANDIDACY

*National Group Expenditures*
Progressive Party, National Wallace-for-
President Committee (from reports filed
with the Clerk of the U.S. House of
Representatives)     $1,260,102.91

*State and Local Expenditures*
Exclusive of Contributions to National Groups (estimated)     1,325,000.00

*Associated Group Expenditures*
Reported (reports filed with the
Clerk of the House)     169,029.79
Estimated: Labor     500,000.00
    Women-for-Wallace     50,000.00
    Miscellaneous (Farm, Busi-
    ness, Student, Veterans)     30,000.00

        *Over-all Total*     $3,334,132.70

estimate. This total is clearly in keeping with Baldwin's mid-September estimate of $2,500,000 of expenditures through that time and is likely to be less, if the total is substantially different, than the actual figure.

Information about where the money went proves even more elusive than that concerning its sources. Full accounting is available for only the million and a quarter reportedly spent by the national committee and party, with only scattered reports to suggest state and local spending. Both committee and party records indicate that the national groups expended very little for local purposes, while substantial state funds were used on the national campaign.

Major national expenditures were for fundraising events ($207,624.50—18.2 per cent), tours ($61,700.27—5.5 per cent), campaign material ($171,589.46—15.0 per cent), and budgetary expenses ($583,484.25—51.0 per cent). The money expended on fundraising events and tours was more than balanced by the income received at these events. The national groups listed gross income of $561,591.70 for a net income of $282,266.93 from such sources. Campaign material was also on a better than self-sustaining basis for the national committee and party, with nearly $200,000 ($198,200.63) realized from sales at cost to local groups, leaving an apparent profit of more than $25,000 on this item.

Travel expenditures were remarkably low—especially in view of the extensive campaign tours undertaken by both Wallace and Taylor, many by planes chartered at high rates. Incidentally, the reports listed disbursements to Senator Taylor for travel but none to Mr. Wallace. This, however, does not indicate that Wallace paid his own expenses as he had in the 1944 campaign for Roosevelt and Truman. The explanation lies in the fact that the Senator traveled on an expense account basis, whereas headquarters paid Wallace's travel bills directly rather than reimburse him later.

The fact that the national group lumped more than one half of their total expenditures under an unrevealing budgetary expenses item makes it impossible to ascertain such items as salary expenses, the cost of office overhead, and the amounts expended on various advertising media. There is no precise way to determine just how much was spent on radio advertising, particularly in the later phases of the fall campaign. Wallace radio talks formed an important part of party strategy in the last six weeks, with some seven fifteen-minute addresses going out over a national network. At an estimated $17,000 per half hour, this represented approximately $60,-000 for this project alone. And, in addition to national broadcasts, there were many local ones employing transcriptions and records. Toward the end of the campaign, the party was so anxious to press the increased use of radio that it agreed to pay 30 per cent of the costs incurred by state and local groups for air time.

For the most part, however, the state groups were expected to contribute to the national, and they did so. Only a very small amount, some $43,000 (3.0 per cent) went from the national to the weaker state parties. According to the recollection of C. B. Baldwin, "most of this money was sent to the southern states for petition campaigns in order to get on the ballot. Also, some funds were sent to West Virginia, for the same purpose." And while an $1,800 contribution was made by the national to the Georgia Committee for Wallace and Taylor, the Georgia Progressive Party contributed $3,000 to the national Progressive Party. In contrast, $14,000 or 39.4 per cent of their total money was contributed by the Washington, D.C. organization to the parent bodies. And Professor T. I. Emerson estimated that some 40 per cent of the Connecticut People's Party expenditures of approximately $75,000 went for similar contributions to the national groups. This practice reversed the major-party pattern of national assistance to weaker state committees, for even the "weak sisters" in the Wallace camp gave more to national headquarters than they received.

What conclusions may be reached from this survey of Wallace party financing? How successfully had this major obstacle been hurdled? The over-all pattern was one of success. The party's national balance sheet was in the black, showing (on the basis of the available figures) an actual surplus of some $20,000, whereas a deficit is usually anticipated—even by major parties.[3] The total monetary goals set earlier in the campaign were achieved before its close. Unlike earlier minor parties, no plans were abandoned because of insufficient funds, no candidate left stranded through inadequate resources. The crusade had extracted the fiscal resources from which to forge its weapons in the "fight for peace."

And even though it had not emerged completely as the popularly supported mass movement portrayed by party publicists, the Progressive group could legitimately lay claim to being, in contrast to its major adversaries, a party of the people—a party of small contributors. Possessing its share of major contributors and first magnitude angels, the Wallace band had relied heavily and successfully on new and daring techniques—on the voluntary contributions of converts to its cause. This was a phenomenon unique—certainly on the scale employed—in American history, in which the true believers backed their faith and conviction with dollars and dimes.

On the other hand, there was the conspicuous failure of labor—both organization and individual alike—to respond

[3] In contrast, the Democratic National Committee reported a deficit of $263,935.59 for the campaign year 1948, and the Republican deficit for the same period was estimated at $300,000. The Dixiecrats reported a surplus of $1,360.42.

*Walt Partymiller,* York (Pa.) Gazette and Daily

*Reproduced from the Collections of the Library of Congress.*
*Cartoon by Dowling,* New York Herald Tribune.

Henry Wallace's third party: varying points of view.

# "Listen! Listen To The People Cheering!"

Reproduced from the Collections of the Library of Congress.
Cartoon by Herblock © 1947 The Washington Post.

*Wide World Photo*

Crowd waving $1.00 bills for collection at the Henry Wallace rally held in the Cow Palace in San Francisco, May 18, 1948.

*Wide World Photo*

Delegates cheering Henry A. Wallace's nomination for President at the Progressive Party's national convention in Philadelphia, Pa., on July 24, 1948.

United Press International Photo

Members of the executive committee of the Wallace Progressive Party meeting on July 23, 1948 prior to the opening of their convention. Left to right, seated: Sen. Glen Taylor, Henry Wallace, Paul Robeson; standing: Rexford G. Tugwell, Clark Foreman, C. B. Baldwin, Albert Fitzgerald, Elmer Benson.

*Wide World Photo*

Henry A. Wallace speaking to a large crowd in Greensboro, N.C., August 30, 1948. Spectators threw eggs at Wallace; note portion of egg and shell in hair back of ear.

*Wide World Photo*

Members of audience gathered at Peekskill, N.Y. Sept. 4, 1949, to hear singer Paul Robeson, watching parade of protesting veterans.

*Wide World Photo*

About 8,000 people jamming 38th St., New York City, in Oct., 1948 to hear Henry A. Wallace.

to the call. Labor's million-dollar investment in the 1948 campaign went to the party and candidate that, lesser evil or not, had a chance of winning. And geographically, financial support for the new party proved extremely narrow—limited for the most part to the coastal, industrial confines and never reaching the main streams of middle America, even in those areas where political dissent had a proud heritage.

But measured by the most critical device of all, ultimate strength at the polls, the Progressives' financial success was to prove completely out of keeping. On the basis of the 1,156,103 votes received in November, the Wallace party had spent an average of nearly $3 per vote—the highest ever recorded in an American campaign. For even in the infamous 1926 Pepper-Vare Pennsylvania primary fight where, according to Professor V. O. Key, "the Pepper supporters set the highest recorded figures for expenditure per vote received," they had achieved an average level of only $2.42. Certainly, if cost be measured in average expenditure per vote, the Progressives had come up with the costliest campaign of American history.[4] As one observer bitingly remarked, not without some measure of truth, "Back where I come from, they could have *bought* their votes cheaper than that."

[4] By way of contrast, the States' Rights Democrats (Dixiecrats) received 1,169,021 votes after their reported expenditure of only $160,081.66—approximately 14¢ per vote.

# CHAPTER 8

# "The Same Old
# Merry-Go-Round"

BY THE close of June, 1948, it began to appear that the Wallace Progressive Party had been waging a losing battle in the spring campaign of its "fight for peace." Despite an occasional skirmish victory, it had been greeted with a discouraging lack of support on the part of an increasingly hostile public, as well as an inexorable flow of world events, draining the vitality from its major thesis—peaceful coexistence. And now with evidences of a renewed liberalism in the Democratic Party, it was faced with the imminent loss of many of its own supporters and workers. Some had already departed, and early in July many more were wavering.

In the light of these trends, and in view of the fact that the third-party candidates and platforms were already decided, party strategists were faced on the eve of their Philadelphia Convention with a set of circumstances unusual to such party assemblages—major or minor. The chief problem was that of attempting to regain lost ground—of renewing public interest, of reviving the failing spirits of party workers, and of countering the press attacks that had proved so damaging during the spring. It should come as no surprise, then, that the Philadelphia Convention ultimately became a propaganda battleground more than anything else. The opposition—both party and press—recognized the situation and unleashed their strongest broadsides against the faltering crusaders.

With the Progressive seemingly accepting Professor Dayton D. McKean's thesis that a national convention is rightfully "a device of propaganda rather than a deliberative assembly," what would they do to sharpen this image, to make more effective the publicity value of their assemblage? Long before July they had evidenced an awareness that propaganda, to be effective, must be well done, both convincing and, if possible, entertaining. They had made good use of their adherents from Broadway to revise drastically the traditional party rally. They had added the professional touch in their staging, lighting, and timing. And they had demonstrated the power of the dollar—the dollar exacted in paid admissions and voluntary contributions—to cement support, to inject religious fervor into their political crusade.

When Beanie Baldwin announced that this would be a "new, streamlined people's convention," it seemed that the Wallace-ites were planning procedural changes in the traditional structure to make their Philadelphia meeting a professionally produced spectacle. The hackneyed form would yield, it was expected, to their dramatic touch and become a more effective instrument.

But, in addition to the publicity value of a national convention, party strategists also hoped to acquire "morale value" from their convention. As E. Pendleton Herring had so cogently outlined this aspect in *The Politics of Democracy:*

> The value of the convention lies in permitting the rank and file of the party to participate physically and emotionally in a common enterprise. Here are the men who must carry the brunt of the campaign. Here they have a chance to meet, to shout together, to act together, to feel together. The excitement and the turmoil of the convenion fulfill a useful purpose. The relationship of follower and leader is

seldom an intellectual bond. A common bond of sympathy, a common symbol, is easily grasped and equally binding.

For a party in the process of formation, with little patronage at its disposal, these factors seemed doubly important in the decision to meet at Philadelphia in July.

Who were these crusaders there assembled? How had they been selected? The chief characteristic of the selection system employed by the Progressives seems to have been an almost complete lack of system. Party affiliates included only one well-established organization, New York's American Labor Party, and only a few relatively well-developed groups such as California's Independent Progressive Party and Illinois, Pennsylvania, and Connecticut groups. For the most part, even as late as July, the vast majority of state organizations and Wallace committees were still in a rudimentary form.

In April a "Call to the National Founding Convention of the New Political Party" had gone out from the Chicago committee meeting to all "state parties supporting the Wallace-Taylor candidacy" and to all "state Wallace-for-President committees." It specified that each party or committee was entitled to send two delegates for each state presidential elector and might send additional delegates not exceeding four plus one alternate for each elector. Later this provision had been modified so that each state might send two more delegates per elector—a total of eight plus one alternate for each presidential elector. According to Campaign Manager Beanie Baldwin, this enlargement was made to accommodate a greater number of party workers in the populous states, such as New York, who were anxious to attend the convention as delegates.

With such a large number of delegates provided for each elector, it was not surprising that a total of some 3,240 attended the Philadelphia Convention.

State delegations were limited to a total vote equal to twice the number of their state electors, regardless of the actual number of delegates sent, thus providing for fractional voting.

Unlike the major parties in recent years, the Wallace-ites made no direct attempt to curtail delegations from areas of weak party support or to increase representation from areas of greater strength. However, this purpose was indirectly served by a provision that members of the National Wallace-for-President Committee (a total of some seven hundred) should be seated as delegates by virtue of their office, although they would not be entitled to cast a ballot in any roll-call vote. Since this committee consisted in part of "functional division" officers from such groups as women, labor, nationalities, and veterans, its membership provided a degree of functional representation new to American politics.

In the selective process itself there was no mandatory provision for rank-and-file participation. These decisions were left to the state parties and committees—a delegation no more democratic than that of the major parties in a state like New York, where selective power rests primarily with the county chairmen.

What of the products of this selective process? Gallery observers at Convention Hall had no difficulty in distinguishing them from their major-party predecessors. The most cursory glance revealed, as Helen Fuller noted in the *New Republic,* that "the average delegate was about 20 years younger and 30 pounds lighter than his Democratic or GOP counterpart."

In fact, the average age of the Wallace delegates was not much more than thirty, and only 40 per cent were over forty, according to party questionnaires filled out by 1,247 of those attending. Furthermore, nearly one third of the total number of delegates present at the convention were women, in marked contrast with the sparse female representation at major-party conventions. In addition, there was a much broader variety of professions represented. More than one third were union members; one fifth were veterans—mostly of World War II. Professional people—doctors, lawyers, artists, actors, writers, and teachers—constituted one fifth, while 9 per cent were businessmen, and only 4 per cent were farmers. Although no racial figures were gathered, the easily noted presence of large numbers of Negro delegates also set the Progressives apart from major-party conventions. Instead of the professional politicians—predominantly lawyers—making up the major-party conclaves, these were amateurs from all walks of life.

There was a sprinkling of familiar political names—Representatives Vito Marcantonio and Leo Isaacson, Rexford Tugwell, Paul Ross, and others—but the preponderance of party wheel horses usually so evident at Democratic and Republican gatherings was conspicuously missing. This fact, combined with the youth of the delegates, led Luther Huston to remark in the *New York Times* that the dominant atmosphere was that of the "soda fountain" rather than the "smoke-filled room." Moreover, the delegates to this convention behaved with a spontaneity markedly absent from the funereal Democratic assemblage a fortnight earlier. Staid Philadelphia received an introduction to party songs as youthful delegates joyously sang their way on buses and streetcars to and from Convention Hall. For, despite their slim hopes of victory—at least in 1948—these Progressives seemed possessed of a sense of mission and filled with the joy of "spreading the word."

But while most correspondents viewed these attributes of the delegates with equanimity and even approval, at least one, Rebecca West, attacked what she viewed as "attempts to sentimentalize the character of the convention by pointing out that it consisted largely of young people." To her, it was "as unappetizing an assembly as I have ever seen in America."

> . . . There were quite a number of young people who were very horrid indeed. They were the ones who were embryo

Babbitts, having their fling before they settled down to safe and narrow lives, stupid young people, too stupid to understand . . . .

. . . I never saw so many boys with the sullen eyes and the dropped chins which mean a brain just good enough to grasp the complexities of life and to realize that it would never be able to master them.[1]

Another distinguishing mark setting the New Party delegates apart from their major-party counterparts was their relative sobriety—in the alcoholic sense—in comparison with the earlier Republican and Democratic conventions. While not generally the subject of public discussion, many observers have pointed out, as has party analyst V. O. Key, Jr., that major parties often attempt to launch their candidates upon a tide of liquid cheer. There may have been several reasons for the Progressives' restraint—a sense of fulfillment in the work of the convention needing no further outlet or perhaps the simple economic fact that the majority could not afford to indulge excessively, for the affluence of the major parties was also conspicuous by its absence.

But at the same time that this "soda fountain" atmosphere, this youthful exuberance, provided a whiff of freshness after Republican and Democratic "smoke-filled rooms," it also demonstrated that the New Party was markedly deficient in political skill and experience. Practical know-how—acquired only through long years in actual campaigning—was possessed by very few. Most significantly, these delegates who had abandoned major parties were only vaguely aware of the important role of compromise in politics—even third-party politics.

---

[1] *Baltimore Evening Sun,* July 27, 1948. Progressive Party sources reported that her columns appearing in British journals were even more venomous.

With the delegates assembled, the "new, streamlined people's convention" opened Friday evening, July 24, 1948, in a profusion of traditional speechmaking. The keynote address was delivered by Charles Howard, former Republican Negro leader from Des Moines, Iowa. Following this, the Progressive label was officially pinned on the New Party in response to the urgings of Secretary C. B. Baldwin:

> Thirty-one New Party organizations have already named themselves the Progressive Party . . . . It has a tradition of independence. It expresses the fundamental spirit of America. I propose that we adopt that name.

The following morning witnessed the election of the permanent convention chairman, Albert J. Fitzgerald, president of the CIO United Electrical Workers. Following his address, the Committee on Credentials reported, as did the Committee on Rules.

The report from the latter resulted in a significant floor fight over proposed representation on the National Committee. Once the rules had been adopted, the Progressives followed the time-honored roll call of the states for nominations. Despite the fact that everyone in the hall already knew the candidate, the usual parade of nominating and seconding speeches followed, with every state present getting in at least one address. Finally, Henry A. Wallace was accepted as the presidential candidate by acclamation. The same routine started once more for the selection of the vice-presidential candidate. But, when California was reached in the call of the states, Paul Taylor, the Senator's brother and a delegate from that state, rose with a welcome motion. Inasmuch as the hour was late and the candidates were waiting to make a brief personal appearance, he urged that the nonsense (though his phrasing was not so blunt) be dispensed with and Senator Taylor's nomination proclaimed without further speeches. The weary delegates were all too happy to accept this revolutionary suggestion, and, for once at least, tradition went by the boards in the New Party Convention.

The candidates, Henry A. Wallace and Senator Glen H. Taylor, appeared briefly on the platform to be greeted by a tremendous ovation. For spontaneity, this demonstration seemed to those in attendance far more convincing than the obviously staged affairs of the earlier Republican and Democratic assemblages. Nevertheless, the enthusiasm was interpreted as sinister by at least some of the reporters present. To Joseph and Stewart Alsop, writing in the *Philadelphia Evening Bulletin,* it was a "macabre spectacle" that had

> not even been entertaining, simply because the well-oiled party machine allowed for no real surprises. The "demonstrations" have had that quality of loudly spurious enthusiasm which prevails in eastern Europe.

However, the high light of the convention—an open-air rally at Shibe Park—was still ahead. This event alone, of all the Philadelphia proceedings, exhibited the professional touch expected but so conspicuously absent in Convention Hall. Moreover, this rally at which the candidates formally accepted the nominations tendered them (despite the fact that they had already been campaigning for several months) marked several innovations for a national nominating convention.

Following their successful practice of charging admission for political gatherings, the Progressives attracted a near-capacity audience of more than 30,000 at prices ranging from $.65 to $2.60. And once they had paid their way in, the spectators were tapped for additional voluntary contributions. In this manner a total of some $60,000 was realized from the Shibe Park rally. In return for their donations, the audience was treated to a well-staged spectacle—designed to entertain as well as convert or further indoctrinate. First a few brief speeches by such party stalwarts as Vito Marcantonio and Paul Robeson. The Negro baritone, as befitting his professional stature, delivered one of the most moving addresses of the entire convention, then wound up his stint with vocal selections called for by the audience. Hand cupped to ear, his rich voice poured out his most famous songs—"The House I Live In," "Los Cuatros Generales" (of Spanish Civil War fame), and, finally, "Old Man River." Then came the inevitable pitch, delivered by William Gailmor, with contributions commencing at the $1,000 level and gradually working down through the loose change. Their participation nailed down financially, the audience was now ready to hear from its candidates.

Senator Taylor, speaking briefly and to the point, told the gathering that he was "proud to be associated with Henry Wallace in the founding of this new party" and "proud to be his running mate on the Progressive Party ticket." He promised a fight against the "forces that would bankrupt America by spending billions in a futile effort to bribe whole nations into becoming our mercenaries in a senseless struggle for world domination." Concluding, he was joined by Mrs. Taylor and their sons in a touching family rendition of "When You Were Sweet Sixteen."

The stage was now set for Henry Wallace's dramatic entrance. Spotlights followed him as, to an accompanying ovation, his car circled the park and stopped before the rostrum. The thunderous applause continued as he strode to the stand and began the feature address of the entire convention. Calling liberally upon the memory of Franklin D. Roosevelt, Wallace detailed his views on the desertion of the Roosevelt position that had necessitated the formation of a new party:

The party Jefferson founded 150 years ago was buried here in Philadelphia last week. It could not survive the

Pawleys, the Hagues, the Crumps, the racists and bigots, the generals, the admirals, the Wall Street alumni. A party founded by a Jefferson died in the arms of a Truman.

But the spirit which animated that party in the days of Jefferson has been captured anew. It has been captured by those who have met here this weekend with a firm resolve to keep our tradition of freedom that we may fulfill the promises of an abundant peaceful life for all men.[2]

Accepting the nomination of the Progressive Party "with pride," he went on to acknowledge the commitments made in obtaining the nomination—commitments to the people of America in hundreds of speeches across the land. These commitments he repeated—pledges of working for the common man, of seeking peace, and of making capitalism "progressive."

Thus concluded the high point of the Philadelphia Convention of the Progressive Party. But before moving on to its closing platform deliberations, a few comments should be made on other aspects of the staging employed by the New Party, as well as the atmosphere surrounding its deliberations.

Above all, there was the use of music. For this was a singing convention—songs of the people, not only of a few star performers, songs of the delegates, songs of the spectators, and even songs of the reporters. Old folk and popular tunes were decked out in new lyrics extolling both party and candidates and promising defeat to the old parties. "Great Day" for instance was reworked to predict: "One of these mornings bright and fair, Harry Truman won't be there." But the popular favorites were a catchy pair composed especially for the Wallace-ites— "The Same Old Merry-Go-Round" and "Ev-

[2] Text of Wallace and Taylor Speeches, U.S. *Congressional Record,* August 9, 1948, pp. A5362–65.

eryone Wants Wallace—Friendly Henry Wallace—Everyone
Wants Wallace in the White House." The latter had a second
chorus which, casting logic aside, wanted *Taylor* in the White
House, too.

Nor did the delegates need any urging to join in the singing.
The spontaneity exhibited in Convention Hall and at Shibe
Park bubbled over into the streets and into the buses and
streetcars of old Philadelphia. In fact, the singing was so con-
tagious that even the minions of a conservative press were
observed joining the tuneful proclamation:

> It's the same, same merry-go-round.
> Which one will you ride this year?
> The donkey and elephant bob up and down,
> On the same merry-go-round.
> The elephant comes from the North,
> The donkey may come from the South,
> But don't let them fool you,
> Divide and rule you
> Cause they've got the same bit in their mouth.
> If you want to ride safe and sound,
> Get off-a the merry-go-round.
> To be a real smarty,
> Just join the New Party,
> And get your two feet on the ground.

Then there was the atmosphere of the convention. The reporter who described it as that of the "soda fountain" rather
than of the "smoke-filled room" captured one aspect—that
of youth. But coupled with this freshness, this spirit of opti-
mism and hopefulness, there was a second and more serious
note—a sense of mission—to be observed in the delegates.
Like the La Follette Progressives of an earlier day, they,
too, felt themselves "born to set it right." In terms of lifted
morale, the convention was clearly a success, with the dele-

gates publicly enjoying a sense of participation hardly equaled at major-party assemblages.

But from the propaganda phase reflected in other aspects of the convention, the Wallace-ites were far less successful. They were consistently represented (or misrepresented) by a hostile press in such fashion as to convince the average voter that Union Square headquarters of the Communist Party in the United States had been temporarily transferred to Convention Hall in the City of Brotherly Love—that the Reds and the fellow travelers were completely running the show. As the Alsops interpreted it:

> The Wallace party convention here has not, of course, been a convention at all. It has been, rather, a dreary and sometimes nauseating spectacle, carefully and quite obviously stage managed by the American Communist Party in the interests of the foreign policy of the Soviet Union.[3]

And with network television coverage still in the future, most Americans had to rely upon similar biased reports for their understanding of the crusade.

Primary target of many newspaper attacks was the platform adopted by the newly titled Progressive Party. Formal work on this policy statement had begun with Wallace's declaration of candidacy. His December speech had designated the main goals to be pursued. First was a secure *peace,* based upon real understanding between the American and Russian peoples. This involved American repudiation of universal military training and removal of "the Wall Street–military team . . . leading us toward war." Second, *prosperity* was to be attained by curbing the "growing power and profits of monopoly" and

[3] Joseph and Stewart Alsop, "Third Party Is Stage Managed by Leftwingers," *Philadelphia Evening Bulletin,* July 24, 1948.

by taking steps to preserve American living standards by providing housing and lowering food prices. Third, *progress* was to be sought in curing some of American democracy's ills, such as racial segregation and curtailment of civil rights.[4]

With this declaration as a basis, the New York City headquarters staff had begun work under Lee Pressman, former CIO general counsel. At the April Chicago meeting, the presidential candidate had further outlined his views, and a platform committee had been established to work along these lines in preparation for the Philadelphia Convention. Professor Rexford Guy Tugwell of the University of Chicago was named chairman and pressman secretary of this committee. The New York group continued to work on its platform, while in Chicago a second draft was entrusted to Professor Richard Watt in consultation with Tugwell.[5]

The week before the convention, an advisory group of some sixteen members met in New York to resolve the differences between the New York and Chicago drafts. In addition to these two documents, the group also had under consideration two preambles, one composed by Paul Sweezy and Leo Huberman, the other by Scott Buchanan. From all these sources, the advisory committee was to arrive at a single document to put before the full platform committee in Philadelphia.

The New York draft emphasized the "anti-monopoly" and "drive to war" planks in terms that one observer, Professor John Cotton Brown, thought "doctrinaire." It was relatively brief—aimed at the man in the street, or, more specifically, the man at the factory gate. On the other hand, the Chicago

---

[4] Text of Wallace's Address, *PM,* December 30, 1947.

[5] For a complete discussion of Progressive Party platform considerations, see John Cotton Brown, "The 1948 Progressive Campaign: A Scientific Approach" (unpublished Ph.D. dissertation, University of Chicago, 1949).

draft was much more detailed, lengthy with economic analysis, its tone more moderate and scholarly.

The Sweezy-Huberman preamble was concerned chiefly with the "growing concentration of economic power," but its language varied considerably from that of the New York draft. The Buchanan preamble, patterned on the Declaration of Independence, used eighteenth-century terminology to attack a "20th Century tyranny of government" which failed to heed the needs of the American people and infringed upon their civil rights.

Inasmuch as all four of these documents were based on the Wallace position, there was relatively little substantive difference among them. Nevertheless, the difference of phraseology, of shading, and of intonation became the subject of dispute in the Advisory Committee. Eventually, however, the first three were compromised into a basic draft submission. Buchanan's preamble received little support, but was filed as a "minority report."

The following week, still in advance of the opening convention session, the full platform committee met in Philadelphia to ready a final draft for the convention. There was now essential agreement between the extreme leftists and the moderates on all major points. Regardless of press insinuations and interpretations, firsthand accounts of the closed committee deliberations agreed that there was no "Communist domination" observable.[6] Rather there was virtual agreement on the issues to be presented to the voters, as was to be expected with the earlier defection of those not in substantial agreement with Wallace's pronouncements.

Public hearings were held but seem to have had little im-

[6] The sole written account—that of Brown—is in full agreement with the recollections of "non-leftist" committee members interviewed by the author, including Professor Thomas I. Emerson and J. A. Keefer, administrative assistant to Senator Taylor.

pact on the platform, despite Dr. Tugwell's statement that
the third party wanted the "ordinary American" to aid in its
drafting. The sole modification was a more conciliatory plank
regarding old-age pensions, resulting from the virtual ultimatum served by Dr. Francis Townsend: "If they'll [the
Progressives] accept our whole program, then I'll be for them.
Otherwise I'll be indifferent toward them just as I am toward
the Republicans and Democrats."

On the other hand, those groups irreconcilably opposed to
the Wallace foreign policy position—the policy which was,
after all, the reason for existence of a third party—seized
upon these hearings to express their view that any opposition
to the Truman doctrine and Marshall plan must be Communist inspired. And since this opposition testimony was played
up by the press, the propaganda value of the public hearings
backfired against the third party.

Headlines heralded the "platform suggestions" of Americans for Democratic Action official James Loeb that "Mr.
Wallace's candidacy does not obscure the fact that the Communists and their collaborators guide the major policies and
word the major pronouncements of this party." Loeb's proposal that the party get rid of its "Communist grip" and
support the European recovery program became front-page
copy—even in the *Washington Post-Times-Herald*. In all,
some seventy-five different organizations and individuals offered testimony, with fifteen representatives of labor groups
and another fifteen from pacifist, world federalist, and related
organizations.

Ultimately, however, the most significant platform devia-
tion from the Wallace program came about as the result of
pressure *outside* the hearings—from the National Independent
Businessmen's Committee for Wallace. Whereas Wallace had
advocated a program of "progressive capitalism," this group
favored nationalization of basic American enterprises such
as railroads, merchant marine, power utilities, and banks.

Earlier, the candidate had offered mild opposition to their proposal, telling them that he was a "little more timid." He had, however, agreed that there was no question of the need to nationalize "all enterprises that depend for their profits on large Government contracts for arming the country," such as the aircraft and munitions industries.

Nevertheless, Wallace exercised no pressure during committee considerations to gain conformance with his own ideas. Professor Frederick L. Schuman brought up the matter of "progressive capitalism" only in the closing hours of deliberation. The committee members had gone without supper; the convention was already opening; and, in the words of Professor Brown, "the great majority of the tired committee members [were] apparently ready to nationalize as a sort of panacea and anxious to get through with the platform as soon as possible." No mention of "progressive capitalism" went into the platform.

In contrast, there were two instances in which the presidential candidate actively intervened in the formulation of the party platform. The first came when Dr. Tugwell and Representative Marcantonio reached an impasse over whether the platform should declare for independence or self-determination for Puerto Rico. This obscure dispute finally reached the stage where Tugwell was reported to feel "so keenly about it that if the present wording [independence] remains he will not present the platform to the Convention." The quarrel was resolved only at Wallace's urging of compromise language employing both words.

The second intervention came on behalf of a proposed world government plank. Professor Schuman, accompanied by Scott Buchanan and two other delegates, pressed his own views in a personal visit to Wallace's hotel room on Sunday morning immediately prior to convention consideration of the platform. He was able to secure the endorsement of the presidential candidate, who then asked Campaign Manager Bald-

win to talk to Lee Pressman as "the only one likely to object."
As a result, this Wallace-backed plank was accepted by the
Platform Committee and adopted by vote of the convention
that afternoon.

Once the committee had agreed on a final draft representing a compromise in tone and language between the militant
and respectable approaches of the New York and Chicago
drafts, it presented its findings to the convention for consideration and amendment. The ensuing session was both lengthy
and tedious—remarkable both for the number of minute
points brought up and for the fact that debate was unlimited
on all of them. Far from being railroaded through, the Progressive Party platform was subjected to a much more democratic, searching, exhaustive—and exhausting—floor scrutiny
than is customary for any similar major-party pronounce-
ment. Chairman Fitzgerald seemed determined that everyone
should have his say, even at the sacrifice of the dispatch with
which skilled gavel wielder Sam Rayburn had handled the
earlier Democratic delegates.

With the platform representing an already narrow viewpoint, most of the points at issue were too trivial to warrant
repetition. There were, however, two amendments of significance offered from the floor, only one of which received press
attention. This was the so-called Vermont Resolution that the
Progressives declare in their platform that it was "not [their]
intention to give blanket endorsement to the foreign policy of
any nation." The Platform Committee had no advance warning that this proposal was to be brought forward. Its presentation caught committee chairman Rexford Tugwell, presiding
at the time, by complete surprise. Following a hurried conference on the rostrum with Lee Pressman, Tugwell reached
a spur-of-the-moment decision to oppose the resolution. Several pro and con speeches ensued, with the main criticism
being that this simple statement might be construed as Red-
baiting. Eventually, the proposal was rejected on a *very close*

voice vote. The press, however, reporting the vote as "overwhelming," seized upon the incident to "prove" that the "Communist-dominated leadership" refused to permit any criticism, no matter how indirect, of the Soviet Union. Actually, the Communist fellow travelers were not the ones to rise in opposition to the Vermont Resolution, according to Ralph Shikes, since this group thought the resolution harmless.

But, once again, it was the press interpretation rather than the observed facts that caught the public eye. Professor Tugwell's snap judgment to oppose the Vermont Resolution was clearly ill-advised rather than "Communist-dictated," but its effect on the party was just as damaging.

The second floor amendment demonstrating significant disagreement in party ranks was that offered by the Pennsylvania delegation. Unlike Wallace, they felt the party plank on industrial socialization was too timid and offered a motion to include steel and coal in the list of industries to be nationalized. Their proposal generated little support among the delegates, however. After a brief discussion, it was decisively defeated.

Eventually, at the end of a marathon meeting some seven and one-half hours long, the platform was accepted by a weary group of delegates. From the staging viewpoint, this was the deadliest session of the entire convention. With Chairman Fitzgerald's reluctance to cut short any delegate wishing to comment at any length on any subject, this was free speech to the point of exhaustion.

What was the net effect of convention consideration upon the earlier announced program of Henry A. Wallace? A point-by-point comparison reveals few alterations. "Peace, Progress and Prosperity" became "Peace, Freedom and Abundance." But except for the spelling out of every point in fullest detail and the inclusion of the nationalization plank, there were few points which had not been specifically stated or clearly implied earlier by the candidate.

The American press, however, pounced upon the platform
as something new and radical. The *New York Times* head-
lined it as containing "Planks Like Those Foster Group
Seeks" that had been adopted "With Communists in Control."
It devoted some four columns to an itemized comparison of
the Progressive platform with that of the Communists adopted
May 30, 1948 in the attempt to press home this point.

More objectively, as Susan W. and Murray S. Stedman
pointed out later in *Discontent at the Polls:*

> With the exception of their foreign policy planks, Wal-
> lace and his colleagues stressed the familiar farmer-labor
> demands: curbing of alleged monopolies, changes in those
> portions of the law dealing with labor relations, public
> ownership of various types of utilities, raising the income
> of the "common man," extension of social security and
> welfare legislation.

Virtually all of these "abundance" planks of the Progressive
Party antedated Wallace and Taylor—as well as the United
States Communist Party—by many years.

The foreign policy planks of the party represented the
views of all those, including the Communists of course, who
had found it necessary to form a new party for their expression. As Helen Fuller commented in *New Republic,* "As an
issue in [the] convention, 'peace' drew strength from pacifism,
isolationism and religion as well as from pro-Sovietism."

A more objective appraisal than that of the contemporary
press would conclude that at this particular time there was no
serious disagreement over substantive matters between the
fellow travelers and non-Communist liberals within the Progressive Party. Once the quibbling over details was concluded,
both groups willingly accepted the basic tenets laid down by
Wallace some seven months previously. Nevertheless, the
press continued to portray the platform of the Wallace Progressive Party as the latest word straight from the Kremlin.

Still another "evidence" of "Communist domination" was uncovered by reporters in a different aspect of the Philadelphia Convention—the adoption of the rules for permanent organization of the New Party. The comments of H. L. Mencken in the *Baltimore Evening Sun,* while more acid than most, were all too typical.

> After lurking in the catacombs and sewers of the hall for three days, the Communists sneaked into the main arena . . . this morning, and put the innocent delegates to the Wallace convention over the barrel.
>
> Tonight the rules of the New Party are precisely what they wanted them to be, and their trusted stooges are sitting on almost every salient stool in the party organization.
>
> The Communists are old hands at such tricks, and get many with them almost infallibly. First they horn into places on the important committees, then they frame the reports thereof after the members have fallen asleep or gone home, and then they come in and bull the reports through in a din of words.

But what was the truth of such charges? The groundwork for the third-party structure had already been laid at Chicago in April. Most of the plan had been generally accepted and occasioned little dispute at Philadelphia in July. The rules battle that erupted involved a proposed alteration in the manner of distributing representation on the National Committee. Unlike their major adversaries who have customarily assigned two national committeemen for each state, the Progressives suggested that the larger states be entitled to an additional member for every five electors in excess of the first ten possessed by the state. There was little disagreement over this suggestion. But the report of the Rules Committee embodied a proposal to establish a sort of corporative representation on the National Committee for the several functional divisions of the party—Women-for-Wallace, labor, professional, veterans, nationalities, and youth groups. There were to be an additional forty members-at-large chosen from these groups by the geographically apportioned members of the committee.

The purpose of this proposal was to encourage greater participation on the part of the specified groups. It was reported by Helen Fuller that "top party strategists [were] aware that their real problem, if the Progressives [were] to survive . . . [was] to reinforce the shaky labor base." Then, too, there were well-known members of the arts, sciences, and professions whose names would lend prestige to the committee.

Far from being Communist-inspired, as the *New York Times* claimed, the proposal for functional representation, according to firsthand observer Brown, was not favored by the fellow travelers.

> The rule establishing this arrangement was originally opposed in the Rules Committee . . . by key left-wingers like John Abt . . . and Congressman Marcantonio, Chairman of the Rules Committee.
>
> The real pressure for the rule came from the labor people who were concerned over the weak participation of labor in building the party.

Marcantonio's reason for opposing the measure was obvious—it would weaken the state parties, including his own American Labor Party in New York—making ward and precinct work unnecessary for a voice in policy councils.

Finally accepted by the Rules Committee, the proposal ran into substantial opposition when it reached the floor. A recommittal motion was so closely contested on voice vote that a show of hands was called for. On his count, the chairman ruled that the proposal had been defeated, ignoring a delegate who persisted in the attempt to secure recognition for a roll-call vote. Toward the close of a turbulent session, with innumerable requests for minor modifications defeated, the convention, faced by its nominating session deadline, finally accepted the rules proposed by the committee.

The chief distinctions in the permanent party organization were two. First, there was the provision that a national convention be held every year rather than every four. This body was to constitute "the highest governing authority of the party." In this the Progressives adopted a plan similar to that of the Labor Party in Great Britain for annual policy discussions by an all-powerful national convention. Second, the rules provided for a large, cumbersome national committee which was to choose a national executive committee, meeting at least once a month. In this manner, it was hoped that a small operating group would constantly guide party policy. Finally, there was to be a slate of party officers with full-time administrative duties chosen by the national convention.

Numerous charges were leveled that this system must inevitably lead to leftwing control of the Progressive Party—under the assumption that the party-line followers would be able to dictate the choice of the strategically located executive committee. On the other hand, the plan was also open to interpretation as an attempt to improve the haphazard national organization methods employed by the major parties in the years between presidential elections. Democratic and Republican national committees, consisting of only one hundred members, have found it necessary to delegate most of their power to officers who have generally been hand-picked choices of presidential candidates rather than popularly selected representatives. In short, while the Progressives' structure was open to valid complaints of lending itself to potential domination by a single group, this risk is inherent in virtually all representative democratic institutions. Where reliance is placed upon popular participation, organized minorities are often able to defeat apathetic majorities. Had the Wallace

Progressive Party ever acquired the hoped-for numbers of active non-Communist supporters, it could never have been subjected on the basis of its structure to extremist control. Rather, it would have been possible for a non-Communist majority to have completely excluded the left-wingers from party councils, had they felt such action necessary to solidify their control.

Nevertheless, to the average newspaper reader, the third party had accepted "Marcantonio Rules"—a "Communist Follower's Code." Its very organization offered proof positive that the Wallace venture was "Communist-dominated."

To firsthand witnesses, other press distortions were glaringly apparent. The *Philadelphia Inquirer* reported the convention was distinguished by "apathy," "empty seats in the galleries," and "an audience that walked out while Mr. Wallace talked at Shibe Park"—"facts" observed by neither those in attendance nor television viewers. For the average citizen, relying on his daily newspaper, the Philadelphia Convention became confirmation of the fact that the whole crusade was only a Communist-inspired plot.

Consequently, from the propaganda view, the proceedings actually had a markedly adverse effect. Instead of gaining new converts, many previously inclined toward the Progressives were alienated by the convention image of the party. Exact measurement of the effect is difficult, since there were no polls taken on a before-and-after basis. However, the downward trend earlier detected by the polls continued unabated. By mid-August the Gallup Survey showed only 5 per cent of the electorate favorable to Wallace and Taylor.

Moreover, the Progressives failed to adopt a salable platform—one lending itself to publicity purposes. Instead of a brief, hard-hitting exposition, they wound up with a lengthy, detailed document far exceeding major-party pronouncements in verbiage. Failing to realize the lack of any necessary conflict between brevity and specificity, they nailed down every loose end in a document immediately relegated to the limbo of other party platforms.

In terms of building party morale, the convention was more successful. With few exceptions (the most notable professor Tugwell), the party delegates departed from Philadelphia in high spirits, confident of their party and candidates and of their own roles in a worthy venture.

On the other hand, the convention failed to reveal Progressive improvements in the national nominating procedure. With the exception of the Shibe Park rally, staging and timing were lost from sight. Party orators, as in major-party conventions, were both repetitious and long-winded. An archaic nominating procedure was adhered to rigidly, despite the fact that the New Party already had its candidates. And "democratic" discussion of a platform already settled upon deteriorated into extended wrangling over minutiae with too little time for major points. Possibly the most significant staging contribution of the Progressives was their use of music—the songs composed for them, the mass singing by delegates and spectators alike.

On the whole, while the Progressives attracted a new, young, enthusisatic, singing group of riders, they took them onto the traditional carrousel of their older adversaries. Instead of blazing a trail to the promised "new, streamlined people's convention," the New Party, too, wound up on "The Same Old Merry-Go-Round."

# CHAPTER 9

# *"The Fight for Peace"—*

# *Fall Campaign*

IN A sense, the fall campaign waged by the Wallace Progressive Party in 1948 was but a second act—a continuation of their "fight for peace" of which the spring campaign has already been described. And yet, by comparison with that earlier phase of the battle, this climactic drive exhibited markedly different characteristics. Whereas the spring campaign had varied considerably from the customary major-party preconvention maneuvering, the fall campaign was much more closely akin to the usual pre-election concentration on the publicizing of issues and the attempt to gain votes for party candidates.

Perhaps the chief distinction between the two phases of the "fight for peace" lay in the fact that by the fall of 1948 the Progressive Party was a going concern. Its organization had been established, its ballot drives for the most part concluded, and its workers already recruited. Thus its candidates were free to concentrate on their campaign tours and the issues they wished to emphasize. Save for the problem of finances— the paid-admission, voluntary-contribution rally remained part of the third-party tours to the end—the fall campaign was, on the surface at least, almost an orthodox American political venture, not too dissimilar to those of the past conducted by major and minor parties alike.

Yet many difficulties encountered by the Progressives remained unique to this party. Events beyond their control—events that bore the stamp of an intolerant America or a "made in Moscow" label—continued to have a marked impact on their success, as much as their own efforts and those of their adversaries. But first their campaign tours held the center of the stage.

On the whole, the pattern of the fall tours of Henry A. Wallace and Glen H. Taylor was quite similar to that of their earlier junkets. In both instances a constant attempt was made to link the over-all program of the Progressive Party to the more immediate issues of local significance.

This aspect was brought into clear focus in the very first speech of the fall campaign delivered by Wallace at Bridgeport, Connecticut on August 21. Speaking to a predominantly urban labor audience, the presidential nominee opened with an attack on the "misleaders of labor [who] have found redbaiting and Russia-baiting just as useful as the reactionary politicians have found it useful in covering their own failures."

Pointing up some of the unsolved problems found in the Bridgeport area, Wallace remarked:

> The old parties promise to build houses—and erect barracks; to curb inflation—and arm you; to expand social security—and draft you; to extend civil rights—and put you in a war economy where all civil rights disappear.

From here he found it but a short and logical step to an exposition of the need for the third-party peace platform.

> I am sure that . . . the common people of America will reject the treacherous hypocrisy of the Democrats as they will reject the more open reaction of the Republicans.

They will see that the bipartisan foreign policy is matched by an equally sinister bipartisan domestic policy.

The two old parties are, after all, the same. Given a foreign policy directed against the common man all over the world, they must combine on a bipartisan domestic policy directed against the common man in the U.S.A.[1]

Peace, then, was the underlying dominant note of the fall campaign, as it had been of the entire spring campaign— peace coupled with the attempt to link lofty and rather remote international theories to the practical bread-and-butter interests of diverse audiences all across the land.

In a series of four major campaign tours, the presidential candidate blanketed the nation, while at the same time his running mate was engaged on an equally extensive scale. In the course of Wallace's tours, the South, New York and New England, the Midwest, Southwest, and Far West, and finally the metropolitan New York–New Jersey–Philadelphia areas were covered by plane, by car, and by train—some 25,000 miles in all.

The first of these tours, through the South during August and September, was in many ways the most significant. Declaring his intention of following his and Senator Taylor's earlier precedent of addressing only unsegregated audiences and of refusing to stay in hotels enforcing discrimination, Henry A. Wallace embarked on August 24 on a tour that took him into seven southern states and twenty different cities in a single week. In Virginia, the first stop southward, all went peacefully, despite a state law banning racially mixed public assemblies. Audiences in Norfolk, Suffolk, and Richmond were not only unsegregated but quietly and courteously attentive.

But with the candidate's entrance into "liberal" North

[1] See the *New York Times,* August 22, 1948, for the text of Wallace's Address.

Carolina, where no legal barrier existed, the fireworks exploded. A near-riot preceded the candidate's Durham armory speech. In the course of the scuffle, a Wallace supporter, James D. Harris of Charlotte, was stabbed twice in the arm and six times in the back. With order restored some time later, the half-Negro audience of 1,500 witnessed the most dramatic entrance of the presidential candidate's career—far more sensational than any conceived by his Broadway staging team. While officials waited at the main entrance, a seldom-used door on the opposite side was thrust open and in strode a uniformed National Guardsman, pistol in hand, followed by an unruffled Wallace surrounded by four plain-clothes men. Admitting to the crowd that this was "the most unique introduction I ever experienced," he proceeded with a speech, interrupted by the intermittent explosion of firecrackers and almost constant heckling. In this speech the third-party nominee outlined for the first time a "real states' rights program" for the South, entailing a billion-dollar development to end the area's "economic bondage to Wall Street."

The next day's tour of the Piedmont area in the same state witnessed an end to the bloodshed but saw the beginning of barrages ranging from eggs and tomatoes to peach stones and ice-cream cones, as Wallace attempted to address crowds in Winston-Salem, Greensboro, and Burlington. While his physical courage proved equal to the abuse, the candidate found a crowd of some 500 so completely out of "police 'control' " that he had to forsake his speech in the latter city.

It was only the following day, in Asheville, North Carolina, that adequate police protection was eventually furnished by the authorities. For the first time in the Tarheel State the third-party nominee was able to deliver a speech audible in its entirety. In it Wallace referred once more to the needs of the South—needs for improved health, education, and housing—which were attainable, he claimed, only with a peace program such as his.

But at Hickory, North Carolina, the same day, the egg and tomato barrage was so intense that Wallace once more had to give up entirely, remarking, "As Jesus Christ told his disciples, when you enter a town that will not hear you willingly, then shake the dust of that town from your feet and go elsewhere."

While President Truman and Governors Cherry (North Carolina) and Wright (Mississippi) issued public statements deploring the violence against the third party and its candidate, local police officials often took a different view. Not only did some refuse to furnish protection or prosecution (reportedly declining to arrest the Durham assailants of the party worker), but they instead accused the Progressives of deliberately provoking the incidents. The Salem, North Carolina, chief of police alleged, according to the Americans for Democratic Action, that it was "Commie John Hunt [publicity director of the CIO Food and Tobacco Workers] who started the 'down with Wallace' cries."

This same suggestion, that the Wallace-ites wanted to incite violence, was played up by the *Washington Star,* whose reporter Neubold Noyes, Jr., quoted party official Clark Foreman as saying, "If we'd had the same kind of quiet reaction here [in Greensboro, North Carolina] as we had in Virginia earlier in the day, then I wouldn't have liked it at all. This is what we wanted." Confirmation of such views is lacking from other sources, however, and while there undoubtedly were elements in the Wallace Progressive Party willing to resort to such measures and methods, most of the party's workers and officials opposed them. The vast majority felt that the prejudices and practices challenged in this southern trip were such as to require no artificial stimulation.

Moving on into Alabama, the Wallace party was courteously received in rural areas by farm groups, but from Gadsden's mayor came a wire that Wallace was not welcome and that segregation would be enforced if he persisted in plans to speak there. Accordingly, the third-party candidate refused to deliver his prepared address and moved on to Birmingham. There awaited another brush with Police Commissioner "Bull" Connor, the central figure in Senator Taylor's earlier encounter. Connor now took action to insure that Wallace, if he spoke, would address a segregated gathering. Retorting that he would not participate in an unconstitutional meeting because "we believe in free speech and free assembly without police restriction or police intimidation," Wallace and his crusaders once more shook the dust from their feet and went elsewhere.

In Mississippi, Governor (and States' Rights vice-presidential candidate) Fielding Wright acted in accordance with his earlier protest against Wallace's North Carolina treatment. Throughout the state police protection was the finest of the tour; Wallace's reception was a "combination of official courtesy and studied public indifference," according to John N. Popham of the *New York Times*. As will be recalled, it was in Mississippi that the state convention of the Progressive Party—a highly informal luncheon gathering at Edwards—was combined with the visit of the campaign party.

Following this, the caravan moved on to Shreveport, Louisiana. Here, on the advice of officials who reported the situation in their city "out of hand," Henry A. Wallace found it necessary to cancel a scheduled public address and speak instead by radio. From Louisiana, the party moved westward into Arkansas.

After another peaceful trip through that state—no public addresses were delivered, but ballot petitions were presented at the state capital—the tour moved on into Tennessee. Here, in the heart of the Tennessee Valley Authority country, Wallace received the first southern welcome that could be described as both warm and friendly. In both Nashville and Knoxville, according to the *New York Times,* the candidate was applauded as he laughingly told audiences:

I am expecting to see the day when every year, chickens, bred by the new methods originated by my son and myself, will return to the South 10,000,000 eggs for every one we have received. I hope they will be used exclusively for food —not politics.

Then, in more serious vein, he remarked that he had been deeply affected by the hatred and violence exhibited, but rather than losing his faith in the South, he had had it "renewed by the great, glorious and God-loving people of the South." Concluding his southern tour in the Volunteer State, the nominee returned by plane to New York to prepare for his next jaunt.

But what of the significance of this trip through the South? Brief though it had been, it had evoked the most violent response of the entire campaign. While Henry Wallace had challenged, successfully in most instances, those violations of the "freedom" plank of his platform—practices dealing with racial segregation and discrimination—he had also brought forth showers of hatred, abuse, and vilification seldom heaped upon a presidential candidate—third-party or not.

But once again the most enduring damage was not to the egg-bespattered candidate or to his party but to American political tradition. The personal indignities were quickly forgotten. The damage to "freedom" was much more lasting. The most devastated target of the southern egg-hurlers was democracy itself, which to endure must be based on the accepted right of all to a full, free, and peaceful expression of opinion—even when that opinion conflicts with the majority.

Senator Taylor personalized the issue, claiming that President Truman "started the whole thing with his remark 'Why doesn't Wallace go back to Russia?'" And while the President's tactics in getting out from under the Communist issue by shifting the onus to Wallace may have seemed sound party strategy for the immediate campaign, they were to prove ultimately disastrous to the Democrats themselves. For the intolerant wind sown in remarks such as these ascribing foreign policy differences to a lack of patriotism was to be reaped later in the whirlwind of emotion, prejudice, and violence of a McCarthyism directed against the administration.

Wallace, reviewing his southern experiences before a Madison Square Garden audience, pointed also to "the economic basis of hate and segregation . . . in the steel towns where it is profitable to keep labor divided." According to him, it was "the owners of mines and mills, the great plantations and newspapers who incite violence." As partial solution he called for enforcement of the second section of the Fourteenth Amendment—reducing congressional representation in states where the right to vote was abridged.

The effectiveness of the southern tour in attracting any great number of votes to the Progressive Party remained highly problematical, but the courageous battle of the candidates to make themselves heard attracted widespread attention. Outside the Deep South, even the bitterest opponents found it difficult to take issue with the party stand on the racial issue. The Americans for Democratic Action had to admit that

> In his *escape* to the South, Wallace made a visible effort to bring conversation around to the *non-controversial* topic of Jim Crow. Liberals applauded his precedent-shattering journey and denounced the attacks on his person and liberties, but . . . .[2]

Following the southern tour, there came a brief trip to Baltimore and Chicago, then through upstate New York and New England, with the emphasis on the "fight for peace" and

[2] Americans for Democratic Action, "Henry A. Wallace—the Last Seven Months of His Presidential Campaign" (mimeographed, Washington, 1948). Italics supplied.

its relationship to local issues. In Buffalo and Rochester, New York, there were attacks on "spending for war" as well as upon the war scares and crises allegedly whipped up by the administration "to help the industrialists." Taking his cue from the title of his earlier book, Wallace told a Buffalo assemblage:

> They have brought us 60,000,000 jobs, but their 60,-000,000 jobs do not bring homes to returning veterans. Their 60,000,000 jobs do not reassure our continuing prosperity. They do not even create the illusion of security. For their 60,000,000 jobs are not 60,000,000 jobs for peace.

In Boston, the Wallace attack on the vested interests continued, this time linked to New England's need for low-cost electric power—a need that must, according to the candidate, go unsatisfied as long as administration spending was for "military aid to a Chinese dictator and a Greek king," and not for the development of America's resources for America's people.

This brief northeastern tour was prelude to the most exhausting part of the fall campaign—a "grand swing" around the nation, covering some 10,000 miles in the next thirty days. By plane, train, and auto, the crusaders wended their way across the Midwest—Ohio, Indiana, Illinois, and Missouri. Wallace was simultaneously on the attack and the defensive. Supporting his party against President Truman's allegations— "The fact that the Communists are guiding and using the third party shows that this party does not represent American ideals"—the former Vice President retorted, "The Communists don't run the Progressive Party and they didn't run the convention." Taking the offensive, he assailed Truman as a "verbal liberal" who had only recently "grabbed at the coattails of the New Deal he did so much to kill." Furthermore, he added, the major parties "as constituted" were "merely

wings of the same party, representing the same interests"—
big business and Wall Street.

From the Midwest, the caravan dipped once more into the
South, this time into Texas. Once more Wallace became the
target for eggs and tomatoes as he spoke in Houston. Nevertheless, he continued his attack on segregation and "recurrent
war scares." Receiving courteous, if less than exuberant, receptions during the rest of its four-day Lone Star visit, the
party then moved on to a nine-day swing of the West Coast.

High light of the Southern California tour was a major address in Los Angeles. Speaking at the same stadium visited a
week earlier by President Truman, former Vice President
Wallace attracted a *paying* audience of at least 4,000 persons
more than were present at the President's *free* one, according
to Gladwin Hill in the *New York Times*. Here Wallace outlined in detail a numerically reminiscent fourteen-point plan
for peace.

1. Eliminate from policy-making power all men who
have a personal financial stake in the policy decisions they
help effect.

2. Take private profit out of the war industry business.

3. Make an international agreement for armaments reduction, in order to strengthen confidence in peace and
produce for human needs and not for human destruction.

4. Stop the exporting of weapons by any nation to any
other nation.

5. Resume unrestricted trade between nations except in
goods related to war.

6. Reaffirm the free exchange of scientific information
and scientific material between nations.

7. Re-establish in a vigorous form the United Nations
Rehabilitation and Relief Administration or some other
international agency for the impartial distribution of relief.

8. Put an end to the exploitation of colonial empires.

9. Reinforce in all possible ways the prestige and authority of the United Nations.

10. Remove occupation forces of all nations from Germany, Japan, Greece, Korea and other countries as soon as possible.

11. Announce a policy of refusing to use economic or financial pressure in order to wield undue power in the internal affairs of other countries.

12. End the peacetime draft and plans for the establishment of universal military training.

13. Work for a United Nations rule prohibiting any nation from terrorizing or intimidating member states by naval demonstrations, the massing of land forces or establishment of bomber bases within easy range of those states. This rule should apply both to the United States and Russia.

14. End the increasing dominance of the military in American foreign policy, thus invoking the wise policy of Clemenceau who said war is too important a matter to be left up to the generals.[3]

Many of these points were similar to those contained in the spring open letter to Stalin. Taken together, they indicated both the approach to and the pre-eminence of the "fight for peace" in the third-party position.

Another major West Coast address, this time in San Francisco, was devoted almost exclusively to American foreign policy—this time in Asiatic affairs. Attacking administration dealings with China since the failure of the Marshall misson, which he referred to as "the last gasp of American liberal foreign policy," Wallace warned:

Great social changes are abroad in the world, all of us know that.

We cannot stop them, not even by raising the cry of

[3] As quoted in the *New York Times,* October 3, 1948.

"communism" and pouring money, guns and bombing planes into the arsenals of Chiang Kai-Shek.

. . . our position in China at the present time is morally bankrupt and indefensible even from the standpoint of practical power politics.

In Indonesia and Southeast Asia our support of the colonial system in opposition to native peoples struggling to free themselves of it seems strange in view of our own beginnings as a colonial people who had to struggle to free ourselves from tyranny.

From Siberia to Siam there are more than a billion people out there in Eastern Asia, just across the Pacific. We and our children and our children's children need them as our friends—and heaven help us if through hysteria and stupidity we turn them into implacable enemies.[4]

These two West Coast statements, constituting the third party's indictment of and alternative to administration foreign policy, climaxed the presentation of issues in the fall campaign. And the Los Angeles and San Francisco rallies marked the high point in the candidate's air-stop tour of the nation. While the "grand swing" continued, through the Pacific Northwest, back across the Midwest, and on into Chicago, the decision had been reached by party strategists that this approach was falling short of the mark and that an increasing use of radio speeches was urgent.

While Wallace had embarked upon a radio campaign in mid-August and had continued a series of weekly talks since mid-September, he had placed supplementary rather than primary emphasis on this medium. However, in mid-October a $100,000 project was launched to bring the candidate's voice to the air twelve times in the brief weeks before election day. While the grand tour continued eastward from Chicago into Pennsylvania, it was no longer the leading device for

[4] Text of Wallace's Address, *New York Times,* October 5, 1948.

attracting attention to the Progressives' candidate and issues.

With personal appearances de-emphasized, the final pre-election days witnessed an abbreviated fourth tour to Philadelphia, New Haven, New Jersey, and New York City—a whirlwind trip with thirty-three speeches, many to street-corner audiences, in four days. Winding up the numerous rallies, Henry A. Wallace concluded the fall campaign of his "fight for peace" at Vito Marcantonio's traditional "lucky corner"—116th Street and Lexington Avenue in New York's Eighteenth District. In these last appearances, he was already looking beyond the election returns and to the continuation of the party, as well as backward over its accomplishments of the past year.

> We have proved that the source of every American trouble is the drive for war, that from this drive stems scarcity and high prices and shrinking wages and assaults on ancient American liberties.
>
> Already we have accomplished much and we have just begun. This campaign is but a single battle in a long war. Until the great issues facing us—peace instead of war, abundance instead of scarcity, health before wealth, men before profit, are solved in favor of the American people, the Progressive Party will remain the great triumphant fact of American life.
>
> And to this continuing fight, to the Progressive Party now and in the future, I pledge all my effort, all my counsel and all my life.[5]

So ended the strenuous series of campaign tours, in the course of which the presidential candidate had traveled more than 55,000 miles—25,000 in the fall campaign alone—and visited nearly every state in the Union. To the utmost of his

[5] Text of Wallace's Philadelphia Address, *New York Times,* October 31, 1948.

ability, Henry A. Wallace had carried the "fight for peace" directly to the people of America.

Meanwhile, vice-presidential nominee Glen H. Taylor had also been engaged in a nation-wide tour of his own. Little noted by press and radio and studiedly ignored by national news services and metropolitan dailies, the Senator, too, had taken to the road. Like Wallace, he soon found himself the target of abuse—both vocal and vegetable. Only the menu varied—in Florida it was eggs, in his native Idaho eggs and peaches.

And just as his receptions paralleled those accorded his presidential running mate, so the issues he presented were similar in all respects. To Wallace's somewhat remote and lofty idealism, however, Senator Taylor added a much warmer appeal—a folksier approach. As much at home on the platform as on the stage, Taylor delivered seemingly homespun performances as professional and polished as the Progressives' staging that accompanied them. And to Wallace's 25,000 miles, the Senator added a roughly equal amount as his contribution to the fall campaign of the "fight for peace."


With its basic emphasis upon rallies and tours, did the third-party campaign differ to any great extent from traditional American counterparts? The chief difference in the rallies lay in the fact that the Progressives charged admission to their events, took up collections, and were able to get away with this unorthodox method of fundraising. A second distinction was that the third party brought to its functions a measure of the professional Broadway touch—in staging, lighting, and planning—in the attempt to make good politics into good entertainment as well. And while the presidential candidate rolled up a new record for mileage covered in a campaign, he confined himself to the more conventional means of conveyance—air liner, special train, and auto caravan. There were no dog sleds or helicopters, and Glen Taylor had abandoned his horse a year earlier.

In addition to this primary campaign emphasis on tours, there was the increasing use of radio in the closing weeks of the campaign. It may well have been that the Progressives delayed too long and thus failed to reach a large potential audience, the undecided who stayed at home listening to candidates Dewey and Truman on the radio, while they were attracting to their rallies only those already convinced.

Perhaps the most distinctive aspect of the third-party techniques was the emphasis upon doorbell ringing both to persuade and to get out the vote. As Ralph Shikes, national publicity director, put it, "Because 99% of the press and radio is against us, the best means we have of reaching the voters with the real issues is through house-to-house canvassing." In this work the Wallace-ites employed the same techniques developed earlier by Shikes and by Lewis Frank for the CIO Political Action School in Washington. Compiled into a workers' manual, *Knock On Any Door,* there were such instructions as:

> . . . Concentrate in those areas where the natural Wallace supporters live . . . working people, minority groups, Negro people, farmers and small businessmen . . . the people whose basic needs are met by the Wallace program.

They also went on to list some "Do's and Don'ts" for volunteer workers:

1. Don't canvass too late, or too early.
2. Canvassers should be neighbors if possible.
3. Be "up" on local issues.
4. Seek points of agreement, not argument.
5. Secure hosts, hostesses for meetings.

Highly effective for the Progressives in certain instances, such as the February Isaacson election, the method proved far less successful for the presidential campaign itself. As Shikes remarked later, the house-to-house emphasis was "both a strength and weakness" of the third party. It had succeeded in getting signatures for the ballot drives—a situation where "legwork" was necessary. But when it came to changing minds of citizens already decided for the presidential contest, it was a different story. The technique evidenced the same shortcomings as the machine performances of the party bosses it had been designed to combat; it was best adapted to elections with small participation. In the face of a large turnout of uninstructed and independent voters, it was subject to swamping.

In addition to house-to-house methods, the Progressives also launched a virtual flood of printed campaign material—an estimated 25,000,000 copies of some 140 different leaflets, pamphlets, brochures, and other handouts. Printed in approximately seventeen languages, including Spanish, Italian, German, Finnish, Croatian, and Greek, they indicated the various minority groups to whom the Progressive appeal was directed.

The most ambitious of these was an eight-page tabloid newspaper, the *Citizen,* which made its first showing at the Philadelphia convention and then appeared sporadically until the close of the campaign. Another, *These 15 Million,* was a four-page tabloid aimed at the Negro voter. Its approach was indicated by a feature story that the "Stevens Congress," denounced by President Truman as the "worst in history" (the Eightieth Congress was only "second-worst"), had done a great deal for Negro rights, whereas the Truman administration had allegedly done nothing.

Much of the printed material consisted of locally mimeographed sheets which emphasized issues of limited scope. According to Publicity Director Shikes, "We frequently [found] such leaflets more effective than slick printed material or radio talks."

In addition to these direct party publicity devices, a new

weekly newspaper, the *National Guardian,* was launched as a result of the Wallace campaign. Originally planned as the *National Gazette* by York, Pennsylvania, publisher Jess Gitt, Progressive Party chairman in that state, the *Guardian*'s mid-October appearance was so belated that it had little, if any, impact on the 1948 campaign.

Far more impressive than the deluge of words in apparent effectiveness was the use that the Progressives made of music and singing throughout the campaign. Carrying on the tradition set at Philadelphia, rallies and meetings invariably opened with a period of audience participation in both folk and campaign songs. "The Same Old Merry-Go-Round" and "Everyone Wants Wallace" were sung out coast to coast in third-party circles with "several hundred thousand" song sheets reportedly sold. In addition, transcriptions and recordings were prepared for broadcast use so that the radio audience might also be introduced to the Progressives' singing campaign. And of course the Wallace-Taylor rallies always featured the rich baritone voice of Paul Robeson or the guitar and ballads of young Peter Seeger.

Completing the range of media employed, more than a dozen films were turned out for the party "on a shoestring by volunteers." These presented in cartoon, comedy, and dramatic forms some of the political issues of the campaign for presentation to home groups and small local gatherings remote from the paths of the touring caravans.

The Progressives left no stone unturned. They neglected no possible technique or medium—old or new, tried or unproven—for publicizing their candidates and campaign. From comic books to billboards, they attempted to blanket the nation.

But how were these efforts received? What responses did they evoke from the public? How did the Progressives' political adversaries react?

In New York State the American Labor Party soon encountered political chicanery from two sources: in Albany the O'Connell Democratic machine succeeded in infiltrating the Albany County ALP to gain Labor nominations for Democratic henchmen. These stooges then withdrew on the last filing day, leaving the ALP line devoid of all local candidates. In this manner the O'Connells expected to make it impossible for backers of the third party to vote a straight ticket and to create an impression of weakness by a nearly blank Row *C,* thus inclining voters to the full Democratic slate. This maneuver, however, was checkmated by New York Supreme Court Justice Isadore Bookstein, who ruled with a closer eye to justice than legal technicalities that the ALP's State Central Committee had the power to fill the vacancies, even though the September deadline for such action was a month past.

A second tricky maneuver came in New York City, where Tammany Hall organized a ghostly United Laborite Party, or ULP, hoping to gain a second line on the ballot for the machine's candidates and obviously expecting that many unwary ALP voters would pull down the ULP lever instead of their own. The courts rapidly rejected this transparent attempt, on the grounds that it violated a state election statute forbidding the adoption by a new party of any portion of an established party's name. This view of the lower court was upheld unanimously by the State Court of Appeals and the ULP died a-borning (*Marcantonio* v. *Heffernan,* 82 N.E. 2d, 298 N.Y. 661).

In the realm of more violent attempts to suppress the third party, further attacks came in the South, where five Progressive Party workers were abducted from the Augusta, Georgia, winter home of Pennsylvania chairman Jess Gitt. Despite the fact that Augusta Chief of Police C. J. Wilson claimed he was unable to find "a single piece of evidence to support their story," Georgia Bureau of Investigation Agent J. P. Hillen (identified by party workers as one of the abductors, yet assigned by the Governor to investigate the case) was reported in the *Baltimore Sun* as saying:

> The incident undoubtedly occurred, but it did not happen just as they stated it to begin with, and, after its commission, these people tried in every way to use the publicity to their advantage.

Furthermore, said Hillen, the abduction had taken place without, "any roughness whatsoever," and, anyway, the party workers "have been openly associating with the colored race in that locality." Such, then, was Georgia justice in the election campaign of 1948.

But the South was not alone in witnessing violent attempts to stifle dissent from the nation's bipartisan foreign policy. In Illinois, members of a Progressive Party caravan of senatorial candidate Curtis MacDougall were stoned near West Frankfort, Illinois, while police refused to furnish protection. MacDougall reported being struck by at least ten stones; a female worker was slugged; and all attempts to speak were suppressed. Following several unavailing phone calls, one party worker sought protection at police headquarters and was, according to the *Washington Post,* told by the Desk Sergeant, "We don't like you any better than they do. Get out of town." Later, Police Chief E. B. Ragland said his reports indicated *"only* that a bunch of fellows broke up the meeting because they apparently did not like what was being said." So much for the First Amendment in Illinois, or at least in West Frankfort!

In many cities less violent tactics were employed, as in Youngstown, Ohio, where a detective attending a Wallace rally compiled a list of contributors to third-party funds or as in Pittsburgh, Pennsylvania, where steelworkers attending Progressive gatherings were checked off on union lists as they entered the hall.

But perhaps the most common method of harassing third-party workers was to challenge their usage of sound trucks, public address systems, and street-corner meetings. Notwithstanding a series of court decisions upholding their rights in virtually every instance, the Progressives found their speeches interrupted and their speakers hauled down off rostrums. If, in the course of the arrest, a disturbance occurred or police instructions were resisted, officials then had a constitutionally airtight case of disorderly conduct against the offender.

A report of one incident in the *New York Times* was revealing.

Some city officials here [White Plains, New York] asserted recently that the police erred in refusing to permit public meetings on public thoroughfares if the meetings would not interfere with traffic. After conference, however, officials agreed to support the position of the police in the current cases, *which involve disobedience of policemen's orders.* [Italics supplied.]

This then was the atmosphere in which the fall campaign was waged—an atmosphere which gave prudent individuals considerable pause before announcing open support for Henry A. Wallace. Opposition forces were making the "fight for peace" a war of attrition rather than a battle for men's minds.

As the fall campaign progressed, it became increasingly apparent to all—observers and participants alike—that the "fight for peace" was not going well for the third-party crusaders. Despite the exhausting tours of the candidates, despite the wealth of funds and the myriad of methods employed to publicize both candidates and issues, it became obvious that new adherents were not flocking to the Wallace banners in any appreciable numbers; in fact, it seemed that the substantial following of ten months earlier was continuing to fade away.

Newspapermen accompanying the nation-wide caravan were quick to herald the decline in attendance at Wallace rallies, and, despite occasionally conflicting stories, they agreed on the trend. So it was with the pollsters. Soon to be discredited in their final forecasts, their surveys nonetheless accurately indicated the Wallace ebb tide. Rather than building to a climax with the close of the campaign, Wallace strength was slumping to an all-time low of only 4 per cent of American voters by mid-October.

As Cabell Phillips noted in the *New York Times:*

> The preponderance of the available evidence suggests that the chill winds of apathy have begun at last to affect Henry Wallace's public. The members of this group have developed an observable tendency to shuffle their feet and to sit on their hands.

Progressive officials publicly derided both the polls and the reports, predicting the turnout of a huge hidden vote. Secretly, however, they viewed with alarm the post-convention slump in the party's fortunes, with the last-minute shift to a radio campaign evidencing their last-ditch attempts to turn the tide of battle.

What were the reasons for the decline? Once again, events beyond the party's control or compass—events in Moscow, Berlin, and Washington—destroyed almost completely the possible appeal of its "Peace, Freedom and Abundance" planks. The remaining coffin nails were supplied by the party itself in its failure to overcome additional internal handicaps.

The final death knell to Progressive hopes of peaceful coexistence was dealt by their Truman-alleged allies in the Kremlin. The May thaw of Joseph Stalin, reflected in the exchange of letters with Henry A. Wallace, had hardened into June's Berlin Blockade. With continued Soviet intransigence during the fall, the cold war had begun in earnest. While Stalin's motives remain an "enigma wrapped in a mystery," his tough policies produced a clear impact on the American voter and on the third party. Instead of creating public pressure on the administration for a relaxation of containment, his actions crystallized support behind the bipartisan get-tougher-still approach of Truman and Vandenberg.

As Cabell Phillips remarked in the *New York Times,* the party had "lost much of its zealous appeal, chiefly because of the paradox of Mr. Wallace's pro-Russian policy in the face of the realities of Russian conduct in Europe and the United Nations." From the viewpoint of Howard Norton in the *Baltimore Sun,* this was the result of "a growing and spreading conviction among New Dealers and other 'liberals' that Wallace, wittingly or unwittingly is playing Moscow's game and is hurting rather than helping the cause of peace." And it was undoubtedly true that Russian maneuvers—during the spring in Czechoslovakia and now, during the fall, continued in Berlin—strengthened the feeling among the better informed that no conciliatory approach was possible. But newspapermen were all too reticent in accepting credit for the role of the press in instilling in the public mind both the view that Henry Wallace was, if unwittingly, a "tool of Moscow" and the concept that the Progressive and Communist parties in the United States were only "two doors into the same house." Nor were the gentlemen of the press quick to assess the part in the decline of third-party strength played by their own constant insistence, direct or implied, that all questioning of the bipartisan foreign policy clearly indicated either a lack of American patriotism, an affinity for communism and Moscow, or both. But, since the American public was acting on the basis of the information most easily available to it, rather than on the full facts in the matter, this continuing smear was undoubtedly a factor in the decline—a factor sufficiently important to warrant treatment in a subsequent chapter.

And while events overseas may have been little noted and not long remembered by many voters, domestic happenings began to attract their attention increasingly. Earlier rent by the centrifugal forces of the Dixiecrats to the right and the Progressives to the left, the Democratic Party finally began to pull its remnants together as an effective political organism for the first time since 1944. Roused from their funereal lethargy by the newly found "give 'em hell" eloquence of their leader Harry S. Truman, they began to fight against the inevitable loss to Republican candidate Thomas E. Dewey. Faced with disaster, the President began to shift his policies to the left. Freed by the Philadelphia walkout from the Dixie-crat restraining influence, he began to invoke the politically potent images of Franklin D. Roosevelt and the New Deal in a dramatic "whistlestop" campaign.

Pushed by liberal Democratic Party elements led by Min-neapolis Mayor Hubert Humphrey, the President adopted for the first time an unequivocal position on civil rights. Whereas only a few months before he had been attacking price controls as "dictatorial" and had been threatening to draft striking railroad workers, he now began to go "all out" to prove that his proposed Fair Deal offered all the features of the New Deal and more. The Truman who, ten months before, had been content to accept an anti-inflation measure virtually identical with that proposed by "Mr. Republican"—Senator Robert A. Taft (Ohio)—now assailed in vigorous terms the "no good, do-nothing Republican-controlled 80th Congress" which had refused to accept his proposals.

Whether or not these were, as Wallace contended, only words—the mouthings of a "vocal liberal"—remained to be proven or disproven by history. But for the moment at least, Harry S. Truman was *talking* virtually all the liberal domestic policies so strenuously advocated by the Progressives through-out the campaign.

Even in the field of foreign affairs, there were indications that the Man from Missouri might be starting to yield. For in the midst of the campaign, apparently hoping to detract from the appeal of the Wallace "peace" plank, the President had suddenly prepared to send Supreme Court Chief Justice Fred Vinson on a new "Mission to Moscow" to explore ways of peacefully ending the cold war with Russia and the Berlin Blockade. Although this peace scare had been rebuffed in no uncertain terms by General Marshall and other State Department advisors, it seemed to indicate that Truman was abandoning the position of personal intransigence that had prevailed since the Potsdam Conference of 1945.

In the face of a third-party campaign which threatened to deprive him of the presidency, Harry S. Truman appeared to be making concessions all along the line, attempting to steal the thunder of the Progressives in the very midst of the campaign. And in so doing he was, in all except foreign affairs, promising to effectuate their advocated policies. Thus, on the domestic scene, regardless of the outcome at the polls, the efforts of Henry A. Wallace and Glen H. Taylor seemed certain to be crowned if indirectly with a modicum of success.

But in addition to the sweep of events outside the party, there were internal frictions and forces at work that may have played a part in the decline. Veteran newspapermen like Cabell Phillips, writing in the *New York Times,* felt that the Progressive Party was "beginning to suffer a certain degree of internal disintegration. Within its own radical constituency it seems to be suffering from the classical and hereditary ailment of all political parties—the incompatibility of right and left." But while it was scarcely to be denied that the left-right cleavage had indeed seriously affected party machinery in several states, this had remained fairly well hidden from public sight.

Such was not the case, however, with the widely publicized argument that the party was "deliberately attempting to split the liberal vote" in order to elect reactionary candidates to senatorial and congressional posts. Phillips argued that the party's "belated withdrawal of opposition to other liberal candidates cannot win back the independents who deserted on this account." According to Howard Norton, misgivings had been created "over the efforts of Wallace earlier this year, to defeat such outstanding 'liberal' Democrats as Helen Gahagen Douglas and Chet Holifield—efforts which cast a shadow on Wallace's claim to be the true prophet of the liberal movement."

Undoubtedly this belief, fostered by the press, had an important effect on Progressive support. For this threat, "The third party is going to elect reactionary Congressmen by 'splitting the liberal vote,' " was the constantly repeated theme of such groups as the Americans for Democratic Action. In the views of some, including CIO President Phillip Murray, there was a deliberate plot to elect purposely a "reactionary Congress" in 1948 so that the Progressives might benefit from a countertrend in 1952.

While the exact degree of influence possessed by this allegation in the decline of Progressive strength in the fall campaign of 1948 is difficult to assess, the truth of the charges may be examined with some accuracy. On November 2, 1948, the Progressives still had in the congressional races of twenty-five states a total of 114 House candidates of their own, plus a total of 9 senatorial candidates. In addition, they had formally endorsed some 14 Democratic candidates who carried both major- and third-party designations on the ballot. Prior to election day, they had, however, withdrawn a number of nominees from various congressional races as well as from the crucial Connecticut gubernatorial contest.

Criticism of their "belated withdrawals" stemmed from a news dispatch of September 30 in which it was reported that the third party was "withdrawing its candidates for thirteen House seats in five states." Actually, according to Ralph Shikes, publicity director for the third party, Campaign Manager C. B. Baldwin had released to the press a *summary* of previous withdrawals at this time in order to counteract the Democrats' and ADA's "splitting the liberal vote" propaganda. But in reporting this release, the press, he claimed, had so distorted the statement as to make it appear that the withdrawals had been newly effected. According to Shikes, the only "new" withdrawals had come some ten days earlier when the national organization had finally been able to convince local officials in Southern California of the need for withdrawing opposition to liberal Democratic candidates Douglas and Holifield.

These two races had been a continuing source of friction between local and national groups since early in the campaign. Following a discussion between Wallace and his campaign manager, the Progressive withdrawals were finally announced, but because of California statute, the third-party candidates' names still appeared on the November ballot, despite their support for the Democratic slate. And as noted in an earlier chapter, Connecticut gubernatorial candidate Thomas I. Emerson had been pledged from the first to withdraw his name if the Democrats nominated an "acceptable" candidate, such as Chester Bowles. As soon as Bowles received the nomination, Emerson *had* withdrawn, although his shift, too, was labeled last-minute.

Concerning the charges that there was a deliberate attempt on the part of the Progressives to "split the liberal vote," an excellent study—both scholarly and objective—was made by John Cotton Brown of ten different contests where this accusation had been made.[6] Brown's findings indicated conclusively that such was not the third-party purpose. Instead, they showed that seven other factors singly or jointly seemed to determine whether or not the Progressives endorsed a Democrat or entered their own nominee in opposition.

[6] John Cotton Brown, "The 1948 Progressive Campaign: A Scientific Approach," Chapter VI.

If the Democratic candidate was (1) *reactionary* by Progressive standards, which included such matters as his vote on the Truman doctrine, the peacetime draft, and the contempt citations of the "Hollywood Ten"; (2) *"unreliable"* concerning attitudes, receptivity to delegations, and liberal "leadership"; or (3) a *liberal with no hopes* of election, the Progressives refused endorsement. On the other hand, if the Republican candidate was a *"moderate,"* or if he would clearly owe his election to the third party's *balance of power* position and hence be likely to moderate his position, then the third party also tended to enter independent candidates. Finally, if there was actually a *chance of victory* for the Progressives or if party *power building considerations* were involved (such as retaining Negro support with a Negro nominee), the third party again refused to endorse Democrats and entered its own candidates.

On the basis of his examination of New York City contests, Brown found that

> The conclusion seems unavoidable that in New York City the ALP, by Progressive standards, did very little "splitting of the liberal vote," and then only for calculated and justifiable reasons aimed at increasing its political power. No evidence was uncovered that the ALP was deliberately trying to elect reactionary congressmen, and there was considerable evidence to the contrary.

In summarizing his findings on the matter of "splitting the liberal vote," both in New York and elsewhere, Brown concluded:

> The 1948 Progressives faced a political dilemma. If they endorsed "liberal" Democrats instead of running their own candidates they were building Democratic rather than Progressive Party power. If they ran their own candidates

against "liberal" Democrats they were "splitting the liberal vote," hence risking the partial achievement of Progressive programmatic objectives to which these Democrats, if elected, would contribute.

This dilemma was confused in the public eye by a general failure to distinguish between conflicting ADA and Progressive criteria of "liberalism" and by unsupportable propaganda charges that the Progressives were deliberately attempting to elect reactionaries through "splitting the liberal vote."

While particularly aggressive, non-compromising personalities of "militant" local Progressive leaders got out of hand, tactical decisions appeared to result more from emotion than from cold calculations of strategy. Latter-day moderation of militant Progressive opposition to "liberal" Democrats apparently resulted from a recognition that such tactics were defeating both programmatic and power-building objectives.

On the basis of these findings it seems clear that this charge of "splitting the liberal vote" was hardly substantiated by the facts, although it may have gained some credence by the sheer force of repetition and thus contributed to the Progressive decline in the fall of 1948.

But what of the press and radio coverage afforded the crusaders? Reference has already been made both to the silent treatment given the spring campaign of the Wallace Progressive Party by the nation's press and to the distortions that stereotyped the Philadelphia Convention as a Communist field day. This same trend continued and was even intensified during the fall campaign.

To cite one example, while the *New York Times* considerably increased its coverage, it continued to relegate news of

the party's tours and speeches to back pages, at the same time
devoting front page attention to Communist charges leveled
against the party or to stories of its decline.[7] And while the
*Times*'s accounts of the national tours were relatively objective, its editorial bias continued to be exhibited in local
dispatches whenever the American Labor Party was mentioned.[8] But by comparison with some of the less responsible
and less restrained journals, the *Times* was a paragon of virtue
both as to coverage and objectivity.

The dangers inherent in such a situation became apparent
in the course of the fall campaign, even to many who opposed the Wallace Progressive Party. Thus, anti-Wallace commentator W. B. Hesseltine felt compelled to protest in the
*Progressive:*

> The conspiracy of silence among the newspapers to sup-
> press news of the party and its activities reveals a danger-
> ous drift towards an un-American totalitarianism.

In addition to their conspiracy of silence and their slanted
news coverage, many American papers employed still a third
technique—the old device of the deliberately selected un-
flattering photograph. Senator Taylor was a leading target
for this method of reporting, beginning with the shots accompanying the story of his decision to run—shots suggesting

[7] For comparison, the story of the abduction of Progressive Party
workers in Georgia occupied a few inches on page 35 (October 3,
1948), while a story of the CIO Political Action Committee's prediction of party decline appeared on page 1 (October 17, 1948).

[8] For example, the following excerpt from an October 21 dispatch
by Douglas Dales: "Fundamentally the difference between candidates
[in New York's Twenty-fourth Congressional District] is the difference between the Communist party ideas of foreign policy as ex-
pounded by Henry Wallace and other ALP candidates in New York
and the bipartisan foreign policy of the Republican and Democratic
parties."

that only a dolt with a vacant expression (and presumably a vacant mind) would make such a choice. While Wallace had received similar treatment ever since entering the Roosevelt Cabinet, with press attacks on his "dreamy," "visionary" schemes, Taylor now received the full impact as the press portrayed him—in word and pictures—as little more than a hillbilly jester, a buffoon in high public office. This then was the "paper curtain" with which the party had to contend.

How may the fall campaign of the "fight for peace" be evaluated? In its effect upon the Progressives themselves and their hopes for a large vote for Wallace and Taylor, the fall campaign, despite the large-scale expenditure of time, effort, and money, failed to gain any substantial number of converts to the third-party fold. While the Progressives were untiring in their efforts to get their views before the American public, public reception of these views—except on the part of those listening directly to radio speeches or personally attending rallies—was another matter. The "paper curtain" proved more than an imaginary barrier—either preventing or making difficult an undistorted image of either crusade or crusaders.

On the other hand, the campaign tours were successful in focusing the spotlight of publicity on some of the things endangering American democracy—particularly in the South. And Wallace and Taylor had the grim satisfaction of seeing their Democratic adversary set forth for the first time a Fair Deal program comparable in liberalism to the New Deal— even while it stole the thunder of their own "Freedom and Abundance" platform. But, just as in the spring, they were helpless in the face of international events—the increasing intransigence of the Soviet Union—that completely debilitated the appeal of the plank encompassing their prime purpose—the promise of peaceful coexistence underlying their "fight for peace."

# CHAPTER 10

# *"Stand Up and Be Counted"*

TUESDAY, NOVEMBER 2, 1948, was to have marked the long anticipated climax of the Wallace campaign. Toward this day all the currents of the preceding two years, all the intensive efforts of the past ten months had been directed. For on this election day, the verdict would be rendered on the "fight for peace"—a verdict arrived at through the votes of jurors all across America. This was the day when the supporters of Henry A. Wallace would have their chance to "stand up and be counted."

Actually the day proved something of an anticlimax. Although few Progressives had seriously anticipated victory at this time, they had looked to other goals capable of attainment. Wallace himself had hoped to create the foundations for a new party—a broad liberal party all across the land that would serve the interests of the common man. The less ambitious had hoped at least to create a cohesive force without whose support the Democratic Party would be unable to win a national election. Thus their bargaining power for the adoption of liberal policies would be substantial.

The immediate objective on which all agreed was the turnout of a substantial Wallace-Taylor vote—a protest vote which would serve to indicate the strength of popular sentiment against administration policies, most of all against the negative Truman foreign policy of containment. To attain the minimal goals, the necessary vote was probably in the vicinity of five to six million—while a ten million turnout would have probably served to insure the party's future as a potent and enduring force. Failing this, if the Progressives' votes spelled the difference between success and defeat for the Democratic Party, their party might then be in possession of a weapon by which to gain policy modifications as the price of rejoining the Democrats.

The verdict of the American people came as a crushing blow to all these hopes. The total popular vote cast for the Wallace-Taylor ticket reached 1,157,140—just past the *one* million mark. Moreover, the Progressives failed to capture the electoral votes of a single state. Nor did they run second, ahead of either major party, in any of the states. In only three states, New York, Michigan, and Maryland, could they claim credit for having shifted the electoral outcome from Truman-Barkley to Dewey-Warren. Despite the Wallace defection on the left and the Dixiecrat defection on the right, Harry S. Truman had led the Democratic Party to victory and had achieved the impossible—re-election as President of the United States.

The depths of the Progressive defeat extended on down into the senatorial and congressional races as well. Only in the Eighteenth New York District were they able to elect a Member of the House. And here the candidate was the incumbent Vito Marcantonio, elected for a seventh term chiefly on the basis of his personal machine and following. The only other third-party Member in the Eightieth Congress, Representative Leo Isaacson of New York's Twenty-fourth District, was soundly beaten by a coalition candidate. And "Marc" himself had acquired only a plurality—a hint as to the future should Democrats and Republicans decide to unite on a single candidate. The completeness of the defeat was indicated by the fact that in only a few districts—two in New York City and several in California, Texas, and Wisconsin—

did the Progressive congressional candidates run second. And in every such instance, the victorious candidate had either received the nomination of both major parties or was unopposed by a major-party candidate. In both the Fourteenth and Twenty-fourth New York districts, however, the American Labor Party (third-party) votes were greater than those received by the coalition candidate on the Republican line.

The thoroughness of their rejection at the polls left little consolation for the Wallace-ites. Nevertheless, an examination of the election results may shed some light on the more prominent factors involved.

While surprising to Progressive Party followers, the magnitude of the defeat had been indicated earlier by the pollsters. Their sampling had shown a steady trend away from Wallace as the campaign progressed. But even they failed to gauge completely the depths to which the party would actually plummet on election day. From an early high of 11.5 per cent in February, the pollsters had charted a decline of popular sentiment to 7.5 per cent in April, 6 per cent in June and again in August, and to a final 4 per cent in the final days of the campaign. The actual Progressive vote amounted to 2.37 per cent of the total cast.

Voluble in their earlier explanations as to the potential errors in these poll predictions, the Progressives were finally silenced by the returns that came in on election night. In the midst of all the gloomy figures, there was but one relatively bright spot—New York State, where the Wallace-Taylor slate received a total of 509,559 votes on the American Labor Party line. While this marked the highest figure ever polled by an ALP candidate in the Empire State, it represented the result of continued organizational strength, rather than any substantial accretion of new voters. For in the 1944 presidential election, the Roosevelt-Truman ticket had polled some 486,405 votes on the ALP line, and in 1946 the Labor senatorial candidate, Herbert H. Lehman, had polled 435,846 votes. Percentagewise, the total in New York was less significant, constituting only 8.12 per cent of the state's vote. However, it was sufficient to transfer the state from the Democratic to the Republican column, the eventual Dewey margin being a scant 60,959 out of some $6\frac{1}{4}$ million votes cast.

By way of contrast, the Progressive performance in some of the states where they had expected to make a creditable showing, such as California and Pennsylvania, was highly disappointing. California had amassed a total of 482,781 petition signatures for the third party but delivered only 190,381 votes, a scant 4.73 per cent of the 4 million-plus turnout. Industrial Pennsylvania, expected to furnish a sizable Wallace following, actually reported 55,161 votes—a paltry 1.47 per cent. Thus the returns went—state after state filing negligible returns for the third-party candidates.

Party officials were quick to raise cries of election fraud. The Progressives had, they claimed, been "counted out." And, certainly, some of the discrepancies revealed by a comparison of ballot signatures and actual votes indicate some grounds for this suspicion, even discounting the proportion of persons who might have signed nominating petitions without thus committing their votes. For instance, in Georgia the party had obtained 60,000 to 80,000 ballot signatures, according to party officials, yet were credited with only 1,636 votes. In Massachusetts a total of some 110,000 signatures produced only 38,157 votes. North Carolina and West Virginia both indicated a "shrinkage" of about one third between petition and ballot. Missouri, with 53,000 signatures, turned in only 3,998 votes.

The nature of some of the claims was indicated in reports published in the *Baltimore Sun*. According to Wallace supporters, in Maryland

Votes were being bought right out in the open wherever you looked . . . . In most precincts the standard price was

$10 per vote. Men stood on street corners passing out dol-
lar bills like they were propaganda leaflets or something.

And, even when Progressive voters, resisting all these
tempting offers, finally got to the polls to cast their votes for
Wallace and Taylor, the party's difficulties were not over, they
claimed, as

Whole sheets of registrants' names were temporarily removed from loose-leaf registers. In Northwest Baltimore,
Dr. Camper [Progressive Party candidate for Congress]
lost thousands of votes through this kind of trick.

Party officials estimated that in Ohio nearly 150,000 ballots were voided as a result of the complicated voting procedure for the "independent" electors listed there.

In Michigan, some substantiation for Progressive complaints was revealed as a result of charges levied by Frank
E. Hook, defeated Democratic senatorial candidate. These
led to an inquiry by a field staff of the Subcommittee on
Privileges and Elections of the Senate Committee on Rules
and Administration. Hook had "reported that he was informed that election inspectors had not counted and he had
not been credited with approximately 36,000 votes representing Progressive Party tickets split in his favor." Interviews by the Senate investigators revealed that a large number
of election officials were ignorant of the law. Some had failed
to count split votes for Hook, as alleged, while others had
voided completely every ballot so marked. Third-party instructions had been to split their votes in this manner inasmuch as it had no senatorial candidate of its own. And while
this was completely legal, the Progressives found it necessary
to call upon roving inspectors to prevent less informed officials
from completely voiding ballots so marked. Complete surveillance had been impossible and many valid ballots thus ruled
void.

Other Progressive claims, lacking senatorial or other confirmation, involved a district in Missouri. Here, it was alleged by party official Ralph Shikes, an estimated 5,000 votes had been recorded as 500-odd. And according to party counsel John Abt, numerous party workers in many states had reported voting for Wallace and Taylor in their own precincts, only to find that their votes had never been recorded.

In spite of all these allegations, and even if one accepts as valid every Progressive claim—and it appears that many could be substantiated—the maximum estimate of votes lost in this fashion would not total more than 2,000,000. And even were these added to the credited total, the net result— a little over 3,000,000 votes—would still represent a dismal showing, an insignificant percentage of the nearly 49,000,000 votes cast.

Keeping in mind that the total Progressive vote was minute on any absolute scale, there may nevertheless be some significant revelations in a comparative examination. What does a sectional analysis indicate? How did they run in comparison with earlier third parties? A marked geographical pattern emerged in the percentage of state votes cast for the Progressives, even though performance on any absolute scale could be rated as only "fair" in the best of them—New York. (See Table 7, Appendix) In the top quarter there was only one other eastern state—New Jersey. All three West Coast states, however, were included—California, Washington, and Oregon. Three Mountain States—Montana, Nevada, and Idaho—and three north central states— North Dakota, Minnesota, and Michigan—were also near the top. The twelfth and final spot was occupied, surprisingly, by Florida—sole southern state in the upper half of the listing.

At the bottom of the list, the lowest 25 per cent was occupied by four border and five southern states in addition to the three states where the Progressives failed to secure a place on the ballot. Of the eight states just above this quartile, five were southern. Thus the pattern revealed strength—on a relative basis—in the Far West and Mountain States and weakness in the southern and border states. The latter was hardly surprising in view of both these areas' recent "orthodoxy" and the Progressive stand on civil rights and segregation. Moreover both anti-Russian feeling and internal anti-Communist hysteria were particularly marked in these same areas at the time.

The failure of the Progressives to capture significant labor or farm support was revealed by the relative showings. Industrial states such as Pennsylvania, Ohio, Massachusetts, and Connecticut were well down the list. And, with the exception of North Dakota, Minnesota, and Wisconsin—all states historically strong in dissent—none of the rich farm states of the Midwest placed highly.

A comparison of their showing with that of earlier third parties clearly revealed the weakness of the Wallace Progressive Party in failing to capture what might be called the "radical" or "insurgent" areas of America—states traditionally responsive to the call of political dissent. A comparison of the state percentages of total votes cast for minor parties from 1864 to 1936 with similar figures for the Progressives is revealing. (See Table 8, Appendix) Third-party planners had deliberately tried to enlist the support of those areas throughout the campaign. For example, in planning the strategy of the petition drives in Oklahoma, Kansas, and West Virginia, the rural areas of 1890's Populist support had been carefully charted and effort concentrated in them rather than in the cities which, on the surface, might have been expectedly more receptive to the Wallace appeal.

The Progressives, however, were almost completely unsuccessful in their electoral appeal to the areas of Populist support a half-century earlier. A unique geographical combination of mountain West and agricultural South had made up the 1890's revolt, the 1892 presidential candidate actually carrying four states, coming within a hair's breadth in three others, and receiving at least 10 per cent of the vote in eleven more for a national percentage of 8.63 per cent of the popular vote. But in 1948 the best the Wallace-ites could do in any of these was less than 4 per cent, and their national figure was only 2.3 per cent.

Nor were they any more successful in tapping the traditional discontent of those states where their earlier namesakes had run well. States like Wisconsin, Minnesota, the Dakotas, the Mountain States, the West Coast trio, and Iowa, where the vision of old "Fighting Bob" La Follette had conjured up a substantial 1924 vote—more than 30 per cent in ten of these—remained unyielding to the crusaders' call. Only in California did their response exceed 4 per cent. And while the La Follette Progressive ticket had carried only one state, it had doubled the Populists' national average, with nearly 17 per cent of the popular vote against Calvin Coolidge and John W. Davis.

Comparison with the Bull Moose venture of Teddy Roosevelt is less valid, since Roosevelt had carried with him much of the organization of a major party. While not a third-party movement, pure and simple, his candidacy received a national popular vote of 29.6 per cent, with only three states where the percentage figure was worse than Wallace's *best* state— New York.

In making these comparisons, it is necessary to keep in mind that while the Wallace Progressive Party hoped to appeal to the same groups reached by earlier farmer-labor parties, it had come into existence primarily as the result of *foreign policy* dissent. Unlike the previous ventures, it was not indigenous to the "radical" heart of the American West, but to the "internationalist" East and West Coast. Even in the latter areas, however, its banners were ignored.

But were there any positive correlations with known party strength? The relationship of Progressive Party votes to reported Communist Party followers will be discussed in some detail in the next chapter, but a statistical comparison is interesting at this point. Ten of the twelve states containing the largest numbers of known Communists were among the top fourth of Progressive Party support at the polls. And the top twelve, which contained 91.23 per cent of known Communist Party members, gave the Progressive Party 86.57 per cent of their popular vote. Caution should be applied in drawing conclusions from this close correspondence, however, since Communist Party membership reflected only one tenth of 1 per cent of the Wallace vote. The presence of both Communist and Progressive strength does not necessarily indicate any causal relationship, but it does suggest that the same conditions, surroundings, or population in these areas furnished atmosphere relatively favorable to both.

Were there any evidences of presidential "coat-tail riding" in the third party? The figures for the congressional and senatorial races are not very revealing, inasmuch as the Wallace Progressives furnished only 9 candidates for the 32 senatorial contests, and only 123 House candidates for the November 2 ballot. Nevertheless, it comes as something of a surprise to note the number of states in which the presidential ticket ran behind the local congressional candidates. There were six such cases—California, New York, Maryland, Oregon, Tennessee, and Virginia. By comparison, however, of the 170 Representatives and 17 Senators elected by the Democrats in 18 states in 1948, only 24 Representatives and 5 Senators failed to run ahead of Truman.

In New York, the difference (with candidates in forty-four of the forty-five districts) was not appreciable (512,148 to 509,559), but in California, where there were Progressive candidates in only fourteen of the twenty-three districts, the congressional aspirants piled up a total of 228,180 votes to only 190,381 for the national ticket. But examination of the situation reveals that in every district where an IPP candidate ran strongly, he was opposed by only one major-party candidate. Thus, under California's unique cross-filing statute then in existence, the only opposition in seven districts to the Democratic-Republican nominees was furnished by the Progressive candidates. Consequently, dissidents had to vote the IPP line if they wished to express their disapproval.

Even more significant is the fact that in not a single district were the Progressive Party votes crucial. Their ballots were insufficient to defeat a single Democratic candidate where they offered opposition, just as they failed, where they supported a liberal Democrat, to furnish him with his margin of victory or to prevent his defeat. Thus the threats of "splitting the liberal vote" to elect a conservative candidate proved as unfounded in the congressional races as they did in the big show—with the Progressive vote equally ineffective in both cases.

Little of significance emerged from the results of the senatorial races, save in Virginia where the votes cast for the Progressive candidate for Senate, like those for the nominees for the House, exceeded the votes received by the presidential ticket.

Endless speculation would be possible upon some of the facets thus revealed, or upon other possible conclusions, but eventually one always returns to the starting point—the poor showing made by the party at the polls.


What were some of the reasons that Henry A. Wallace received such an insignificant percentage of the popular vote? The more pertinent causes may be summarized under four broad headings. First, there were the handicaps under which the Wallace Progressive Party was launched and which limited its following at the outset. Second, there were some relatively constant conditions which prevailed throughout the campaign and which *prevented* the accretion of any large numbers of new supporters. Third, there were the developing conditions throughout the campaign which caused a considerable decline in numbers as 1948 progressed. Finally, there were other causes which might be classified as contributory rather than critical.

As will be recalled, the Wallace venture was launched without the support of any substantial segment of American labor and with virtually no support from farm groups. Moreover, the basic disagreement leading to the Wallace decision had centered about foreign policy—a situation unique in American history. For the Wallace Progressive Party offered the sole instance in which a new party had been formed on this basis, rather than borne in on some wave of popular discontent with more closely felt domestic problems.

Moreover, the socioeconomic climate into which the infant endeavor was brought was one hardly calculated to make it thrive. Throughout the campaign, three main currents of America remained relatively steady, none of which served to sustain the Wallace endeavor. Quite the contrary.

First there were the conditions of economic prosperity, full employment and high farm prices. Despite the inflation which greatly diminished the purchasing power of the dollar, there was more money in circulation. Of greatest importance to labor, there was work to be had and wages were moving upward even if prices were also moving upward at an even more rapid pace. From the vantage point of the farmer, the world provided a still voracious market, with resultant high prices for expanded production. And for the future there was the promise that price support schemes would never allow agriculture to fall again into the despair of the late 1920's and early 1930's.

In short, with factories humming and business good, why risk upsetting the apple cart? Historically, the ranks of the discontented and thus of third-party voters, have always been swollen by periods of economic crisis. Regardless of the weakness of its footing revealed only a year later, 1948 was a period of prosperity rather than crisis.

Second, there was the social climate of the times, best described as one of postwar reaction and mounting hysteria. The seemingly inevitable moral letdown was evidenced by increasing crime rates across the nation. Hostile sentiment was being whipped up by both press and radio against our recent wartime ally—the Soviet Union. Without attempting to disentangle economic aspects of governmental control from totalitarian actions of a one-party dictatorship, the same Red brush was applied to everything Russian, and "Communist" became the most vituperative of epithets. In such an atmosphere, as invariably happens, a premium came to be placed upon *conformity*—a blind, unreasoning acceptance of the dogma of the times. One who dared disagree with the accepted norm became immediately suspect, unless perchance the witch hunts he proposed were more violent than those already in effect.

Obviously, such was not a time for dissenters to rally adherents to a new party—the more so when the party's candidates bent over backwards to avoid any appearance of the intolerance that had become part and parcel of the era. Consequently, adherence to tradition in voting was something which stamped the citizen as "respectable." Commenting upon the La Follette Progressive campaign, the Lynds had observed in *Middletown:*

In 1924 it was considered such "bad business" to vote for the third party that no one of the business group confessed publicly either before or after the election to adherence to this ticket. "If we could discover the three people who disgraced our district by voting for La Follette," declared one business-class woman vehemently, "we'd certainly make it hot for them!"

The United States in 1948 was *Middletown* multiplied a thousandfold.

Finally, the war-fostered interest of the American people in foreign affairs entered a new—a *defensive*—phase. While the traditional isolationism of the Midwest slowly regained strength in some areas, elsewhere the shibboleth became "containment." Instead of further progress or a positive expansion of democratic ideals, the status quo was now to be preserved against Communist iconoclasts seeking to demolish a structure so laboriously erected and perfected. Acceptance of this doctrine also served to relegate foreign affairs to a position of secondary importance for the average person. Even though it might be "One World," Greece and Turkey and China were far away, and a show of military might by the admittedly greatest power in the world would keep the Communists "in their place." Meanwhile, the transition to a peacetime economy at home offered the really pressing problems. All sights were leveled on the maintenance of American productivity, employment and farm prices on the new plateau to which they had climbed in the postwar era. And since the areas of traditional "radicalism" were among the most contented and the least interested in foreign policy, the climate of 1948 America was hardly an ideal one in which to cultivate an internationally-oriented crusade such as that of Henry Wallace.

But, in addition to these constants of the year 1948, there were also numerous variables—factors whose alteration with the progress of the campaign contributed to the steady decline in Progressive Party strength.

One of the most significant was the "shift to the left" of the Truman administration in domestic policy. By the close of 1947 the Democrats had moved in action, if not in words, far to the right of the Roosevelt New Deal. They now espoused many causes nearly identical with those of the Republican conservatives, such as the administration's anti-inflation program which was, in the words of one high governmental economic analyst, "99 per cent identical with Senator [Robert A.] Taft's proposals for 'voluntary control,' which is no control at all."

Linked to such programs, there came a succession of Truman personal decisions—the reliance upon the generals and the admirals, the appointments of the Pawleys and the Krugs, the removal of the Landises and the Ickes. All these suggested a marked change from the personnel—and also from the outlook—of New Deal days.

With Wallace's campaign attacks upon these administration tendencies there had come a marked reversal. First at the Philadelphia Convention, and at every "whistlestop" thereafter, Harry S. Truman had undertaken a vigorous advocacy of a Fair Deal program, as he attempted to don an outsize Roosevelt-style mantle. A revitalized program had been submitted to a specially summoned session of Congress late in July. When this conservative-dominated body had failed, as anticipated, to adopt the plans, the Truman attack upon the "no-good, do-nothing, Republican-controlled 80th Congress" had begun in earnest. Forgotten in the attack were the President's own actions that had helped scuttle price control in 1946, his 1947 threats to draft striking railroad workers, and his consistent series of "incredible" first-term appointments.

The Democratic National Convention had also marked the onset of a new and vocal attack by the administration against racial segregation and other discriminatory practices. Led by Hubert Humphrey in a spectacular floor fight, a liberal faction had forced the adoption of a strong platform plank supporting such controversial matters as anti-lynch and anti-poll tax legislation and promising a nation-wide fair employment practices act. While the close convention decision had led to the immediate defection of southern delegates who proceeded to form a *fourth* party—the States' Rights Democrats, or Dixiecrats—it had also had a telling effect on the third party. For this new position cut much of the ground out from under the Progressive Party's "freedom" pledge. Large numbers of Negro voters came to feel that they could accomplish more by working and voting for a Democratic Party which now promised just as much as the third party, and which, in addition, had some chance of being elected to carry out its promises.

Regardless of the absence of action, the words of this new dynamic Presidential attack upon the "vested interests" and upon discriminatory practices brought a last-minute shift of independent voters to the Truman banners—too late, in fact, to be caught by any of the pollsters. Faced with the imminent threat of a Dewey-Republican victory, even Wallace supporters at the last minute held their noses, swallowed the "lesser-evil" doctrine, and voted to re-elect Harry S. Truman.

The story was related in Progressive circles of the girl worker-for-Wallace-and-Taylor who had labored strenuously all through the campaign for the Progressive cause. On election morning, so the tale went, she burst into tears upon returning from casting her own vote. Queried as to the cause of her dejection (the returns were not yet coming in), she replied that after she had entered the booth, pulled the curtain, and was alone with her thoughts of "the little man on the wedding cake"—Tom Dewey in the White House—she simply couldn't pull the Wallace lever but instead had voted for Truman. This episode was undoubtedly repeated many times over on November 2, 1948, with thousands of voters ultimately choosing the "lesser evil." Some of the pollsters, including George Gallup, later voiced their belief that the vast majority of their million-odd "missing Wallace votes" represented last-minute shifts that contributed to the upset victory of the President.

Of at least equal importance with the domestic "thunder-stealing" by the Democrats that undercut the "abundance" promises of the Progressive platform, there were the unfolding events in Europe during 1948 that had vitiated the appeal of the "peace" plank. The most significant of these had been the Czechoslovakian coup of March, whereby the Communists had gained control of the previously democratic coalition government. This was a shattering blow to those who had hoped that it was possible to permit Communist cooperation and still retain Western-style democracy. To many it was also convincing proof that the Soviet was embarked upon a course of world conquest and that no bridge between East and West was any longer possible.

This fact alone would have been sufficiently damaging to Progressive proposals for United States–Russian negotiations, but in addition Wallace had been caught off base when questioned by reporters. His remarks had seemed to indicate a belief that *American* intervention had been the fundamental cause—a conclusion highly unacceptable to most observers. The combined effect of both the incident and Wallace's observations had been to reduce the numbers of Progressive followers very sharply at a critical time in the preconvention campaign. Short months after this had come the Berlin Blockade with its continuing reminder throughout the campaign of the intransigence of the Russian leaders for any form of coexistence implicit in the "peace" plank.

A third factor of increasing importance as the campaign progressed was the Communist link attributed to the Progressive Party. Early in the year, Gael Sullivan, at the time acting chairman of the Democratic National Committee, had suggested that the Wallace candidacy would actually help the Democrats, inasmuch as it would unload from their backs the Red label with which the Republicans had so successfully tagged them in the 1946 off-year campaign. This prediction was borne out to no small extent. Few serious and sustained charges of communism were leveled against the Democrats, and most were disregarded. Communism never became a vote-losing issue for the Democrats in 1948, as it did later and as it did for the Progressives in this campaign.

The third-party presidential candidate himself estimated that acceptance of Communist support probably cost his party 3,000,000 votes. But the matter became one of principle from which no retreat was possible, and the Progressives were on the defensive throughout the campaign. They failed to adopt a clear-cut line of counterattack such as that offered by Senator Glen H. Taylor. In his acceptance speech, the vice-presidential candidate had announced:

> I am happy to have the support of all those who go along with our program. But just let me say to the Communists so there will be no misunderstanding, my efforts in the future as in the past will be directed toward the goal of making our economy work so well and our way of life so attractive and our people so contented that Communism will never interest more than the infinitesimal fraction of our citizens who adhere to it now.[1]

But with the Progressives' failure to follow up on this approach, the popular impression of the third party as "Red-dominated" continued to grow. By mid-July a majority of Americans (51 per cent) questioned in a public opinion poll "agreed" that "Wallace's third party is run by Communists." And while the precise figure might be suspect because of the loaded question, there was little doubt as to the general sentiment revealed.

Regardless of validity, the popular view of the Progressive Party as little more than a Communist front had a damaging effect—on voters and workers alike. Progressives (with a small *p*) who might otherwise have been attracted to the Wallace camp stayed away, and considerable numbers of those who had gathered later departed—both groups repelled by

[1] Text of Senator Taylor's remarks published in *PM*, February 24, 1948. Other journals failed to include this paragraph in their excerpts.

the Red light in which the crusade's banners were bathed as
the campaign went on.

The part played by the American press in the fostering of
this conception was highly significant. As a member of the
New Deal administration, Wallace had always been a leading
target for conservative attack. With his candidacy on a third-
party ticket, the vilification had assumed unprecedented pro-
portions. Reporters, even some who privately admitted sympathy to the candidate, turned out reams of bitter, sarcastic
copy—playing up every remark, every shred of evidence
which could be manipulated to prove that the Progressive
candidate was (a) a dreamer, a visionary, and an idealist
completely devoid of practical knowledge, and (b) a dupe,
wittingly or not, of Joseph Stalin, the Soviet Union, and the
Communist Party in the United States. Little acknowledgment
was given that this "dreamer" had created fortunes, for others
as for himself, through agricultural developments, had served
as capable administrator of the largest branch of the peacetime government—the Department of Agriculture—and during his term as Vice President had enlisted notable popular
support for the United States throughout the world—particularly in Latin America. Press coverage was instrumental
in presenting a pink-hued, vote-costing version of the Philadelphia Convention to the American public. And this was the
constant portrayal throughout the campaign to discredit the
third party. An adequate method of response was simply not
available to the Wallace-ites.

Nor did they benefit in any marked degree from the traditional American sympathy for the underdog. For theirs was
indeed a quixotic crusade—a crusade based upon a combination of moral and idealistic principles, rather than upon hope
of winning the election. And in 1948 the voters' emotional
response was to the battling underdog, and the candidate
whose "just plain folks" approach was so clearly genuine,

rather than to the hopeless if intellectual appeal of a Quixote.

Finally there were many minor causes, contributory rather than crucial, which played their part in the small vote received by the Progressives. First there was the organizational failure. The fact that no sound machine was firmly established down to the ward and precinct level was evidenced by the weak showing everywhere except in New York, where such a structure, that of the American Labor Party, had already been built. The areas making relatively better showings were those where relatively stronger organizations had been established, as in Southern California. The other significant organizational flaw was the failure to build a working labor organization— a defect clearly indicated by the weak showing in the industrial states. Second there were the ballot problems already discussed in detail. The two most damaging failures were those in Illinois, which may well have cost the Progressives a quarter of a million votes, and Ohio, where the necessity of marking twenty-five separate $X$'s on a ballot to vote Progressive was estimated to have taken a toll of 150,000. Finally there was the matter of election frauds, mentioned earlier in the chapter. Difficult to measure with any degree of accuracy, this "counting out" undoubtedly deprived the Wallace ticket of many votes, though hardly the 2,000,000 estimated by party publicist Ralph Shikes.

But what of the impact of this dismal performance? Nothing succeeds like success, and the Progressives had failed to establish even a working basis for the 1952 election. Their failure was not only an immediate one, but it also posed increasing difficulties for the four-year period up to the next presidential contest. Workers who had in so many instances sacrificed time, money, social standing, and even long-held positions had little to look forward to on the basis of the general apathy exhibited their endeavors.

The vote was enough for Senator Glen H. Taylor—sufficient indication of the complete lack of support for both party and policies. He promptly notified party secretary C. B. Baldwin that it was not his "intention to quit politics," hence he must leave the party. This attitude was typical of many moderates who now departed less formally than did the vice-presidential candidate. And one of the ultimate effects of their departure was to give the extreme leftists increasing control of the organization by default.

Moreover, the small vote achieved by the Progressives' candidates indicated that the administration foreign policy was accepted, if not endorsed, by an overwhelming majority of the American voters. While the interpretation of the election outcome as a "mandate" in favor of the Truman get-tough-with-Russia policy seems unwarranted, the fact that it had failed to arouse significant opposition meant endorsement of a negative sort. If the voters felt any great qualms over the wisdom of President Truman's doctrine abroad, they had been calmed by the tides of economic pressure and the ground swell for conformity at home.

Finally, the fact that the Democrats had gained victory without the Wallace forces meant that the Progressives had failed to gain even a staying power, let alone *balance* of power. Their unsuccessful quest for votes had openly exposed the weaknesses of their position.

In short, then, Henry Wallace, having taken his "fight for peace" to the highest tribunal of the people, found himself rejected in no uncertain manner. Those willing to "stand up and be counted" had proved disappointingly few.

The defeat at the polls suffered by the Progressive Party on November 2, 1948, was such as to virtually sign its death warrant, barring either of two possible contingencies—a major depression at home or an overwhelming defeat for the containment policy abroad. Regardless of the complex causes, there was little evidence in the election returns of sufficient vitality to allow the Wallace Progressive Party to endure in such a hostile climate.

## CHAPTER 11

# Communist Bogey

"WALLACE'S COMMUNIST Front Party," "The Pink Façade," "How the Reds Snatched Henry Wallace"—titles such as these and repeated epithets of "Communist-dominated," "dupes of Moscow," "fellow travelers" were indicative of the invective hurled at the Wallace Progressive Party in 1948. Reaching their high-water mark at the Philadelphia Convention as noted earlier, such charges constituted a powerful current all through the campaign. How valid were these charges? What role *did* the Communists play in the party? What was the effect of their participation?

The press generally reflected the opinion expressed by the professedly (and professional) "reformed Communist" Louis F. Budenz in *Collier's* that "the Communists conceived the idea of a third party . . . organized it, named it and chose [Henry A. Wallace] as their candidate." This view was identical with that earlier voiced by Americans for Democratic Action, the anti-Communist Liberal group which supported the Democratic ticket. In a document aimed at proving "It All Goes Back to Frère Jacques," (the reference being to Jacques Duclos, French Communist leader) the ADA stated:

It is fair to say that the core of the Wallace's supporters [*sic*] is composed chiefly of those individuals and unions which in the period of the Nazi-Soviet pact were the spear-

252

head of the Wallace opposition the only other time he ran for public office.

The Communist Party itself, while not taking *sole* credit for the Progressive Party, was far from modest in its claims as to its role. In a draft resolution for its 1948 national convention, the National Committee of the Communist Party admitted, according to the *New York Times,* that

> The Communist party, from the earliest days after the end of the war, understood that its traditional fight for a new people's party directed against the two-party system of the monopolies had once more been placed by events as an immediate practical question before the American people, and, acting upon this understanding, it boldly proclaimed the need for such a new people's party.
>
> Because of its correct line, the party was able to carry on effective mass work and make significant contributions to the struggle for peace and democracy and to the forging of the new political alignment and people's coalition.

On the other hand, the presidential candidate himself asserted repeatedly:

> I am not a Communist, have never been one and never expect to be one.
>
> The Progressive Party is not controlled by Communists nor was its convention or program dictated by them.

And Professor Rexford Guy Tugwell, who had reportedly absented himself from the party's fall campaign because of Communist domination, concluded some months later in the *Progressive* that "no matter how it may be represented, I believe [the Progressive Party] to be genuinely Progressive and not Communist."

In the midst of all these conflicting statements, what measure of truth can be found? With the press so universally opposed to recent third-party candidates, its reporting in 1948, as in 1924, tended to depart from objective standards and include editorial material. It accepted as fact some of the more violent claims of an opposition united in trying to pin the Red label on the Progressive Party. On the other hand, the Communists were elbowing for a position in the forefront of the new coalition. Hence they might well exaggerate the extent of their participation to better advance their claims within the party. And from a third viewpoint, non-Communists in the party could be expected to play down as much as possible the actual degree of Communist participation, since common knowledge of such support might prove costly in votes.

With all the available source material subject to these many possible distortions, the obvious necessity is for a valid criterion by which to make an objective appraisal of both sources and material. Unfortunately, there seems to have been no such clear-cut standard in 1948. In the realm of policy there simply did not exist, at the time, any sharply defined differences within the Progressive Party by which to distinguish Communists and party-line followers from non-Communist Liberals. Both groups had expressed their willingness to accept the "Peace, Progress and Prosperity" program of Henry A. Wallace.

In 1941, it would have been possible to separate isolationists and pacifists from Communists on the basis of their views toward World War II. The former groups consistently opposed hostilities, while the latter exhibited an overnight change in attitude toward the "imperialist war" following the invasion of the Soviet Union. And in 1950, it became possible to distinguish Communists and "party-liners" from Liberals in the Progressive Party on the basis of their respective attitudes toward the action of the United Nations to halt Red aggression in Korea. Indeed it was the division in the party over this issue that was finally to drive Wallace, as well as most of the remaining non-Communists, from the party's failure-thinned ranks.

But in 1948 no such significant criteria existed. True, there were some differences of opinion over policy, but these tended to be of an inconsequential nature. Thus, as has been observed in an earlier chapter, such matters as the Vermont Resolution and the report of the Rules Committee at the Philadelphia Convention found reputed "fellow travelers" on the unexpected side of the ideological fence, while persons obviously non-Communist favored what should have been, in theory, the "party line." The underlying difference over the issue of "progressive capitalism" never came to the fore.

In a dispassionate report of what actually went on "behind the scenes" at Philadelphia, one *firsthand* observer, John Cotton Brown, concluded that "there was no greater behavioral unity among those members of the Platform Committee whose reputations and vocabulary suggested that they might be Communists than there was among the others." While seeking to prove his hypothesis that the Progressive Party was "principally controlled by a minority of Communists and left-wingers," Brown, careful to avoid factual distortion, reported further:

> Prof. Frederick L. Schuman told me . . . that he had carefully watched for signs of Communist tactics, but had observed none.
> I thought I detected several instances of Communist tactics during the four days of committee sessions, although I must confess that on several of these occasions, though by no means all, certain evidences of Moscow plots were subsequently vitiated by the behavior of those who impressed me as suspect-Communists.

The same commentator, having attempted to set up six contrasting "Left-Wing" and "Non-Left-Wing" beliefs, finally reached the conclusion that

> A "common left-wing system of beliefs" rendered the Progressive Convention behavior of Communists and non-Communist left-wingers indistinguishable.
>
> By contrast it was not possible to locate any sort of right wing.

In short, the program established by the Progressives' presidential candidate had, much earlier, eliminated virtually all those not in substantial agreement. Consequently, debate over adoption of a platform at Philadelphia centered around minute detail, language shading, and emphases, rather than around fundamental policy disputes. Therefore, any criteria for distinguishing Communists from non-Communists in the 1948 Wallace Progressive Party on the basis of policy were so tenuous as to be virtually worthless.

On the other hand, there were some organizational evidences that, as has been suggested, served a better means of distinguishing between the Communists and their followers and the moderates in the party. Thus the former were generally united in supporting and working for a narrow, restricted group with a hard core of support which could be tightly organized and closely disciplined. The moderates, on the other hand, believed in setting up as broadly based an organization as possible. To this a great mass of American voters would be able to attach themselves loosely, subject to little discipline, as is customary with American major parties.

Despite early claims by A. B. Magil in the Communist *New Masses* that "Since *we want a mass party and not a sect* we must operate through organizational forms that will unite rather than divide the labor and progressive movement," the Communists and fellow travelers, once the Progressive Party had been organized, apparently proceeded to operate in given localities on an opposite assumption. As noted, in Colorado and New Mexico open rifts between the moderates and the extreme leftists developed over this policy. And in New York the policy of exclusiveness was abetted by the adamant refusal of state ALP chairman Vito Marcantonio to allow a "fifth" or Progressive Party line on the ballot. Moreover, scattered reports from local organizations with strong Communist membership indicated that similar tactics were generally pursued by the "party-liners."

Opposition to these methods was voiced by Wallace at various times, but he failed to take vigorous action to curb the techniques of his more extreme followers. Consequently mass action tactics, deliberate law violations to invite arrest, and similar methods continued throughout the campaign. They served in no small part to repel many prospective followers who came to fear a loss of "respectability" in third-party participation.

Outside the realm of policy and organizational evidence, there was little but hearsay, accusation (most of it undocumented), and the admissions of self-confessed former Communists. Relatively little light was shed by these disclosures on 1948 Communist Party policies, but some evidence was thereby made available as to the earlier political affiliations of some of the party's leaders. Thus, Lee Pressman who served as secretary of the Progressive Platform Committee later revealed in 1950 testimony before the House Committee on un-American Activities that at one time he had been a Communist. Similarly, he claimed that John Abt, party counsel, had been a "member of a Communist group."

The attempt to identify Communists by means of their "reputation and vocabulary" and their use of "Communist tactics" proved uniformly unrewarding to those who attempted to utilize such means of examining third-party members. Senator Taylor remarked that in all the meetings he attended he had noted "no evidence of any Communist tactics, steamroller or otherwise." In his opinion there had instead been "complete freedom of discussion" and "scrupulous adherence to the rules" of democratic procedure. Nevertheless, the fact that Communists were present was admitted freely by all concerned. This being the case, what was the effect of their presence on the Wallace Progressive Party? What were the factional lines within the party?

At one pole were the extreme leftists, three closely related groups—admitted Communists, past and present; the party-liners and fellow travelers who failed to differ noticeably with the Communists as to either policy or principle; and finally those non-Communists who, in the period under surveillance (1944–50), failed to take issue with the Communists on policy, but whose underlying principles seemingly differed. Lee Pressman, Vito Marcantonio, and C. B. "Beanie" Baldwin offered examples within the party leadership of each of the three respective groups. It was to this group as a whole that Wallace later applied the appellation, the "Peekskill Boys," on the basis of their endorsement of the mass action tactics similar to those employed in connection with the Peekskill, New York meeting for singer Paul Robeson which led to a full-scale riot.

In the middle were grouped an apparently large majority of Progressive Party followers—the moderates. Exemplified by both national candidates, these individuals were willing to accept Communist support, because they felt that it was inconsistent, in the light of their ideals, to oppose Red-baiting by others, yet attempt to read Communists out of the new party.

At the right were arrayed those who, feeling that Communist support should have been disavowed in no uncertain terms, yet were unwilling to adopt the ADA tactic of violent attack on the Communists. This group would have approved making the Progressives "non-Communist" rather than "anti-Communist," excluding but not assailing the Reds. Most persons sharing this view had, like Max Lerner, completely avoided the party, but others like Rexford Guy Tugwell joined and stayed, if reluctantly, through the campaign. While few in this group favored, as did Tugwell, the Marshall plan, they were all agreed on the necessity for a third party in the face of totally repugnant Truman-Dewey alternatives.

In the period following 1948, these groups tended to leave the party in the order of their views from right to left. Most of the rightists departed during or shortly after the campaign, accompanied by many of the moderates. And the moderate defection, so marked following election day, 1948, became a nearly complete walkout in the summer of 1950, with the policy rift over Korea and Wallace's departure. Consequently, by the close of 1951 the few remaining portions of the Wallace Progressive Party were composed almost exclusively of the earlier extreme left group. These were the ones who had favored a "narrow" organization; after the Wallace break, they finally achieved this goal, with the departure of almost everyone else.

But while these may have been the facts with respect to groupings within the party, they were ultimately far less important than the public image—the stereotype projected by press treatment of the issue. For what the public *thinks* is often far more important than what *is*. And in 1948, 51 per cent of the American public, in a poll conducted by the American Institute of Public Opinion, "agreed that" the Wallace third party was Communist-dominated.

The tenor of the press portrayal was illustrated in many publications, including the weekly news magazines. Journalists for *Time,* reporting the Philadelphia Convention in their own inimitable fashion, opined:

Henry Wallace, the Iowa horticulturist emerged last week as the centerpiece of U.S. Communism's most authentic-looking façade. The façade was Wallace's helter-skelter following, assembled under careful Communist supervision at a founding convention in Philadelphia and brazenly labeled the Progressive Party.

A similar approach was employed by *Newsweek:*

The Communist Party boasted that it had decided that Wallace would run for the Presidency even before Wallace did, and that Sen. Glen Taylor, the self-styled "Singing Cowboy" from Idaho, would be his running mate. It had done much to organize the party for them and even picked the name.

The position taken by these and other journals was that the failure of Wallace to repudiate Communist support constituted overwhelming evidence of Communist domination. The conclusion was simple: "No repudiation, therefore domination." Actually there were grounds for believing that even had the third party denounced Communist support as strongly as did Robert M. La Follette in 1924, large segments of the press would have continued to call it Communist-dominated, averring that the disavowal was merely camouflage. For all during 1948 the ADA, despite the vigor of its anti-Communist attacks, continued to be branded as "pink" in both conservative and irresponsible circles. In short, a "status quo" group shortsightedly viewed all attacks upon its entrenched position as "Communist-inspired." The general effect of this approach was noted by sociologist C. Wright Mills commenting on the labor picture in his *The New Men of Power:*

The greatest success of the Communist Party in the United States has been accomplished with the active aid and support of conservatives and reactionaries. Together they have made the mass public think that "Communist" is a synonym for "left" in general and "radical" in particular.

In 1948 there were evidences of this same unwitting co-operation by both right and left extremists to impress upon the average voter the fact that the Wallace Progressive Party could be nothing but Communist. The candidate's own view was that this concerted attack indicated that the press was "not after the Communists but after the whole Progressive movement." Regardless of their motivation, these views and their "documentation" were much the same wherever found. First summarized by the ADA in mimeograph form, the opposition "line" may be sketched as follows:

The idea for a third party originated at a meeting of the Communist Party national board in 1946—a meeting whose location was variously described as West 12th Street, the home of Frederick Vanderbilt Field, and "a mid-Manhattan apartment near Bellevue Hospital." Unfortunately, such detailed (though conflicting) reports were not available for the date of the meeting which was set at sometime in 1946. The exact date, if provided, might have been significant, as will be noted below.

At this meeting, so the version went, the decision was reached to form a third party for 1948 with Henry Wallace at its head. This verdict was then communicated to the several Communist-dominated unions of the CIO, ordering their support for a third party. Following this, a group of progressive organizations—all of which were subject to Communist dictation—were directed to unite in the Communist-dominated PCA. The chief purpose of PCA was to be the building of machinery and organization for a third party, without clearly revealing the intent.

Then, according to this interpretation, when the time

seemed propitious, the "heat" was turned on Wallace to announce his candidacy. While "not a Communist himself," the former Vice President clearly became the tool of these leftists when, spurred on by their urgings, he announced his intention to run for President on a third-party ticket. At the same time he accepted, perhaps unwittingly, the entire program of the Communist Party in the United States as his own.

Third-party opponents also claimed that during the course of 1948 the Communists used typical tactics—"going to meetings early, staying late"—to insure their control of local Wallace groups and state parties. At the Philadelphia Convention, they ran roughshod over all opposition, forced acceptance of a platform virtually identical with their own, and put through rules which would insure their control of party organization in the future. Finally, according to these reports, the Communists were quick to silence even the faint note of protest emitted by a Vermont delegate hopeful enough to bring to the convention floor an innocuous resolution stating that the party platform was not to be construed as an endorsement of Soviet foreign policy.

In brief, then, according to this opposition view, Henry Wallace, Glen Taylor, and the whole Progressive Party were little more than muddle-headed dupes of a Soviet plot organized through the Communist Party in the United States. Unfortunately this view, while long on "interpretation," proved somewhat short of facts that would hold up under investigation.

But what of the evidence supplied by the Communists themselves? Examination of their writings makes it relatively easy to plot their shifting course, but fails to shed much light on the actual extent of their influence. Publicly, the Reds claimed credit for participation in the Progressive Party's formation, but disclaimed any intention of seeking a "special position" within its ranks. They boasted—after the fact—in an Arnold Sroog article in the *Worker Magazine,* July 25, 1948, that

> The Communists had long known—and stated publicly —that a new party was essential to America, if its people were to move forward along the path of peace and security.
>
> So it was that the Communists, armed with their Marxist understanding of American history, renewed their traditional call for a new people's party at the time of Wallace's ouster by Truman.

Discounting the inherent braggadocio and attempting to fill in the important omissions, this was indeed a rather accurate résumé of Communist action with respect to a third party. In 1944, as already indicated, the Communists had been one of the firmest if weakest components of the vice-presidential support for Henry A. Wallace at the Democratic National Convention. At this time, it will be recalled, the Communist Party in the United States, under the leadership of Earl Browder, had been operating within the American two-party system—attempting to gain an influential position within the Democratic Party. Ever since the attack by Nazi Germany on Soviet Russia in June, 1941, it had been vigorous in its support of President Franklin D. Roosevelt.

It should be noted, however, that this position represented the latest wartime reversal of a much older view of the Marxists concerning American politics. The earlier policy, which had enjoyed an off-again, on-again popularity in Communist ranks through the 1920's and early 1930's was that of the "popular front." As outlined by Georgi Dimitrov to an assemblage of the Comintern in 1935:

> The establishment of unity of action by all sections of the working class, irrespective of their party or organiza-

tional affiliation is necessary even before the majority of the working class is united in the struggle for the overthrow of capitalism and the victory of the proletarian revolution.[1]

In America, the popular front was to be advanced through the medium of a new farmer-labor party which would challenge the inherently conservative position of both old major parties. During World War II, this approach had been shelved in favor of accepting the Democratic Party, and trying to influence its views from within. Consequently, when at the end of the war, Earl Browder was ousted from his position as head of the CPUSA, the party line seemed to revert to the earlier popular front orientation. As Robert Minor, writing in the *Daily Worker* on the 1948 Communist Convention, remarked:

> The resolution [proposing Communist support for the third party] gives a correct picture of the New Party movement as the beginning of a break up of the "Two-Party System." This is a further development of the correction made by our emergency convention three years ago which discarded one of the most dangerous mistakes we made when we accepted the anti-Marxist theoretical proposition made by Browder that the political struggles of the country could be fought out within the two-party system.

Thus it seems clearly indicated that a 1945 meeting of the party's national committee was responsible for resumption of a policy calling for an attempt to break down the American two-party system. The best way to achieve this, the Communists now believed, was by introducing a third party—with both labor and farm support—into the American political scene. While this new party might not achieve immediate suc-

[1] Georgi Dimitrov, *The United Front* (New York: International Publishers Co., Inc., 1947), p. 29.

cess at the polls, it still might gain a balance-of-power position in presidential elections comparable to that of the American Labor Party in New York State contests.

Nevertheless, there was little evidence in party-sponsored literature indicating that the decision had been made that the time was yet ripe for the actual formation of a third party. Eugene Dennis had remarked in February, 1946 that the Communists must proceed

> to lay the foundation now to establish in time for the 1948 elections a national third party—a broad people's anti-monopoly, anti-imperialist party . . . . If possible—and it is preferable—steps toward forming a third party should be taken early in 1947.[2]

But both the *Daily Worker* and *New Masses* had remained reluctant to take up the cudgels, making only infrequent references to a third party during the latter part of 1945 and the first eight months of 1946.

Yet during this period there were evidences of Communist political activity and of Communist tactics in organizations not too far afield. One of the most significant was their operation within the American Veterans' Committee. An article concerned with this problem, "Why I Broke with the Communists," shed considerable light on CP organizational tactics. Writing in *Harper's,* Julian H. Franklin described the operation of the Reds in forcing moderates and non-Communist liberals out of local AVC chapters.

> They said they were quite glad they were driving out "the fascist opposition." They said they didn't care how small AVC became as long as it remained ideologically

[2] Eugene Dennis, *What America Faces* (New York: New Century Publishers, 1946), pp. 37–38.

correct. Rather a chapter of two members and a national AVC of 40,000 that would hew to the party line. "Then when the depression comes," they predicted with relish, "we will attract a vast following."

Comparison of these sentiments and techniques with later reports from the Progressive Party indicates a striking similarity of approach. Still, in 1945 and early 1946, there was no positive indication that the Communist board of strategy felt the time yet ripe for a serious third-party attempt.

But, in September of 1946, with the delivery of Henry A. Wallace's Madison Square Garden speech, came the overnight shift to a new positive plan of action. Or, more properly, the transformation came with the belated observation of the effect of the Wallace speech on both Truman administration and American press and public. It will be recalled that the Communists' first reaction to Wallace's remarks had been one of disapproval, or at best, of faint praise. It required several days for the light to dawn that this event could be adapted to their purposes, that it had elevated Henry A. Wallace into a prominent position as potential leader of a new party. While it is interesting to speculate on the sources of Communist illumination, it is virtually impossible to pinpoint them. Louis F. Budenz in his *Collier's* article blithely ascribed the shift in CP line to a *Pravda* dispatch of September 16 which reportedly supported Wallace. The fact of the matter was that the shift in position of the CPUSA came in the *Daily Worker* on September 15. Hence, if the decision originated abroad (as it may very well have done), it was transmitted by some other and less public means.

Regardless of origins, the fact remains that the party line did change, and Henry A. Wallace became the man to whom the Communists turned as the prospective leader of a new party. Moreover the timetable was to be speeded up. Appearing in an article by A. B. Magil, published almost immediately

after the shift in policy—October 8, 1946—in *New Masses,*
the new interpretation followed these lines:

> The Wallace episode has widened popular dissatisfac-
> tion with the two major parties. It has thereby provided an
> opportunity for accelerating a political realignment which,
> under labor's leadership, can in the post-election period
> bring this simmering discontent to the point where it boils
> up into a new vigorous people's party.
>
> The ALP . . . is the nucleus of the broad anti-
> monopoly party which on a national scale still lies in the
> future.

Also establishing the party line for the 1946 election, the
article went on to say, "To reject a Mead or Lehman because he doesn't talk like a Wallace is just as unrealistic as
to reject a Wallace because he doesn't talk like a William Z.
Foster." In other words, while Wallace might be far from
the ideal party-line candidate, the Communists must be real-
istic and take advantage of the furor caused by a speech
which they hadn't liked particularly. They immediately set
to work, as suggested, to build fires under the discontent.
Party publications, not yet openly embarked on a third-party-
in-1948 trend, began to throw broad hints in this direction,
with the emphasis on building a "coalition," a "popular
front."

"Since Henry Wallace [had] come to symbolize the fight
against the reactionary foreign policy of the Wall Street-
controlled Republican Party which the Truman administration
[had] made its own," according to Magil one week later in
*New Masses,* he might be accepted as the leader, "not that
the conference [of the Communist Party] committed itself to
his leadership or that its program was identical with his."

This decision having been reached by the CP conference,
the party apparently then embarked upon the initial phases

of their new tactics at the Conference of Progressives, held at Chicago in October, 1946. The Communists, however, may scarcely be said to have dominated—or even excessively influenced—this assemblage, since its ranks included a far greater representation of non-Communist liberal thought. Included in the Conference of Progressives were many individuals later found in the ranks of the ADA, as well as significant leaders from American labor—the Political Action Committee of the CIO and the Railway Brotherhoods. As noted earlier, there was at this time substantial opposition on the part of liberals of all hues to many aspects of both foreign and domestic policies of the Truman administration.

It was reported that the Communists were strongly represented at Chicago in such organizations as the NC-PAC and the ICC-ASP. But objective criteria were lacking whereby their actual influence in these groups could be measured. Subsequent developments failed to bear out the contention that these groups were nothing more than "Communist fronts" as their opponents charged. When, shortly thereafter, the NC-PAC and the ICC-ASP merged to form the Progressive Citizens of America, this same problem carried over into any attempt to determine the exact extent of Communist influence within the new body. Like its predecessors, the PCA failed to bar Communists from membership as did its newly organized opponent, the ADA. This latter group accepted at face value the "Communist presence, hence Communist control" dogma. It assailed non-Communist liberals who joined the PCA, ignoring the fact that ADA acceptance of the Truman doctrine type of foreign policy, even as modified by the Marshall plan, left dissenters no place else to go.

Following the establishment of the PCA, the Communists began, early in 1947, to work in earnest for a third party. It soon became apparent, however, that they were moving away from the broad people's coalition of which they had spoken so recently. A narrowing influence was taking hold, and party spokesmen began to assail "the illusion that middle class liberals can be both the brains and body of a broad people's movement. This illusion," so the new line ran according to A. B. Magil in *New Masses,* January 14, 1947, "helped shipwreck the third party movements of the past and if allowed to gain ascendance can have no happier results in the future. It is only the working class which . . . can challenge the power of big business."

At the same time, the Communists were seemingly aware that they could not rely solely upon those of socialistic persuasion in "the political coalition that can become—and should become by 1948—a new anti-fascist, anti-monopoly people's party." They entertained, according to the same article, hopes of eventual conversion for these capitalistic infidels, however, concluding that

> One can be critical of Communists, as Communists are critical of other progressives, and still see that the two can and must work together if reaction is to be defeated . . . . In this fight the bonds that tie so many to faith in the capitalist "promise" will loosen and the socialist truth will take root in the minds of millions.

By the summer of 1947, the Communists had become absolutely convinced that the time for a third party was now at hand. "When it is already so late, the new party that *must* come cannot come too soon," said Magil on June 3 in the same party organ. At the same time he more clearly indicated some of their goals.

> While [a new party] may not succeed in winning power on its first try, [it] will nevertheless become a power capable of influencing whatever administration takes office and capable, moreover, of achieving its highest goal in 1952.
> 5,000,000 votes to start with is a very substantial num-

ber . . . *enough to be the balance of power* in most national elections. [Italics supplied.]

Their decision finally having been made, the Communists turned their full attention to fomenting, as best they could, action leading to a third party—trying to bring the discontent of which they were aware "to a boil." The PCA, in which they were permitted to participate, was one means of accomplishing their goal.

The exact role of the Communists in pushing the PCA decision to support a new party is difficult to assess. Certainly they exercised every possible means of enlisting support for the venture. And yet, in this formative stage, much of the third-party pressure within PCA ranks came from the non-Communist group. Testimony to this effect was given by a journalist who had opposed PCA support for a third party. Writing in *PM,* Albert Deutsch commented:

> While I disagree with the PCA decision on the Wallace candidacy, I believe it was made by a group of sturdy Americans according to the dictates of their democratic and patriotic consciences. To suggest that their decision was made in Moscow is nothing less than irresponsible balderdash.
>
> I am frankly dismayed by some of my shifty-eyed fellow-liberals who seem unable to form a conclusive opinion without first looking over their left shoulders to see what the Communists think . . . dutifully reading the *Daily Worker* to find what they should oppose.
>
> If a cause seems right to [the true liberal], he does not discard it because others may follow the same path for longer or shorter distances for their own reasons.

According to Wallace, non-Communist PCA leader Frank Kingdon had "put more pressure on [him] to run than anyone else." Nevertheless, when the decision was finally reached,

Kingdon conspicuously absented himself and in fact denounced the new party, in his *New York Post* column.

> Who asked Henry Wallace to run? The answer is in the record. The Communist Party, through William Z. Foster and Eugene Dennis, were the first . . . . I was finally convinced when the steamroller ran over me the night PCA became the second organized group to demand the Wallace candidacy.

According to Mrs. Elinor Gimbel, also a member of the PCA Executive Board which made the decision, Kingdon submitted a statement of his new position just prior to their meeting, following which the sixty-odd members of the board voted, with only three abstentions, to support the Wallace candidacy.

Once the new party had been launched, it became quite apparent that Communists were participating fully in its organization, its drives to obtain a place on the ballot, and in its campaign. Numerous reports from moderate leaders attested the fact that the extreme leftists, whether actual Communist Party members or not, were among those most willing to get out and work for the Progressive Party, putting in long hours for little or no compensation. Yet at this very time that the Communists were working so vigorously in behalf of the Wallace Progressive Party, there were significant long-range policy differences between them and the moderates. Perhaps the most significant was the fundamental cleavage over "progressive capitalism." Despite the fact that there was little open dispute during 1948 over this concept supported by the presidential candidate, it was one to which no Marxist could subscribe. As Adam Lapin wrote in the Communist *Masses and Mainstream,* October, 1948:

> [The Progressive Party] is not . . . free of the illusion that capitalism can somehow be made "progressive" and subordinated to the interests of the people.

Here is the measure of the difference between the Progressive party and the Communists. It is a difference which extends to some tactical questions, but even more to fundamental objectives. The Communists reject utterly the theory of a "progressive capitalism."

Nevertheless, this fundamental difference of principle remained submerged in the short run of 1948. The general agreement on immediate policies, most of all the similarity of views on foreign policy, meant that for this period at least, Communist and non-Communist were moving in the same direction. With the Communists willing to subordinate their economic tenets, the Progressive Party, narrow as it was, was still broad enough to accommodate both groups. It should be noted, however, that this era of agreement was to be relatively short-lived. Those moderates who remained in the Progressive Party after the disastrous 1948 election returns soon found differences increasingly difficult to resolve.

Early evidence of the growing rift came in September of 1949 when, at a New York City Conference on the Bill of Rights, Professor Thomas I. Emerson offered a resolution favoring a pardon for a *Trotskyite* group convicted of violation of the same Smith Act under which the Communists' own leaders had been indicted. Opposition to the act was widespread in liberal circles, and party moderates, including such leaders as Henry Wallace and Professors Frederick L. Schuman and Harlow Shapley, felt that it should not be employed to suppress the civil rights of *any* group. On the other hand, the extreme leftists opposed the pardon, feeling that a selective application of the rights of free speech was desirable to protect only *Stalinists*. Communist Benjamin Davis phrased it in no uncertain terms according to Gus Tyler in *New Republic:* "Free speech is not for those who come among us as disrupters."

Further indications of growing disunity were observed at

the second national convention of the Progressives in February, 1950. Eventually, however, this assemblage adopted a compromise position, accepting Wallace's lead to agree that the foreign policies of both the United States and the Soviet Union were subject to valid criticism. But the final split came in the summer of 1950, when the Progressive Party failed to accept Wallace's support of U.N. action against Red aggression in Korea. Here the Communist line could brook no compromise. For the first time, the left wing in the third party stood clearly apart on a matter of substantive policy. While the Wallace position supporting American defense of *Formosa* might have been open to non-Communist doubts, there were few moderates who could go along with the refusal of the extremists to support the United Nations action in Korea. Party ranks, vitiated by continued failures which had discouraged most of the moderates, were now susceptible to domination by the extremists. Wallace's position thus made untenable, he withdrew from the party he had founded, accompanied shortly by most of the remaining non-leftist Progressives. Not only had the Communists achieved their narrow, ideologically correct organization, but in the process they had also alienated virtually all the moderate elements which had earlier been willing to cooperate with them.

But what of the "Communist acceptance" stand taken by various non-Communists in the Progressive Party's earlier history? What were their views, their reasons, and their reasoning?

Factors both ideal and practical influenced the decision of the moderates not to disavow Communist support. First, it was, as Wallace observed, a matter of preserving one's "fundamental integrity." While both he and Senator Taylor would have preferred that the Communists stay out of the party, they felt it impossible to live up to an ideal that opposed Red-baiting by adopting tactics that smacked even slightly of the same thing. Any form of intolerance in an organization based on the promotion of tolerance and understanding was to them both incongruous and deplorable. As an official of the American Labor Party expressed it, there could be no "loyalty test" for membership in the party.

Moreover, it did not necessarily follow that adherence to this ideal must automatically lead to Communist domination. For, despite the stereotype of the Reds as political super-Machiavellis, and their own claims to "superior understanding of American history," the verdict of most who worked with them was that they were, on the whole, "eager and willing but lacking in political sense."

Party leaders were hopeful of creating a flood tide of major-party dissent on the part of moderates and non-Communists that would swell new party ranks and completely dominate it, submerging the Communist participants. As Rexford Guy Tugwell commented in the *Progressive,* April, 1949:

> If there had been a flood of Progressives [to the party] —energetic, determined, dedicated—where would the Communists, about whom we hear so much, have been? . . . They would have been lost as they were always lost when they tried to claim President Roosevelt . . . . The reason Communist workers were so prominent to the Wallace campaign was that the Progressives were . . . sitting it out; wringing their hands; and wailing.

As it turned out, the Communists, instead of being submerged, became sufficiently prominent, aided in no small part by press dispatches concerning their prowess, to keep many moderates away from the party. A spectral "Red domination" became the bogey that had a greater influence on the destiny of the Progressive Party than did the actual presence of the Communist Party members.

In this sense it proved unfortunate that Wallace did not see fit to pursue a more vigorous policy, completely disclaiming Communist support, or even, as Senator Taylor had done, pointing out to the Communists that their own long-run interests would not be served by his program. Instead, the defensive attitude, adopted in the face of constantly harrying press questioning, turned out to be ineffective. Nor did the presidential candidate inject himself sufficiently into the organizational details of the party to avert Communist domination in several localities. Admittedly, this would have been difficult and might have deprived the Progressives of some of their most conscientious workers. Nevertheless, the long-range effects of such a course would have proved beneficial—certainly in retaining the full support of the moderates who had joined the party.

But, turning from such speculation, what evaluation may be made of the Communists' role in the crusade? What impact did they have on policy, organization, personnel, and candidates of the Progressive Party?

In the realm of actual party formation, they undoubtedly played an active part in getting the drive under way. But, notwithstanding the fact that they were among the earliest exponents of the idea, they constituted only a relatively small segment of a broad liberal group with an early interest in third-party action. It was only as increasing numbers of Progressives ultimately decided against this course of action that the Communists gained a more conspicuous position. At no time in this formative period did they actually attain the dominant position attributed them by the press.

It was Henry A. Wallace himself, rather than the Communists, who constituted the decisive factor in the determination that there was to be a third Progressive Party. Had Wallace not delivered his Madison Square Garden speech, with its resultant repercussions, it seems hardly likely that the Communists would have united on a third-party drive as early as mid-1947—or that they would even have entered the 1948 campaign. Had Wallace not eventually decided to run in December of 1947, it is even more doubtful that the Communists could have agreed on any other national figure around whom they might rally the discontented. It is equally doubtful that they could have seriously considered such a course of action had Wallace not decided as he did. Rather, the Communists pursued an opportunistic course in attempting to employ Wallace for their own particular purposes.

Nor does it seem likely that the Communists exercised any preponderant influence on the decisions leading to Wallace's activities. Certainly the Reds were not the instigators of the 1946 Madison Square Garden speech which they initially found so distasteful. And while they contributed their voices to the cries of "Wallace in '48," they formed but a small part of a much vaster group—non-Communists all—which also looked to the Wallace program of "Peace, Freedom and Abundance." The audiences attracted by Wallace during his PCA-sponsored 1947 tour were much more than "drummed up left-wing demonstrations lacking in political significance," despite Carey McWilliams' label in the *Nation*. Admitting, as seems proved, that the Communists were present en masse at these meetings, whooping things up, there was also present in far larger numbers a broad cross section of America—people from all walks of life hopefully turning their faces to new answers to problems so long bungled by both traditional parties.

Long after the campaign Wallace, realizing that he had been moved by urgings less spontaneous than they had appeared at the time, still felt that his decision had been finally swayed by real issues that could not have been answered, or even compromised, within the framework of the two major parties. It was his reluctant conclusion that the Truman administration could not have been forced to budge an inch upon the vital issues of foreign policy which led primarily to the third-party decision. The pressures exerted by labor and progressive groups, and by friends and advisers, especially Frank Kingdon and Beanie Baldwin, had been only secondary in his decision. Personal antipathy toward the President, said Wallace, had not entered into his decision. But as non-Communist support for a third party began to fade in 1947, the Communists were among the leaders in keeping the façade of support intact. They may not have built the Potemkin village, but they were persistent in keeping the candidate's attention focused on it.

In terms of policy, there was little viable evidence of Communist influence actually resulting in basic shifts during 1948. The original planks set forth by Wallace formed the platform of the party adopted at its convention. "Peace, progress and prosperity" became "Peace, Freedom and Abundance." Regardless of personality clashes (such as Marcantonio versus Tugwell over Puerto Rico), minor semantic battles over specific wording, and the omission of specific planning for "progressive capitalism," there was little to indicate Communist dictation, or even domination, in the spelling out of the Progressive Party's stand. Rather, 1948 was a period during which Communists and non-Communists in the Wallace party could, without serious difference, advocate a single program. The orbits of the two groups, divergent earlier and later, lay in the same plane for the campaign year.

Consequently, the greatest extent of Communist activity in 1948 was to be found not in policy but in the organizational sphere of the Progressive Party. Extreme leftist victories resulted in the domination of several local groups. State organizations in New York and Colorado bore the leftists' stamp. And Wallace's failure to intervene organizationally left his New York headquarters subject to overly strong "party-liner" influences.

But perhaps the most significant conclusion concerning the whole Communist issue was that reached by so many leaders—among them candidates Wallace and Taylor and Professors Tugwell and Emerson—with apparent validity. These moderates felt that the extent of Communist influence exerted—most particularly in the local organizations—was primarily the result of default. The failure of non-Red-hued progressives to rally to the banners, thus placing undue emphasis upon the Communist role, was the most significant single factor.

Nor was there anything in the organizational structure of the Wallace Progressive Party that would have led to Communist domination, had there been any sizable influx of moderate support. Even as it was, domination by the extreme left did not occur, save in isolated instances, until 1950. It was only then that the policies of a skeleton party, decimated by nearly two lean years—years of continuing moderate withdrawals—could be swerved from a strictly *Wallace* party line.

If, then, the Wallace Progressive Party was Communist-influenced but *not* Communist-dominated in the 1948 election campaign, what further conclusions may be drawn from its experiences? In attempting to make any over-all appraisal, it seems pertinent to recall the comments of Henry Wallace himself that a new party must build upon a broad base if it is to have any chance of success. It must be rooted in middle-class America rather than limited to any sharply defined or exclusive group. The experience of the 1948 party bore out this view, yet at the same time it indicated the paradox— the two horns of the dilemma involved. The broad, amorphous group whose participation was vital to success failed to sense sufficient urgency or the imminence of any disaster that would overcome their inherent inertia and bring them to the point of action. On the other hand the narrow, rabid group that sensed a need for action and responded to the Progressive Party, by its very response, and by its vigorous action, kept the others—the moderates—away.

In the light of Wallace's belated and futile attempts in 1950 to finally rid the Progressive Party of its Communist label, it is clear that more decisive steps should have been taken in 1948. Substantiation is also lent this view by the conclusions of O. John Rogge in *New Leader,* January 29, 1951, that

> The Progressive Party, by allowing a small organized minority to have a voice in its councils, had too difficult a time in trying to maintain its independence.

As Max Lerner had commented in *PM,* there had been a need for a non-Communist rather than an anti-Communist party. With a clear disavowal of both Communist support and red-baiting, it might have been possible to temper some of the hysteria of the times. Whlie it is unlikely that any large segment of the American press would have ceased its attacks on the party as "Communistic," "radical," and "Red-dominated," support from other sources might well have been forthcoming. Many Liberals sincerely opposed the Truman foreign policy and were unwilling to "go along," like the ADA, with what they considered a course toward war. Yet the Communist bogey kept them from the new party.

And in the final analysis, it was this Communist bogey, rather than the Communist Party itself, that had the greater influence on the destiny of the Wallace Progressive Party.

# CHAPTER 12

# *"More Than a Single Campaign"*

LONG BEFORE election night brought the gloomy tidings of overwhelming defeat to the camp of the Wallace Progressive Party, the decision had already been made that this was not to be a single-campaign party like so many minor contenders of the past. As early as mid-September, Henry A. Wallace had publicly declared that his party was "not going to die out in 1948." In the final week of the fall campaign, the presidential nominee had promised that this Progressive Party would stay and expand "until the war for peace and abundance is finally won." He continued, "We are not fighting a single campaign. We have organized ourselves into a party that will endure until the American people control this land their work has built."

And on the eve of the election, the quasi-official party organ, the *National Guardian,* had pointed out editorially that the "fight for peace" was more than a single battle, that "the Progressive Party, unlike the two old organizations, had its sights fixed on Wednesday as well as Tuesday. 'First battle in a long war' was the way Wallace put it."

Consequently, when Cabell Phillips, writing in the *New York Times* some weeks after the election, remarked that "the Gideon's Army that Henry A. Wallace led through ten months of spectacular campaigning is bivouacked today on the Plains of Indecision," he was voicing better metaphor than fact. The decision to continue the "fight for peace"

280

after November 2, 1948, had long since been reached. Nor was there any apparent questioning of this decision. However, Phillips was on much sounder ground when he observed: ". . . It is widely agreed that the Progressive Party will need hidden springs of strength to survive as a factor four years, or even two years hence." The final episodes of this particular political saga—the "fight for peace"—were about to unroll.

In the last week of the campaign, third-party manager C. B. "Beanie" Baldwin had issued a summons to an immediate post-election meeting of the party's National Committee in Chicago, saying, "the fight for peace and for an America governed in the people's interest has just begun." It was intended that this conclave should plan both political activity looking toward the 1949 state and municipal elections and a legislative program aimed at influencing the course of congressional action in the months ahead.

Assured of one senatorial seat (so they believed), the Progressives had hoped also for a substantial House delegation in the coming Eighty-first Congress—a hope doomed to disappointment, as we have seen, with the election of only one third-party candidate, Vito Marcantonio.

Notwithstanding the party's repudiation at the polls, the National Committee met as planned to see what could be salvaged for the future. Presidential candidate Wallace made a personal appearance to assure his associates of continued assistance, even to the point of again running for the Presidency in 1952 if that seemed "the best thing" for the party. Wallace promised:

> I intend to continue to support the Progressive Party. I don't know what form it will take. I will do anything that will help. I feel that I want to fight harder and more effectively than in the past.

On the other hand, only a few weeks after the Chicago meeting, vice-presidential candidate Glen H. Taylor indicated in a letter to Baldwin that it was his "intention to quit the party, not politics." And in a public statement Senator Taylor declared: "I was elected from Idaho as a Democrat and sit as one." Moreover, while he expressed a determination to carry on his attacks on American foreign policy at every opportunity, the Senator indicated that he would, as in the past, probably "go along with all the President's liberal domestic programs." And while his formal reconciliation with President Truman was delayed for nearly a year, the erstwhile third-party nominee from this time forward resumed his Democratic Party label.

While any precise numerical estimate is completely lacking, there seems little doubt that many of the rank and file had, with Senator Taylor, read the handwriting on the election wall, and in the weeks immediately following the second of November, moved informally, if reluctantly, toward the re-establishment of their major party ties. At the same time, however, segments of the right wing, as well as virtually the entire left wing of the Progressive Party offered renewed pledges of support in a series of state committee sessions across the nation.

The National Committee continued to meet at regular intervals throughout the winter months that followed. In the course of these meetings various standing committees—on foreign policy, civil liberties, housing, labor legislation, and the like—were appointed to keep abreast of current happenings; plans were laid for the future; and continuing opposition to the Truman foreign policy was voiced.

Thus, in January, 1949 the Committee called upon President Truman to implement his statement that "peace is all we want" by concrete action. They urged that he meet the Russian Premier personally to negotiate the differences separating the U.S. and U.S.S.R. and that he refuse to place the United States in the North Atlantic Pact. This Progressive

Party request for a top-level meeting received prominent display in all the leading Moscow newspapers, and there were indications that an American bid would be favorably received in the Kremlin itself.

President Truman's reply to these unofficial advances was characteristic of his previous comments on the subject: "I would be delighted to meet with Premier Stalin—any time he cares to come to Washington." Negotiations leading to NATO continued unabated.

In response to queries by an American newspaperman, Premier Stalin replied that, on doctors' advice, he was unable to make sea or air trips, but that he would be willing to meet with the President at any of five Soviet cities or in Poland or Czechoslovakia. President Truman remained adamant: "Washington and nowhere else—not even Alaska." And "nowhere" it remained.

To Secretary of State Dean Acheson's objections that these Russian feelers were merely "political maneuvering" and that the United States would not negotiate outside the United Nations, Wallace retorted:

> It was said that we could not consider bypassing the United Nations by engaging in peace talks with Russia. This from a Government that has bypassed the United Nations with the Truman Doctrine and the Marshall Plan and is doing so again in preparing a North Atlantic military pact and to arm Western Europe for war.
>
> . . . Section 33 of the charter itself specifically directs that nations in a dispute threatening the peace shall meet together to discuss and settle their differences.
>
> The rejection of the Stalin offer has been followed by a new wave of hysteria against the so-called menace of Communism.

In addition to voicing continued opposition to the cold war, the Progressive Party also offered related proposals for the solution of domestic problems. Their efforts to publicize this aspect of their program were highlighted by the presentation of a Wallace "budget for abundance" as opposed to the Truman "budget for war." The underlying premise of Wallace's fiscal proposals was that slashing "cold war" expenditures of some 21.1 billions to 7.2 billions for "defense" would make it possible to increase expenditures for "better living" —housing, education, social security, atomic energy for peace —from 12.0 to 26.85 billions.

Moreover, the Wallace budget promised a "more equitable distribution of the tax load"—outright exemptions for individuals in the lower income brackets (under $4,000 for a family of four) and an increased burden on corporate incomes. While this budget had slim chances of adoption by a Democratic Congress, its presentation was designed to bring home graphically a more realistic idea of the cost of the cold war in terms of services left unsupplied and the better living for all that might otherwise be had.


Throughout the spring of 1949 the Wallace Progressive Party continued to make use of two of its proved devices of the campaign a year earlier for propagandizing its position— congressional committee testimony and the national tour. Thus in February, former presidential candidate Wallace led off with testimony before the House Foreign Affairs Committee opposing extension of the Marshall plan.

Wallace argued that the European recovery program had failed in four main points:

1. In the "barriers imposed" on trade between Eastern and Western Europe.

2. In the lack of provision for a necessary increase in Europe's industrial capacity.

3. In the "cold war drive" to rebuild Germany at the expense of Western European allies.

4. In the "policy of cold war and the maintenance of the colonial system" that are "saddling Western Europe with an intolerable burden of armament expenditures."

He also concluded that the proposed North Atlantic Pact would undoubtedly "provoke heavy counter measures" and that in his opinion American policy was demanding "unconditional surrender" on the part of Russia as the price of peace.

This attack on American foreign policy in general and the Pact in particular continued in May before the Senate Foreign Relations Committee with Wallace again advancing as alternative the points proposed a year earlier in his open letter to Stalin. He continued to press for a Truman-Stalin meeting as the best possible method of initiating a new policy of friendship toward Russia. At the conclusion of his testimony, the following exchange occurred with Senator Brien McMahon (Democrat, Connecticut):

> Senator McMahon: My summary of what you have really charged is that your country and my country is [*sic*] in a gigantic conspiracy to make aggressive war upon the Soviet Union.
>
> Mr. Wallace: We are in very grave danger of getting into that position. With the adoption of the Atlantic Pact we would be in substantially that position. I do not use the word "conspiracy" because that implies something subterranean. The pact is open. We are whipping up another holy war against Russia.

Once again, as in 1948, this committee forum produced widespread publicity for the party's views, even though it gained no better a press, nor even any marked abatement of the smear tactics employed during the campaign. Thus C. P. Trusell of the *New York Times* wrote of the hearings: "After

several poses a photographer suggested that Mr. Wallace give
the closed fist salute of the Soviets. Mr. Wallace obliged."
While the *Times* two weeks later publicly, if inconspicuously,
apologized for this misstatement of fact, other papers continued unimpeded in their presentations of the "fact" of
Communist domination of Wallace's mind and party.

A second substantial similarity to the spring campaign of
1948 was the nation-wide "peace tour" of the Progressives in
the spring of 1949. Focal point of this transcontinental trip
was their vehement opposition to the proposed North Atlantic
Treaty.

> The pact is proposed in the name of peace. In fact it
> would lead to war. It is a flagrant violation of the charter
> of the United Nations. It would replace the United Na-
> tions' concept of one world with two irreconcilable blocs
> of nations.

The "peace tour" was the Progressives' method of taking
this issue to the people of America. Planned along the basic
lines of the 1948 campaign tours, this 1949 jaunt added an
international touch with the presence of members of two
European parliaments—British Laborite H. Lester Hutchinson and Italian leftwing Socialist Michelo Giua. Originally
it had been planned that Pierre Cot from the French Chamber
of Deputies and Konni Zilliacus, like Hutchinson a leftwing
M.P., would also accompany the caravan. But the latter two
found their entrance into the United States blocked by a
ruling of both State and Justice departments which, for un-
disclosed reasons, labeled them "inadmissible."

The *New York Times* questioned the wisdom of this action
editorially:

> The good words [about Communist Russia] and the bad
> words [about the "Western Imperialists"] will be said, any-

how, by individuals who are Americans in the legal sense, if not in other senses, and who cannot be excluded. No further harm could have been done if they had been said by Mr. Cot and Mr. Zilliacus.

Cot and Zilliacus were, quite naturally, enraged by this open affront to legally elected members of the duly constituted parliamentary bodies of powers friendly to the United States. The Briton, blaming the "outrage" on the "idiotic arrogance of the State Department," was quoted in the *Times* as saying:

> The United States claims to be the savior of Western democracy and civilization but the State Department deprives the American people of the right to hear both sides and consider all the facts before making up its mind on matters that are life and death issues for all of us.

Despite the exclusion of these two guest speakers, Wallace embarked on his transcontinental peace tour with Hutchinson and Giua. During a three-week visit to some fifteen cities, the three presented their views to some 100,000 persons. Reverting to the six points of his year-earlier open letter to Stalin, the former Vice President offered his own plan as a workable alternative to the North Atlantic Pact with "its certainty of war." To Wallace there was no doubt that

> As America becomes the military arsenal for the Atlantic military pact, more and more liberties and rights will be lost.
> For every dollar spent for arms, for every dollar you lose in welfare, you lose its equivalent in human freedom.
> Nobody gets the freedom, nobody gets the welfare and the arms are a complete and utter waste.
> The reactionaries know that if the Administration wants

an armed pact and an arms economy, it must demand the right to control labor, the right to interfere with labor's rights.

Under the cloak of an anti-Communist crusade, it is the right that threatens our institutions and our most precious liberties.

And just as these words of Wallace had a familiar ring to them, so the techniques employed in the course of the "peace tour" were similar to many utilized in 1948. As was the case a year earlier, this 1949 caravan was financed by the paid admission-voluntary contribution method. However, with audiences substantially smaller than during the presidential year, their contributions were also markedly less. Whereas a year earlier the pitch had usually opened with a call for $1,000 contributions and had generally secured several of that size, this year the starting point was a more modest $100, with relatively few donors at that level. Nevertheless, gross receipts from the fifteen-day tour totaled more than $150,000, with an additional $25,000 realized from a $50-a-plate dinner in New York and a $25-per-plate affair in Newark.

And once again the same general staging technique was utilized—preliminary speakers to "warm up" the audience; Pitchman Gailmor again on hand to extract every possible dollar; then the offstage voice, the darkened hall; and finally, the spotlighted appearance of Henry A. Wallace. While it was Wallace's nominal task to introduce his foreign guests, his address actually remained the feature presentation of the series of rallies, just as it had been a year earlier. However, one marked difference stood out in comparison with the 1948 mass meetings—the general composition of the Wallace audiences. Whereas a year earlier large numbers of teenagers had been attracted by the third party's presidential candidate, this year they were conspicuously missing. While numbers of young people still attended, the average audience age had shifted upwards considerably.

And once again in 1949 the forces of intolerance were abroad in the land. Dissent from the Truman-Vandenberg bipartisan foreign policy was more than ever before evidence of "un-American" activity. Criticism was to be suppressed at all costs. Not only the South, but also the North responded to increasing violations of the Bill of Rights. In one of the more famous cases, a Syracuse University student, Irving Feiner, member of the Young Progressives, stood convicted of disorderly conduct for having refused to heed a police officer's request to cease his street corner attack on President Truman as a "bum" and the city's mayor as a "champagne-sipping bum."

His conviction and jail sentence were upheld through the courts of the state and ultimately by the Supreme Court, notwithstanding a bitter and eloquent dissent by Associate Justice Hugo Black, joined by his colleagues William O. Douglas and Sherman Minton. "Even a partial abandonment . . . marks a dark day for civil liberties in our nation," said Black (340 U.S. 315).

> . . . this conviction makes a mockery of the free speech guarantees of the First and Fourteenth Amendments. The end result . . . is to approve a simple and readily available technique by which cities and states can with impunity subject all speeches, political or otherwise, to the supervision and censorship of the local police . . .
>
> . . . today's holding means that as a practical matter minority speakers can be silenced in any city. Hereafter . . . the policeman's club can take heavy toll of a current administration's public critics. Criticism of public officials will be too dangerous for all but the most courageous . . . .

But while the Wallace "peace tour" influenced few minds not already favorable, it did serve as a measure for continuing that party organization still operative across the nation. Despite the dismal showing at the polls and the substantial defections of the post-election period, this spring tour indicated that it would be a grave mistake to count the Wallace Progressive Party out as long as American foreign policy remained in dispute, with "peace" a crucial issue. Moreover, with an economic recession beginning, and unemployment already becoming a serious problem in the "indicator" areas of New England and upstate New York, it seemed as though the Wallace crusade might be about to acquire new converts from a source denied it by 1948's prosperity—the ranks of the domestically discontented.

But while the testimony and tours offered by the Wallace Progressive Party in the spring of 1949 closely paralleled their preconvention campaign of 1948, happenings within the party fold were soon to blot out those rather feeble rays of hope. First, came another crushing repudiation at the polls— in New York's Twentieth (Manhattan) Congressional District where the seat long occupied by the late Representative Sol Bloom was at stake in a special election. A year earlier the American Labor Party candidate had scored a sweeping victory in a Bronx by-election, thus lending considerable support to party morale. During this year and this district, however, the special election proved a damaging blow to party hopes of resurgence. Nor could Progressive spokesmen ascribe the defeat to "ganging up" by the other three parties involved (Democrats, Republicans, and Liberals), as had been the case in several fall contests in the metropolitan area. In a four-cornered race, a third-party candidate was the victor, but he was the candidate of the Liberal and Four Freedoms parties—Franklin D. Roosevelt, Jr. The ALP nominee, Dr.

Annette T. Rubinstein, ran a sorry last, garnering only 6.6 per cent of the total vote.[1] And while the special conditions that had prevailed to aid the Isaacson Bronx victory a year earlier were not repeated in this predominantly Irish section, still the returns were disappointing. For the third party had conducted a vigorous campaign, once more bringing in its name speakers, Henry A. Wallace and Vito Marcantonio, to assist the local candidates.

Disheartening as this defeat was, its damage to party hopes was slight compared with that rendered by the growing internal rift that appeared as the summer of 1949 wore on. The first indications that all was not well within the ranks of the third party's remaining faithful had come earlier in the year with the coolness reported in New York's ALP between Representative Vito Marcantonio, state chairman, and Eugene P. Connolly, New York County chairman. Warren Moscow reported in the *New York Times* that Connolly was spokesman for a faction opposing the "continued open participation of Communists on the ground that the future of the ALP lies with the future of the national Progressive Party and that the Communist bridge hurt the Wallace candidacy immeasurably in the last national election." Other rumors indicated that O. John Rogge, militant leftwing non-Communist and unsuccessful ALP contender for the office of surrogate in 1948 was up in arms following reports of "vote trading" in a Harlem area that had aided the Marcantonio candidacy at his expense.

[1] Results in the Twentieth District election, May 17, 1949, as published in the *New York Times,* May 18, 1949, were: Franklin D. Roosevelt, Jr. (Four Freedoms–Liberal), 41,146, 50.9 per cent; Benjamin H. Shalleck (Tammany Democrat), 24,352, 30.1 per cent; William H. McIntyre (Republican), 10,026, 12.4 per cent; Annette T. Rubinstein (American Labor Party), 5,348, 6.6 per cent. A year earlier, Eugene P. Connolly, the American Labor Party candidate, had received 15,727 votes—12.6 per cent of the total cast in the Twentieth.

Nor was the Connolly-Marcantonio split long in reaching
the surface. With a municipal election pending, and Marcantonio ready to run for Mayor, Connolly refused to accept the
state chairman's designee for the post of Borough President
of Manhattan. Instead he declared his own candidacy for the
office, thus forcing the ALP into a primary battle. With hopes
of victory in the fall election already slim, it was clear that
the real issue at stake was future control of the Labor Party
organization, with New York County the immediate target. A
bitter battle ensued. When the smoke had cleared away following the September primary, it was found that the Marcantonio slate had triumphed by an overwhelming 5 to 1 margin.
The defeat at the polls of the moderate Connolly faction
meant that Vito Marcantonio had now acquired virtually un-
challenged control of the entire New York State branch of the
third party.

This achievement was closely followed by rumors of an
impending Wallace-Marcantonio split. The Congressman had
been urging the former presidential candidate to enter the
special New York State senatorial election occasioned for
November, 1949 by the resignation of old line New Deal
Senator Robert F. Wagner. It was expected that Wallace, on
the basis of his 1948 Empire State showing, would run a
strong race, thus lending support to Marcantonio's mayoralty
candidacy. When Wallace declined repeated urgings that he
enter the lists, it seemed that he might be on the verge of a
break with the party organization in New York.

These rumors were only partially controverted by a speech
of the former Vice President at Madison Square Garden on
the third anniversary of his 1946 address in the same arena
that had marked the initiation of the "fight for peace." In
his remarks Wallace indicated an increasingly critical attitude toward the Soviet Union, noting pointedly that the "welfare state" cannot be achieved by "police state methods."
Moreover he warned, ". . . if anyone should try to use

the Progressive Party for Communist Party purposes, he would be doing the cause of peace a distinct disservice." Nevertheless, he promised his full support for Marcantonio in the mayoralty race.

The following night at a dinner in Wallace's honor, the Congressman announced that there would be no state ticket because:

> We deem it important to win the municipal election . . . such a victory can be achieved only by following a policy of concentration which was adopted by the *National Committee of the Progressive Party*. For the ALP to nominate [state candidates] would detract from the policy of concentration and would only diffuse our strength from the important major objective of winning in the municipal campaign. [Italics supplied.]

With this bow in the direction of the national party, it appeared that the Wallace-Marcantonio rift had been either originally exaggerated or presently healed. This view was seemingly substantiated by a two-day meeting of the National Committee in Cleveland at which "Marc" was named head of a campaign committee to plan for the 1950 congressional races. At the same time Wallace's views were embodied in a six-point plan to combat what the Progressives termed a "growing economic crisis."

Nevertheless this surface appearance of unity was not heightened by the single speech during the course of the New York mayoralty campaign which the former Vice President delivered in behalf of ALP candidate Marcantonio. While Wallace declared that "Marc" had advanced the cause of peace and understanding and disarmament in a "war-mad world" and bore the Progressive banner in this race, still the fact that Wallace spoke only once in the course of the campaign seemed significant.

However, it was only after the November election in which Marcantonio, while running well for a minor-party candidate, was defeated (receiving 356,423, or 13.8 per cent as against Wallace's 423,424, 15.2 per cent in 1948) that a marked coolness between Wallace and leftwing officials of the party he had founded became quite apparent. Informed observers including Helen Fuller of *New Republic* predicted a gradual parting of the ways that would put an end to the party in less than a year.

It was, however, nearly a year before Wallace finally divulged some of the reasons for his growing dissatisfaction during the summer and fall of 1949. First, he said, reports reaching him throughout 1949 from Communist-dominated Czechoslovakia had gradually convinced him that political cooperation with the Communists was impossible. Second, he had become increasingly aware that, with few exceptions, it was only the extreme leftists who had remained fully active in the Progressive Party following the 1948 election. Third, he deplored the continuing and even increasing use by these leftwing groups of tactics that tended to drive away the very groups on whose support Wallace felt a lasting party must be constructed.

The Peekskill incidents involving Paul Robeson were typical of the sort of activity which, in his view, served to permanently alienate large segments of "Protestant middle class America" which he had hoped to attract to his Progressive Party. These Peekskill events began in August, 1949 when a group of veterans' organizations in that Hudson Valley city undertook to prevent a scheduled open-air concert by Negro baritone Paul Robeson for the benefit of the Civil Rights Congress (a group listed as "subversive" by the Department of Justice). When the veterans "paraded" in mass formation back and forth in front of the park entrance to prevent the Robeson audience from entering or leaving, a riot occurred—cars were overturned and several people injured. The concert was called off.

In the words of Milton Flynt, commander of Peekskill Post 274 of the American Legion, as quoted in the *New York Times:*

> Our objective was to prevent the Paul Robeson concert and I think our objective was reached. Anything that happened after the organized demonstration was dispersed was entirely up to the individual citizens and should not be blamed on the patriotic organizations.

This rather warped view of the proper function of a patriotic organization was almost universally assailed in the days after the incident—both by national leaders of the veterans' groups involved and by citizens interested in protecting the rights of all—even the most detested—to a full and peaceful expression of their views.

As the *New York Times* commented editorially:

> Sympathy for Paul Robeson and his followers, after their interrupted concert near Peekskill last Sunday was not increased by their threat to mobilize "20,000 strong" this Sunday and their protest against a permit for the anti-Communist veterans to stage another parade. But sympathy or lack of sympathy has nothing to do with the case. Mr. Robeson has a right to assemble his followers peaceably, sing and, if he wants, make a speech . . .
> . . . The truth is, of course, that civil rights are rarely threatened except when those who claim them hold views "hateful" to the majority.

Not content with similar verdicts indicating wide disapproval of the veterans' actions, Robeson, supported by much of the left wing of the New York City ALP, vowed that the concert would be held—that he would be back the following Sunday with his own protection. The Peekskill veterans' groups replied in kind—that they, too, would be back. With the stage seemingly set for a battle royal, Governor Thomas E. Dewey ordered all available state police to the scene. Local police officers from the near-by communities were dep-utized into a total force of nearly one thousand.

This mobilization proved adequate to keep the groups apart as some 15,000 persons—Robeson-ites, Communists, ALP members, Wallace-ites, and liberals merely interested in personally protesting against suppression of free speech— filed into place. The concert proceeded with only a few minor disturbances. Once the performance ended, however, the police force proved insufficient to patrol the roads leading from the grounds. Mass stoning began as the audience de-parted, bus and auto windows were shattered, and a total of 145 persons (according to impartial reports) were injured, several seriously.

Widespread protests by such groups as the American Civil Liberties Union against the local officials' handling of both policing and prosecution led to an eventual order for a grand jury probe by Governor Dewey. The report filed by a Westchester County "blue ribbon" group the following year concerned itself primarily with what it felt was a carefully planned Communist use of Westchester as a proving ground for mass mobilization tactics. Moreover it attacked the ACLU for an earlier report in which this nonpartisan body had ascribed the riot to local anti-Negro and anti-Semitic sentiment as well as to anti-Communist animosity, and in which it had charged that local and county police "permitted the assault upon the Robeson supporters." More objective in-quiry indicated a clear-cut violation of civil liberties on the first occasion by the veterans' groups alone, but a substantial contribution to the second riot by the attitude and conduct

of the Robeson-ites. Despite the complete legality of their assemblage, their "we dare you" approach, when coupled to
the "you're on" response of the veterans had led to the second bloody affray.

While Wallace publicly deplored violence of the sort exhibited here, resulting in restrictions of freedom of speech
and assembly, he later privately criticized the intemperate
speeches and actions on the part of his more extreme followers calculated to hurl a virtual challenge to interference
and violence. He was particularly critical of threats such as
that voiced by Robeson that his group would, if denied adequate police protection, take the law into its own hands.

At the same time the Peekskill violence was erupting in
New York, there was evidence elsewhere of a growing rift
between the moderates and the extreme leftists of the Progressive Party. In New Jersey, state party leader and gubernatorial candidate James Imbrie flatly refused to accept the
proffered support of the New Jersey Communist Party in his
campaign. In Washington, Senator Glen H. Taylor's complete
return to the Democratic Party was heralded by a White
House conference with President Truman. Indicating that his
views on administration foreign policy had not changed, the
Senator commented, according to the *New York Times:*

> I wish I could go along with the President [on foreign
> as well as on domestic policy]. It would be much more
> pleasant. I can't get it out of my head that we can't get
> along with the Russians and make agreements. The Presi-
> dent believes in a tough foreign policy.

Coupled with these various incidents of 1949, there were
other indications early in 1950 that Henry A. Wallace was on
the verge of a complete break with his Progressive Party. In
both speeches and committee testimony it seemed that
Wallace was adopting a position that was primarily indi-

vidualistic, rather than reflective of a party stand. Thus, on the very day that a party program looking forward to the 1950 elections was being issued from the National Committee in the name of Secretary C. B. Baldwin (previous reports had been in Wallace's name), the erstwhile presidential nominee was delivering an address to a church group in which, completely ignoring party affairs, he dealt with the much broader over-all problem of the need for an understanding between communism on the one hand, and capitalism and Christianity on the other.

Shortly thereafter the former Vice President voluntarily appeared before the House Committee on un-American Activities to defend his personal position and reputation against charges hurled that he had been responsible for wartime shipments of uranium to Russia. Regardless of his justification and motivation in this matter, it was rather unique for the third-party spokesman to be appearing in such a role. For this marked the first time since the inception of the "fight for peace" that Wallace had utilized congressional testimony as a method of personal defense against the unrelenting attacks on him rather than as a national forum for his party's views.

In the face of these internal difficulties a second national convention was called to Chicago in February, 1950 by the National Committee of the Progressive Party to adopt a comprehensive program and a plan of action for the coming fall congressional elections. Most observers, however, expected that the assemblage would develop into a final showdown between the leftwing and the remaining rightwing elements in the party, with Wallace's continued membership and leadership at stake.

Some 1,200 delegates from thirty-five states gathered February 24 in the drafty expanse of Lakeland Auditorium. The anticipated duel began at once as Wallace opened proceedings with an address reported by W. H. Lawrence of the *New York Times* as an "attempt to remove the Communist label from the Progressive Party." He proceeded to assail "with equal fervor" the foreign policies of both the United States and the Soviet Union, which he claimed, "stand out as the big brutes of the world."

> Each in its own eyes rests on high moral principles—but each in the eyes of other nations is guided by force and force alone.

Indicating that he was not urging a purge of party ranks "because of past or present labels," Wallace said flatly that the third party couldn't tolerate "organized factions or groups" within its ranks, and that Communists in the party couldn't be permitted to place first emphasis on any allegiance to Moscow. We must convince the people, said the former Vice President, that

> We are fighting for peace, not because any foreign power wants us to fight for peace, but because we understand the deep needs of the American people and the world.
>
> Our principles are vastly different from those of the Communist Party. We do not believe in the one-party system of government for the United States. Our philosophy is not based upon the principles of Marxism or Leninism. Our program is based upon reform by constitutional and democratic processes. We believe in progressive capitalism not socialism.
>
> The Progressive Party stands for civil liberties *for all.* Civil liberties, like peace, are indivisible. We believe in civil liberties in Eastern Europe, but we recognize that except in the case of Czechoslovakia there has been no democratic tradition on which to build.
>
> The Communists have their party; we have ours. We agree with the Communists that peace with Russia is

possible—but that doesn't make us Communists. We agree
with the Democrats and Republicans that capitalism can
be made to work—but that doesn't make us Democrats or
Republicans.

Offering a ten-point program designed to keep America
from "falling into monopoly fascism, war and communism,"
the former presidential candidate called upon the party to
abandon its present "narrow range of support" and to become "a new broader forward-looking party." Having thus
placed the issue squarely before the assembled delegates, Wallace departed for Des Moines, Iowa, to await the verdict of
the convention in its remaining sessions.

The following day a protracted floor fight ensued over the
proposed Wallace planks on the Soviet. The battle between
left- and rightwing groups ended only when it was announced
that Representative Vito Marcantonio was in agreement with
Wallace on the issue. With the left wing thus brought into
line, the two camps were apparently reconciled, and the following statement was written into the 1950 Progressive platform:

The Progressive Party recognizes that while the United
States and the Soviet Union have both made mistakes in
foreign policy, these two great countries can rise above
their respective shortcomings, to work together fruitfully
for international peace and cooperation.

We are not apologists for Russia, but in so saying, we
want it understood that our supreme objective is one world
at peace, and to that end it is essential that an understanding be reached between the United States and the Soviet
Union.

This language seemed to temper considerably the more
vigorous tone employed by Wallace in his address. Nevertheless, he indicated from Des Moines that the platform was

"generally satisfactory" to him and substantially in accord with his demands.

In addition to these foreign policy pledges, the Progressives' 1950 platform reiterated the domestic planks adopted at the 1948 convention. As for the strategy to be employed in the fall campaign, the party indicated that it would concentrate "in selected areas where the candidates of the old parties offer the voters no real choice and where a victory or balance-of-power vote for our candidates will help unite and strengthen the Progressive forces."

By comparison with the first national convention at Philadelphia in the summer of 1948, this Chicago assemblage in mid-winter 1950 clearly indicated the state to which the party's fortunes had been reduced in the intervening two years. Instead of some three thousand exuberant singing delegates from forty-seven states, there were less than half that number, representing thirty-five states, at Chicago. Instead of the buoyant enthusiasm of two years earlier, hanging over their heads was a pall produced by their failures and by the basic disagreement in their ranks. Whereas in 1948 non-Communists and Communists alike had seemed in basic agreement on most major points of policy, this time evidences of a growing rift were termed an "uneasy truce" between right and left; this was to later prove a short-lived attempt at final reconciliation.

While labor representation at Philadelphia had been limited to the leftwing CIO unions, at Chicago it had dwindled to the vanishing point. Gone from the chair was Albert J. Fitzgerald, United Electrical Workers' president who had served as permanent chairman at Philadelphia. And gone from the floor were the members of his once third largest CIO union. For the UE itself had been torn asunder in the intervening period by the CIO's "purge" of leftwing unions and leaders who had violated national policy to support Henry A. Wallace in 1948.

But, while this second national convention of the Progressive Party showed clearly the stresses and strains that had developed, it also indicated that there was a still substantial structure available for future campaigns. After all, this was not a presidential year, a national party in an off-year was a novelty on the American political scene, and the actual election date was some nine months in the future. Consequently it was hardly to be expected that interest would be at the same fever pitch earlier reached in Philadelphia. Time alone would determine whether this was the first step in the party's fight back, or merely another stage in a gradual decline.

Despite the appearance of unity attained at Chicago, events during the early part of 1950 indicated a continuing coolness between Henry A. Wallace and the party he had founded. While the former Vice President continued to call for a Truman-Stalin meeting in the interests of world peace, and while he continued to press for such measures as an International Development Corporation to invest in the "basic economy of the underdeveloped and over-crowded areas of the world for the specific purpose of increasing world output, stimulating world trade, and satisfying human need," his addresses were becoming more and more expressions of individual position rather than party pronouncements.

In fact, portions of one radio address indicated a virtual abandonment of the party organization, as Wallace called upon the American people to form "Progressive Capitalism clubs . . . for the purpose of saving capitalism in the United States by making it serve the people rather than exploit them." Moreover, while the third party once again resorted to congressional committee testimony for publicity purposes as it had in 1948 and 1949, it no longer presented the former Vice President as its spokesman. Hearings of the House Committee on un-American Activities considering the proposed Wood and Nixon bills (whose features were later embodied in the McCarran Act) saw Progressive Party opposition led by Professor Thomas I. Emerson of the Yale Law School.

Meanwhile, from New York came word that Wallace had once again declined to become an ALP nominee in a state contest—this time for the governorship of the Empire State— but that nevertheless the party was planning to run a gubernatorial candidate to maintain its legal status. Thus, as late as June, 1950, it seemed that there was little prospect of a clean break between Wallace and his Progressive Party. Rather it seemed that their association would weaken gradually through the course of time, with no clear point of separation.

All this changed overnight with the invasion of the Republic of (South) Korea by North Korean Communist troops and the decision of President Truman, quickly backed by the U.N.'s Russian-less Security Council, to oppose the aggression with armed force. The National Committee of the Progressive Party met in New York to consider its policy toward the situation. Over Wallace's objections, the Committee reached the decision to press for the admission of Red China to the United Nations and the return of the Soviet Union to the Security Council as prerequisites for ending the conflict. Their conclusion was:

> With the effectiveness of the United Nations restored through the admission of the government of China and the consequent return of the Soviet Union to the council table, the Security Council will be in a position to take measures to preserve the peace.

Meanwhile, Wallace had been in touch with Secretary General Trygve Lie of the United Nations and had been given access to U.N. reports coming in from the thirty-eighth parallel. There was no longer any doubt in his mind as to the nature of the conflict or Soviet intentions. When the Committee refused to modify its statement in line with his views, the former presidential candidate refused to go along, countering with a public statement of position.

> I want to make it clear that when Russia, the United States and the United Nations appeal to force, I am on the side of the United States and the United Nations. Undoubtedly the Russians could have prevented the attack by the North Koreans and undoubtedly they could stop the attack any time they wish.
>
> I hold no brief for the past actions of either the United States or Russia but when my country is at war and the United Nations sanctions that war, I am on the side of my country and the United Nations.

But while declaring his support of the American–United Nations position, the former Vice President at the same time warned:

> The United States will fight a losing battle in Asia as long as she stands behind feudal regimes based on exorbitant charges of land lords and money lords. Russia is using a mightier power than the atom bomb as long as she helps the people to get out from under their ancient aggressors. But we in the United States have a still mightier power if we will only use it for the people. I refer to our modern technology and our huge reserves of capital, when and if applied to solving the problems of poverty and hunger.

For the first time in its brief history the Progressive Party was faced with a substantive difference over policy. For the first time it became possible to single out those third-party members willing to follow the Russian-inspired decision for war and against the United Nations rather than continue to back the Wallace program for peace and support of the United Nations. For the first time since the overnight reversal of the Communist Party line with the 1941 German invasion of Russia, it became possible to separate American Communists and pro-Communists from non-Communist dissenters and anti-war elements on a definite policy basis.

Wallace indicated that he would wait for rank-and-file support of his position to develop within party ranks. Should this fail to materialize, thus leaving the National Committee decision as the official policy of the Progressive Party, he would resign as the party's leader. Opposing camps were quick to respond. The Communist Party press turned on the man who had been its darling since September 15, 1946, and assailed him in no uncertain terms. Editorialized the *Daily Worker:*

> The thinking and policies which dragged Wallace into the position supporting an aggressive colonial war were indicated when he attacked the Communists some time ago and sought to equate Soviet and Wall Street policies.
>
> When Stalin accepted Wallace's bid for negotiations with the United States, Wallace was denounced by the Wall Street buccaneers and the cold warriors of Washington for his pains. Now Wallace has joined these same forces who vilified and traduced him throughout the period of the cold war.

On the other hand, non-Communist leaders of the Progressive Party rallied to Wallace's support. Both O. John Rogge and James Waterman Wise of New York announced their agreement with his stand as did James Stewart Martin and Dr. John E. T. Camper in Maryland. Professor Thomas I. Emerson of Connecticut, who had cast one of the two pro-Wallace votes in the National Committee, announced that he was in wholehearted agreement with the former Vice President on Korea, even though he was unable to join him in support of a "status quo" neutralization of Formosa by American naval forces.

In the course of the following weeks, the mail reaching Wallace indicated a substantial majority of the party rank and file in favor of the position he had adopted and in opposition to the National Committee. Despite this, most of the state party committees endorsed the national party stand. In Connecticut a two-day convention of one hundred delegates adopted a resolution condemning Wallace for his support of the United Nations action. In Maryland, announcement of a similar state party stand came from executive secretary Harold Buchman, rather than from chairman Camper or vice chairman Martin. Buchman was quoted in the *Baltimore Sun* as saying of Wallace:

> I feel he made a valuable contribution to the subject of peace [before his stand on the Korean crisis].
>
> I regret his failure to agree with the resolution which is actually a compromise of all the divergent positions in the Progressive Party.
>
> I hope the course of events will convince him of the correctness of the stand of the majority.

In New York, the third party's most important state organization, now firmly in the hands of Representative Vito Marcantonio, censured Wallace. But signs of dissension were clear as former Representative Leo Isaacson announced that he would accept the ALP gubernatorial nomination tendered him only if he would be assured of Wallace's support. On the West Coast, 150 delegates to an Independent Progressive Party state convention in Sacramento tried to straddle the issue, adopting what the *New York Times* called a "conspicuously guarded stand."

But this was not an issue that could be straddled. The lines were drawn. Convinced that the still active party officials represented a viewpoint originating in the Kremlin rather than among the party's followers, Henry A. Wallace decided now on the final break. As he remarked later, he could see that many of his associates placed Moscow ahead of the United Nations, and that others whom he felt were clearly non-Communist had been in association with the "party-liners" so long they seemed to have soaked up similar views.

In a two-paragraph note to party secretary C. B. Baldwin, so long his personal associate, Wallace revealed his decision.

> In view of the actions recently taken by the national committee of the Progressive Party and the various state committees, I am convinced I can more effectively serve the cause of peace by resigning from the national committee and the executive committee of the Progressive Party.
>
> You will, therefore, take this letter as my formal resignation from the party.

In a later message, prepared for Pathé Newsreel, Wallace expanded somewhat on this brief note.

> I resigned from the Progressive Party because I felt the party should support the United States and the United Nations in the Korean war. My mail convinces me that fully half of the rank and file of the party is with me but I also know that the top leadership is almost 100 per cent against me. Therefore I could no longer serve the cause of peace through the Progressive Party. It had become clear to me that victory in Korea for the United States and the United Nations was the absolutely essential first step on the road to peace. The second step which in the long run is far more important is planning both while we fight and after we win to gain the friendship of the people of Asia. Only through Asiatic friendship and cooperation can we prevent successful Russian aggression. The common man is on the march

all over the world. It is our job to help that march to expand and enrich human values, not to destroy them. In action this means a program of economic help to a united Korea by the UN after the war stops. We can and must do a better job than Russia in helping the common man to help himself all over the world. This is the only possible road to safety for the United States, the United Nations, for your children and my children. I still hope Russia will cooperate with us through the United Nations to help the march of the common man to become constructive not destructive.

But the first brief notice had served as death warrant for the party whose cause he had served ever since he had announced its formation on December 29, 1947. For without the man around whom the "fight for peace" had centered, around whose views workers of both right and left wings had been hitherto able to rally, the Progressive Party was obviously doomed.

Its already depleted ranks were immediately subjected to a mass exodus that left them bare of virtually all except the disciplined "party-liners." From all across the nation, those non-Communist liberals still in the party began announcing their resignations. Professor Thomas I. Emerson had already, on August 3, taken his departure. With the Wallace announcement, countless others—Martin and Camper in Maryland, Corliss Lamont in New York, and practically all the non-Communist name figures—followed suit. Admitted former Communist Lee Pressman, accused by the press in 1948 of leading the "left-wing, pro-Communist policies" of the party, announced that he was resigning from the ALP because its policies now reflected those of the Communist Party. The consensus of opinion was that the party had been so weakened by the constant defections ever since 1948 that it no longer possessed an organization whose control was worth contesting. The Communists, pro-Communists, and other "party-liners" who remained in the no-longer-Wallace Progressive Party were left to pluck its bones at will.

Only in New York, where the ALP still possessed a well-grounded firmly established ward and precinct organization, was there disagreement with this view. O. John Rogge, who had previously taken such a firm stand in support of Wallace's *policy* position, announced that he thought Wallace was making an error in leaving rather than pressing for the adoption of his views within the party. Rogge was confident that with the former presidential candidate as a rallying point for the weakened forces of the right it would still be possible to take over from the extreme leftists. Former Representative Leo Isaacson indicated that he, too, while agreeing with the Wallace policy views, would not resign from the party, but would continue to press from within for modification of its attitude.

Those who supported this Rogge-Isaacson position soon found just how hopeless was their task. At a sparsely-attended National Committee meeting the following month in Chicago, Rogge saw his call for a special national convention to review the party's position on foreign policy defeated by a decisive 41 to 2 vote.

It thus became evident that the scattered remains of the third-party venture were at last in the hands of the extreme leftists. On its deathbed the organization had finally succumbed to their almost complete control; it had been "narrowed" in accordance with their earlier hopes to the point where they were clearly supreme. But theirs was the control and the supremacy of a party that no longer boasted Henry A. Wallace, former Vice President of the United States, as its leader; of a party that no longer could claim spiritual affinity with American Progressives of the past. With Wallace gone, with the native Progressive elements gone, the Wallace

Progressive Party had faded from the American political
scene, leaving behind only a crimson shadow.

Where once it had stood proudly on the ballots of forty-
five states, now only scattered remnants, either captive of or
clearly addicted to a Communist Party line (despite an occasional remaining non-Communist leader) were visible. Such
was the case in California, in Connecticut, in Maryland, and
in a few other states. Elsewhere the third party had vanished,
leaving hardly a trace. Only in New York where the American Labor Party had preceded the Wallace Progressive Party
by some eleven years were there indications that the rightwing elements still fought on within the party—challenging
the increasing one-man control of Vito Marcantonio and his
fellows of the farthest left.

And even in the Empire State, the "triumph" of the extreme leftists was to prove both hollow and short-lived. Shorn
of the support of Henry Wallace and many of the moderates, the party's 1950 gubernatorial candidate, John T. Mc-
Manus, received only a little more than 200,000 votes, in
contrast to the more than half a million received by Wallace
two years earlier. And in this same election, the "unbeatable"
Marcantonio came to the end of the congressional trail in
his own Eighteenth District, falling before a coalition candidate, James G. Donovan, backed by Democrats, Republicans,
and Liberals.

Within half a dozen years both Marcantonio and the state
party he had helped found would be dead—but not before he
too had ultimately come to the parting of the ways with the
Communists in the party's ranks. In 1949 with "Marc" as its
mayoralty candidate, and Wallace still in the fold, the ALP
had polled more than 350,000 in New York City. Four years
later with Clifford T. McAvoy as candidate for the same post,
it could do no better than 54,372. A day later, "Marc" resigned as state chairman, blasting the Communists for their

support of Mayor Robert Wagner instead of the ALP nominee, and prophesying:

> The ALP will become more and more a pressure group with the issue unresolved. It will become more and more a mimeograph machine rather than a political party. This role is inescapable, it is inherent in the present house divided condition of our party.

The handwriting was clearly on the wall, and the 1954 gubernatorial campaign wrote "finis" to the history of the American Labor Party as a legal political entity in the state. Its candidate, once again John T. McManus, this time received only 46,886 votes—not up to the legal minimum of 50,000 for retention of the party name and place on the ballot. But Vito Marcantonio had not survived to see his party succumb, for in August, at the age of fifty-one, he had passed away.

Interment of the ALP was delayed nearly two years, but in October, 1956, state chairman Peter J. Hawley announced its final dissolution—ascribing its decline to the cold war and to the loss of labor support. Significantly, however, the Communist Party in the United States had decided a month earlier on a new "party line"—to renew its independent fight on the grounds that it had previously placed "too much reliance" on the Progressive Party venture.

In the meantime there had been little to show nationally for third-party efforts once 1950 had raised the uncompromisable policy barrier between the extreme leftists and the much larger majority of party moderates. The attempt to wage a second presidential campaign in 1952 went almost unnoticed. From the ranks of California's Independent Progressive Party came Vincent William Hallinan, San Francisco lawyer, to carry on the tattered, shrinking, now crimson-hued banner. A thirty-state campaign tour with running mate Mrs. Char-

lotta Bass, was rewarded with little more than fringe votes
—140,023 all across the nation, with nearly half concentrated
in the Empire State. So vanished the last remnants of Wallace's crusaders. Like the ALP in New York, the national
party, bereft of the dominant figure of Henry A. Wallace, died
not with the bang of Korea, but with a fading whimper at
America's polling places.

The prophetic words of Fiorello H. La Guardia once more
resounded in the minds of those who watched the final rites:

> The new progressive movement, when it comes, will
> come from the Main Street of thousands of Prairie Junc-
> tions, and not from Union Square in Manhattan.

# CHAPTER 13

# *Road to Disenchantment*

IN 1947 a motley array of crusaders had taken to the third-party road. Hopes had been high, theirs was a vision of a better world—a world of peace, freedom, and abundance. By the end of the trail, their hopes had been shattered—their independent political path had become a road to disenchantment—disenchantment for the candidates, disenchantment for their fellow politicians, disenchantment for the followers of whatever motivation and persuasion, disenchantment for more objective viewers of the American political scene.

For Henry A. Wallace, with his vision of a broad people's party to wage the "fight for peace" on behalf of the common man, the blow was most shattering of all. For he had staked his reputation—a reputation based on a lifetime of service in the public interest—on the outcome of his personal crusade against the Truman-doctrine style of foreign policy. And only in the most limited sense was there achievement of his basic goal, that the people might have a choice—an alternative to the bipartisan get-tough-with-Russia policy. The people had their choice, and they rejected it in no uncertain terms.

But the factors accompanying the defeat were far more tragic than defeat itself. For victory in the immediate sense of a triumph at the polls had never been expected. Instead, the hope had been to demonstrate a substantial discontent—

discontent with the abandonment of Franklin D. Roosevelt's foreign policy, discontent with the termination of the Democratic Party's New Deal outlook. Embarking on the third-party course without the firm backing of either farm or labor segments had seemed foolhardy from the beginning. Indeed it had been early labeled "quixotic politics." Nevertheless, a major show of support for a third-party venture had been maneuvered by long-time friends and trusted advisers to convince the former Vice President that he must make the political sacrifice. But once he had been convinced, once his decision had been announced, many of these friends and advisers had rapidly retreated to the storm cellar of political conformity. Others turned their backs on him as the campaign progressed. Henry Wallace soon discovered that the waging of a *losing*—or even worse, a *hopeless*—political campaign is one of the real tests of friendship.

Nor did the people themselves, the common man in whom he placed such reliance, respond in any numbers to his call. Faced with more imminent domestic issues, the American voter turned his back on the "remote, unrealistic" national scene. Faced with a third-party promise of negotiations with the Russians, he found increasing signs of Soviet intransigence throughout a complex hostile world. Faced with the prospect of a Dewey Republican victory, he turned to the lesser evil —an always human, newly vigorous and hard-hitting Harry S. Truman. At least he turned in terms of a small plurality of the scant 51 per cent of qualified voters who actually took the trouble to go to the polls—thus casting a quavering mandate for a Fair Deal program that was to be so little realized.

But the ultimate in disenchantment for the man who had so increased the stature of the vice presidency in his many wartime services—the man who as Secretary of Agriculture had been both the experimenter and creator of a model administrative order, the man who had been the philosopher spearhead of the New Deal—was not the anticipated though untimely termination of his political career. Rather it was the smearing of his entire record, the attempt to cast into disrepute the accomplishments of a lifetime in the service of humanity. No *de la Mancha* in his earlier jousts, he became the disillusioned victim of those who had earlier urged upon him this third-party course of action.

The ultimate post-Korean capture of the party he had founded by the extremists of the left came almost as an anticlimax to the quiet, graying, friendly man who had attempted to embody in practice the most basic tenets of his fundamental Christianity.

To Glen H. Taylor, too, the Progressive Party path had proved a road to disenchantment. Far more the practical politician than his running mate, he had nevertheless made his decision, not on a politically rational basis, but on the basis of conscience. Realizing the likely sacrifice of the "best job [he'd] ever had," he too had hoped to stir the conscience of the American public by his part in the crusade. But the public had cast him in the buffoon's role—that of a "singing cowboy"—a role that TV could cast much better. Seeking, perhaps, to use the Communists for the advancement of a more democratic capitalistic society, he found that they had used and destroyed him in the process. For his "leftwing" association—an association viciously misrepresented to the voters of Idaho in his fatal 1950 primary battle—returned to haunt Taylor.

A similar fate lent disenchantment to many other "professionals" who had taken to the third-party road. Rexford Guy Tugwell, Elmer Benson, "Beanie" Baldwin—all emerged with reputations tarnished, political careers ended with the added embitterment that it had been in a hopeless cause. Even Vito Marcantonio, that long-time tightrope walker of the extreme left, came ultimately to the end of the rope—and eventually to the point where he could follow the "party line" no longer.

What of the crusaders themselves—those who had embarked with hopes so high, with naïveté and amateurism blazoned so clearly on their shields, on this holy war for a more peaceful world? Disillusionment was the lot of all—public rejection, hostility in an ever increasing period of conformity. Economic sacrifice, the loss of jobs, the scorn of neighbors was in store for many. But even worse was the public reaction that greeted their endeavor—a crystallization, a hardening of opinion against the ideas they advocated, the solidifying of support for a peacetime militarization which they fought. Not only was the fifteen-billion-dollar defense budget soon to climb to the permanent forty-billion-dollar level, but the peacetime draft which they opposed as "un-American" was to become so accepted a part of the scene that Congress could easily re-enact it within short years as "noncontroversial."

Even the Communists emerged among the disenchanted. Their "superior understanding" of American history had once more led them astray. The universe of America had proved larger than the world of Union Square. And even in New York, the balance-of-power position so carefully built over the years by the American Labor Party was soon in ruins about their heads as they pursued their policy of narrowness and exclusion to its logical and suicidal conclusion.

But there was still a broader aura of disenchantment to those who watched as more objective outside observers. Those who viewed the bipartisan foreign policy with grave reservations—the same reservations attached to any democratic policy adopted without discussion, opposition, or presentation of alternatives—saw as the ultimate outcome of 1948 a minimization and termination of opposition to the Churchill-Truman-Dulles "line." Indeed the mere presentation of contrary views moved into the realm of treasonous or at least "un-American" activity. The witch-hunting of the postwar period became more and more pronounced, with political for-

tunes sought and found by opportunistic self-seekers willing
to whip the hysteria into ever greater frenzy.

Nor was the damage limited to the realm of the politically
active. Free speech everywhere—on campus, in lecture hall,
at city desk, in classroom and city hall all across the nation—
fell prey to the hostility unleashed by shortsighted political
demagoguery. Conformity was advancing inexorably, moving
on to overwhelm not only the positions abandoned by the
Wallace crusaders but those still occupied by their adversaries
of the ADA and the Democratic Party. The unleashed tide
failed to distinguish between liberal friend and foe. Under its
wave went those who had looked to 1948 as the beginning of
a realignment of the parties into more meaningful issues-
based groups.

And to those still waiting hopefully for "the coming of a
third party," the Wallace experience was bitter confirmation
of the insuperable barriers in the way of any group hoping to
emulate the British Labour success. True, the ballot obstacles
had not proved as impassable as expected for a party launched
in sufficient time with adequate breadth and organization to
wage a ballot drive all across the land—provided it was able
to pick up a degree of undercover support from a major adversary hoping to profit by its presence. True, the financial
hurdle had been well overcome by the unique voluntarism of
the fundraising ventures, but—as had been observed—only
Henry A. Wallace could get away with it—only zealous crusaders were likely to respond to such persuasion.

Organizationally, however, the Progressive Party had
merely added another exclamation point to the political tru-
ism "It takes a machine to beat a machine." More than zeal,
ambition, and the willing support of amateurs is necessary to
establish even the foundations of a lasting party structure.
Above all, success at the polls and favorable conditions of
the times exist as the bare minima on which a lasting organization may be built. The Jim Farleys, who had claimed that

given time and workers they could build viable machines without patronage, had never been faced with that dire necessity—either in New York or nationally.

The third-party path on which the crusaders had embarked with such high hopes had then become the road to disenchantment by the end of 1950. But were there any contrary signs to be observed along the way? Like many another minor party of protest, the Progressives had served both immediate and less visible long-range functions. From the short-range partisan standpoint of the Democrats, the Wallace party temporarily attracted the albatross-like "Communist issue" that was to prove so damaging only four years later. But beyond that, the domestic shift of the Truman administration and the beginning of the attacks on the "no-good, do-nothing 80th Congress"—a Congress in whose first session the minority Democratic Senate leadership and House rank and file had sided with the majority—were clearly attributable, in part at least, to the Wallace attraction for old line New Dealers. The 1947 threat of labor and liberal defections had not been an idle one. Nor had it gone unnoted by Democratic Party strategists. For the first time in American history, a minor party saw its thunder stolen in the very midst of the campaign, rather than four or forty years later. In unexpected fashion, the philosopher of the New Deal had served to father the Fair Deal of his opponent.

Foreign policy, on the other hand, provided no similar instance of an equally remarkable, radical, and rapid policy shift by Harry S. Truman. Containment remained the dogma of the day. And yet, in his 1949 inaugural, once established policy had been covered in the major (but now forgotten) first three points, the President came to point four. A thrill ran through the rain-chilled crowd in Capitol Plaza as the victorious candidate announced a plan of technical assistance that, save for its bilateral nature, might clearly have been inspired by the dismissed cabinet member who had kept insisting on the need for an American foreign policy promoting the interests of people, rather than governments.

From the vantage point of a decade later, the ultimate contributions of Henry A. Wallace to American foreign policy had emerged as even more pronounced. A different time, a different President, a different Premier—all these were obviously true. And yet the rapid shift within a short year from the continued containment and non-negotiation of a Dulles to the summits and visits of an Eisenhower who had become his own Secretary of State had much of the Wallace hue about them. (Indeed, the illness-aborted display of 1955 with its Geneva summit had convinced the erstwhile Republican Wallace to return to his *first* party—at least for the 1956 presidential campaign.)

And IDA—the International Development Authority so long espoused by Senator A. S. "Mike" Monroney and so unexpectedly adopted by the administration in early 1960—was clearly a refinement of the 1949 Wallace proposal for a similarly named multilateral approach to the problems of those nations with great need, but less than sound banking collateral, for capital development. The renewed interest during the late 1950's of so many Democratic Senators and Congressmen in a return to multilateral assistance, and in a changed emphasis upon economic rather than military assistance, was reminiscent of the speeches ten years earlier of the former Vice President. His very words—"We shall never be able to rely upon allies bought with our arms"—became the basic argument of many who at an earlier time had supported the Truman doctrine.

By late 1959, the American policy of "firmness" toward Russia had lost support not only in domestic circles but even abroad in the mind of its coauthor, former Prime Minister Winston Churchill, who, citing "changed circumstances," supported British abandonment of the concept. And in America its firm supporters remained a handful of those who had participated in its formulation—Truman, Acheson, Dulles, and Harriman. Policy planner George Kennan—the "Mr. $X$" of its earliest defense—had moved completely over to a "disengagement" position.

And so the "fight for peace" of Henry A. Wallace had been vindicated in a sense. Under different sponsorship, under more favorable circumstances, with more amenable principals, and under the more urgent threat of the H-bomb, his basic ideas were being adopted by way of ushering in his "Century of the Common Man." The road to disenchantment had proved to have another turning; in the long run, Wallace's crusade would prove to have been more than just quixotic.

# *Appendix*

## TABLE 1

1948 STATE REQUIREMENTS FOR QUALIFYING PRESIDENTIAL
ELECTORAL CANDIDATES FOR PLACES ON BALLOTS *

I. PETITIONS

    A. *Required Number of Registered Voters' Signatures Determined by Percentage of Vote in Prior Election for Specified Office*

| | | |
|---|---|---|
| Arizona | 2 | of vote in last gubernatorial election (from each of at least 5 counties). |
| California | 10 | of vote in last gubernatorial election.† |
| Connecticut | 1 | of vote in last presidential election. |
| Georgia | 5 | of registered voters.† |
| Indiana | ½ of 1 | of vote for Secretary of State in last election. |
| Michigan | 1 to 4 | of vote for Secretary of State in last election. |
| Nevada | 5 | of vote in last congressional election. |

TABLE 1 (*continued*)

| Ohio | 1 | of vote in last gubernatorial election (to qualify independent electors). |
|---|---|---|
| or | 15 | of vote in last general election (to qualify as third party). |
| Oregon | 5 | of vote in last congressional election.† |
| Pennsylvania | ½ of 1 | of highest vote for any state office in last election (State Judge—1947). |
| South Dakota | 2 | of vote for Governor in last election (qualify as independent). |
| or | 20 | of vote for Governor in last election (qualify as third party). |
| Vermont | 1 | of vote for Governor in last election. |
| West Virginia | 1 | of vote in last presidential election. |

B. *Required Number of Registered Voters' Signatures Determined by Statute*

| Arkansas | no specified number | |
|---|---|---|
| Colorado | 500 | |
| Delaware | 750 | 250 in each of 3 counties. |
| Illinois | 25,000 | at least 200 from each of 50 counties (of 102). |
| Kansas | 2,500 | separate petitions for each of 8 electors. |
| Kentucky | 100 | |
| Louisiana | 1,000 | not affiliated with any major party. |
| Maine | 1,000 | |

| | | |
|---|---|---|
| Maryland | 2,000 | |
| Massachusetts | 50,000 | |
| Minnesota | 2,000 | separate petitions for each elector. |
| Mississippi | 50 | |
| New Hampshire | 1,000 | |
| New Jersey | 800 | |
| New York | 12,000 | at least 50 in each county. |
| North Carolina | 10,000 | nonaffiliated. |
| North Dakota | 300 | |
| Oklahoma | 5,000 | |
| Rhode Island | 500 | |
| Tennessee | 1,425 | 15 from each of 95 counties.† |
| Utah | 300 | |
| Virginia | 250 | |
| Wisconsin | 1,000 | separate petitions for each of 12 electors, plus 1 each for presidential and vice-presidential candidates. |
| Wyoming | 100 | separate petition for each of 3 electors. |

## II. CONVENTIONS

*Delegates Required*

| | |
|---|---|
| Alabama | no designated number of delegates. |
| Idaho | 200 |
| Iowa | 2 (1 to sign as chairman, 1 as secretary.) |
| Montana | no designated number. |
| Nebraska | 750 |
| Oregon | 250 † |
| Tennessee | no designated number.† |
| Washington | 25 |

## III. OTHER METHODS

### A. *Change of Registration*

| | |
|---|---|
| California | 1% of voters in last gubernatorial election.† |
| Florida | 5% of registered voters.‡ |

TABLE 1 (*continued*)

B. *Miscellaneous*

| | |
|---|---|
| Mississippi | any group may name slate. |
| New Mexico | formal organization and filing. |
| South Carolina | print and distribute ballots at polling places. |
| Texas | formal organization. |

\* This table was assembled primarily from newspaper sources. The *New York Times,* January 2, 1948, published a summary as compiled by the Associated Press. This was corrected in the light of later reports and information. The most recent scholarly works in the field at the time were an article by Joseph R. Starr, "The Legal Status of American Political Parties," *American Political Science Review,* June and August, 1940, and a compilation, "Legal Obstacles to Minority Party Success," published in the *Yale Law Journal,* July, 1948.

† Alternate methods provided.

‡ Law amended in course of 1948 campaign to allow presidential electoral nominees to file without meeting formal requirements.

## TABLE 2

Combined Totals of Contributions and Expenditures for the Progressive Party and the National Wallace-for-President Committee

| | Total Contributions * | Adjusted Total, or "Actual" Contributions † |
|---|---|---|
| Progressive Party | $ 382,825.12 | $ 491,090.84 |
| National Wallace-for-President Committee | 578,370.47 | 789,188.65 |
| | $ 961,195.59 | $1,280,279.49 |

| | Total Expenditures * | Adjusted Total, or "Actual" Expenditures |
|---|---|---|
| Progressive Party | $ 535,050.13 | $ 490,385.61 |

|  | Total Expenditures | Adjusted Total, or "Actual" Expenditures |
|---|---|---|
| National Wallace-for-President Committee | 813,532.67 | 769,717.30 |
|  | $1,348,582.80 | $1,260,102.91 |

|  | Refund of Expenditures * |
|---|---|
| Progressive Party | $ 152,920.24 |
| National Wallace-for-President Committee | 254,633.55 |
|  | $ 407,553.79 |

| *Net Expenditures* | 941,029.01 | |
| *Surplus* † | $ 20,166.58 ‡ | $ 20,176.58 ‡ |

* Figures as filed with the Clerk of the House.

† These figures were arrived at by breaking down the party's "Refund of Expenditures" item as follows: "Admissions less than $100" and "Sale of Campaign Material at Cost" were added to contributions; "Advances," "Redeposits," "Exchanges," and "Reimbursed Expenditures" were deducted from expenditures.

‡ The $10 discrepancy arises from what appears to be an incorrect addition in the report of "Refund of Expenditures" for the Progressive Party during the period Oct. 29–Dec. 31, 1948. The reported total is $51,523.43, but the figures submitted actually total $51,-533.43.

## TABLE 3

REPORTED CONTRIBUTIONS BY ASSOCIATED GROUPS TO THE PROGRESSIVE PARTY AND TO THE NATIONAL WALLACE-FOR-PRESIDENT COMMITTEE

*Labor*

Fur and Leather Workers Committee for Wallace,
Taylor, and Progressive Candidates                    $5,000.00

TABLE 3 (*continued*)

*Labor*

| | |
|---|---|
| Independent Political Committee of the Greater New York Council | 1,425.00 |
| Committee for Wallace, AFL Food, Hotel and Restaurant Workers | 1,000.00 |
| PAC (Local 1139, Minneapolis and Chicago Joint Board, IFLW) | 500.00 |
| Labor Committee for Wallace, New York City | 500.00 |
| FTA-CIO Wallace Committee, Philadelphia | 500.00 |
| Labor Committee for Wallace and Taylor, Local 430 | 100.00 |
| | $9,025.00 |

*Nationalities*

| | |
|---|---|
| Armenians for Wallace | $1,648.00 |
| Greeks for Wallace | 443.20 |
| Irish-American Committee for Wallace | 100.00 |
| Italian-American Committee for Wallace | 300.00 |
| Lithuanian Wallace Committee | 200.00 |
| Romanians for Wallace | 120.00 |
| Russian Club for Wallace | 100.00 |
| Serbian-American Committee for Wallace | 309.00 |
| Slovenian-American National Council | 1,887.00 |
| Ukrainians for Wallace | 100.00 |
| Yugoslav-Americans for Wallace | 200.00 |
| | $5,407.20 |

*Progressive Citizens of America (PCA)*

| | |
|---|---|
| California Chapters | $1,350.00 |
| New York Chapters | 1,298.90 |
| Other Chapters | 1,456.00 |
| | $4,104.90 |

*Women-for-Wallace*

| | |
|---|---|
| Greater New York Branches | $ 782.85 |

## TABLE 4

DISTRIBUTION OF REPORTED STATE AND LOCAL ORGANI-
ZATIONAL CONTRIBUTIONS TO THE PROGRESSIVE PARTY
AND TO THE NATIONAL WALLACE-FOR-PRESIDENT COM-
MITTEE IN COMPARISON WITH DISTRIBUTION OF VOTE

| State | Amount Contributed | 1948 Votes for Electors | Rank in Total Organizational Contributions | Rank in Total Vote |
|---|---|---|---|---|
| New York | $76,466.85 | 509,559 | 1 | 1 |
| Pennsylvania | 56,734.00 | 55,161 | 2 | 3 |
| Illinois | 46,450.63 | * | 3 | |
| California | 38,864.00 | 190,381 | 4 | 2 |
| Missouri | 14,500.00 | 3,998 | 5 | 22 |
| Texas | 14,375.32 | 3,764 | 6 | 24 |
| Indiana | 13,173.00 | 9,649 | 7 | 16 |
| New Jersey | 12,650.00 | 42,683 | 8 | 5 |
| Minnesota | 12,543.10 | 27,866 | 9 | 9 |
| Ohio | 12,250.62 | 37,596 | 10 | 7 |
| Colorado | 12,000.00 | 6,115 | 11 | 19 |
| Maryland | 8,980.00 | 9,983 | 12 | 15 |
| Connecticut | 8,450.00 | 13,713 | 13 | 12 |
| District of Columbia | 7,650.00 | † | 14 | |
| Michigan | 6,475.00 | 46,515 | 15 | 4 |
| Wisconsin | 5,400.00 | 25,282 | 16 | 10 |
| Iowa | 4,996.43 | 12,125 | 17 | 13 |
| Idaho | 4,200.00 | 4,972 | 18 | 20 |
| Florida | 4,000.00 | 11,620 | 19 ‡ | 14 |
| Oregon | 4,000.00 | 14,978 | 19 ‡ | 11 |
| Washington | 3,683.30 | 31,692 | 21 | 8 |
| Georgia | 3,000.00 | 1,636 | 22 ‡ | 35 |
| Massachusetts | 3,000.00 | 38,157 | 22 ‡ | 6 |
| Kansas | 2,416.30 | 4,603 | 24 | 21 |
| Nevada | 1,900.00 | 1,469 | 25 | 38 |
| New Mexico | 500.00 | 1,037 | 26 | 41 |
| Utah | 385.00 | 2,679 | 27 | 29 |
| Virginia | 200.00 | 2,047 | 28 ‡ | 31 |

TABLE 4 (*continued*)

| State | Amount Contributed | 1948 Votes for Electors | Rank in Total Organizational Contributions | Rank in Total Vote |
|---|---|---|---|---|
| Puerto Rico | 200.00 | † | 28 ‡ | |
| Montana | 111.02 | 7,313 | 30 | 18 |

Note: These totals represent only contributions from the various state parties and committees. Other group contributions will be found in Table 3.

  * Wallace electoral slate did not appear on ballot.

  † No vote in presidential elections.

  ‡ Tie.


## TABLE 5

CONTRIBUTIONS AND ADMISSIONS REPORTED IN THE PRESS FOR RALLIES AND DINNERS

RALLIES

| Date (1948) | Place | Attendance | Admissions | Contributions |
|---|---|---|---|---|
| Jan. 18 | Chicago | | | $ 3,300.00 * |
| Feb. | Minnesota | 16,000 | $ 15,000.00 | 20,000.00 |
| Apr. 10 | Chicago (2 rallies) | | | 70,000.00 |
| Apr. | Midwest, East (10 rallies) | | | 10,000.00 |
| May 12 | New York (Madison Square Garden) | | 50,000.00 | |
| May 17 | Los Angeles | 31,000 | 30,000.00 | 20,000.00 |
| May 21 | San Francisco | | | 40,000.00 * |
| May 30 | Denver | 3,200 | | 5,000.00 * |
| June 25 | Philadelphia (Shibe Park) | 25,000 | | 60,000.00 |
| June 26 | Washington, D.C. | | | 22,000.00 * |
| Sept. 20 | New York (Yankee Stadium) | 60,000 | 78,000.00 | 52,000.00 |
| Oct. 27 | New York (Madison Square Garden) | 19,000 | 23,000.00 | 24,000.00 |
| | | | $196,000.00 | $326,300.00 |

### DINNERS

| Date (1948) | Place | Attendance | Admissions | Contributions |
|---|---|---|---|---|
| Jan. 17 | Chicago | | | $ 32,200.00 |
| Apr. 20 | New York ($100.00 a plate) | 1,400 | | 100,000.00 |
| June 22 | New York (Businessmen's Lunch) | 600 | | 25,000.00 |
| Sept. 22 | New York ($100.00 a plate) | 400 | | 35,000.00 |
| Oct. 2 | Hollywood ($12.50 a plate) | several hundred | | 2,000.00 |
| Oct. 20 | Philadelphia ($25.00 a plate) | 425 | | 8,500.00 |
| | | | | $202,700.00 |

### WOMEN-FOR-WALLACE DINNERS

| Date (1948) | Place | Attendance | Admissions | Contributions |
|---|---|---|---|---|
| Feb. 26 | Brooklyn | | | $ 5,000.00 |
| Apr. 21 | Bronx | | | 2,000.00 |
| Oct. 27 | New York ($100.00 a plate) | 250 | | 20,000.00 |
| | | | | $ 27,000.00 |
| | *Grand Total* | | | $752,000.00 |

* Identification of separate figures impossible for Admissions and Contributions.

## TABLE 6

COMPARISON OF EXPENDITURES BY NATIONAL GROUPS AND
A LOCAL GROUP

| | NATIONAL WALLACE-FOR-PRESIDENT COMMITTEE AND NATIONAL PROGRESSIVE PARTY * (Jan. 1–Oct. 31, 1948) | | | PROGRESSIVE PARTY DISTRICT OF COLUMBIA † (Apr. 1–Dec. 31, 1948) | |
|---|---|---|---|---|---|
| *Item* | *Expenditures* | *Percentage* | *Item* | *Expenditures* | *Percentage* |
| Advertising, Mail Solicitations | $ 18,311.60 | 1.6 | | | |
| Tours (Wallace, Robeson, Taylor) | 61,700.27 | 5.5 | Travel | $ 693.94 | 2.0 |
| Fundraising Events | 207,624.50 | 18.2 | Meetings, Rallies, and Special Events | 4,682.42 | 13.2 |
| Cost of Campaign Material | 171,589.46 | 15.0 | Publicity | 3,525.14 | 9.9 |
| Non-Fundraising Events | 55,622.70 | 4.9 | | | |
| Direct Contributions to State Campaigns and Candidates | 43,312.67 | 3.8 | Contributions (of which $14,000.00— 39.4 per cent— was to national groups) | 14,612.00 | 41.1 |
| Budgetary Expenses | 583,484.25 | 51.0 | Salaries | 5,082.65 | 14.3 |
| | | | Office Supplies | 2,519.54 | 7.1 |
| | | | Telephone and Telegraph | 1,144.51 | 3.2 |
| | | | General | 351.61 | 1.0 |
| | | | Taxes | 919.34 | 2.6 |

| Item | Expendi-tures | Per-cent-age | Item | Expendi-tures | Per-cent-age |
|------|------|------|------|------|------|
| | | | Non-Itemized (expenditures of less than $10.00 each) | 2,003.93 | 5.6 |
| Total Ex-penditures | $1,141,645.45 | 100.0 | Total Ex-penditures | $35,535.08 | 100.0 |

\* Figures for the expenditures of the Progressive Party (national) and National Wallace-for-President Committee from Consolidated Surplus Statement prepared for national headquarters.

† Figures for the expenditures of the Progressive Party of the District of Columbia taken from report filed with the Clerk of the House, Rept. 1987.

## TABLE 7

PERCENTAGES OF STATES' VOTES RECEIVED BY 1948
WALLACE PROGRESSIVE PARTY

| State | Percentage | State | Percentage |
|-------|-----------|-------|-----------|
| New York | 8.12 | Maryland | 1.67 |
| California | 4.73 | Connecticut | 1.55 |
| North Dakota | 3.81 | Pennsylvania | 1.47 |
| Washington | 3.51 | Ohio | 1.28 |
| Montana | 3.27 | Colorado | 1.19 |
| Oregon | 2.86 | Iowa | 1.17 |
| Nevada | 2.37 | South Dakota | 1.12 |
| Idaho | 2.32 | Vermont | 1.04 |
| Minnesota | 2.30 | Utah | 0.97 |
| Michigan | 2.20 | Wyoming | 0.92 |
| New Jersey | 2.19 | New Hampshire | 0.85 |
| Florida | 2.01 | Rhode Island | 0.79 |
| Wisconsin | 1.98 | Delaware | 0.76 |
| Arizona | 1.87 | Louisiana | 0.73 |
| Massachusetts | 1.77 | Maine | 0.71 |

TABLE 7 (*continued*)

| State | Percentage | State | Percentage |
|---|---|---|---|
| Alabama | 0.71 | Texas | 0.33 |
| Kansas | 0.58 | Arkansas | 0.31 |
| Indiana | 0.58 | Missouri | 0.25 |
| New Mexico | 0.56 | Kentucky | 0.19 |
| North Carolina | 0.49 | Mississippi | 0.12 |
| Virginia | 0.49 | South Carolina | 0.11 |
| West Virginia | 0.44 | Illinois | * |
| Georgia | 0.39 | Nebraska | * |
| Tennessee | 0.34 | Oklahoma | * |

* Progressive Party did not appear on ballot.


## TABLE 8

COMPARISON OF PERCENTAGES OF STATES' VOTES
RECEIVED BY SOME MINOR PARTIES

| State | Wallace Progressive Party, 1948 | All Minor Parties, 1864–1936 | La Follette Progressive Party, 1924 | Roosevelt Progressive Party, 1912 | Populist (People's) Party, 1892 |
|---|---|---|---|---|---|
| Alabama | 0.71% | 4.8% | 4.9% | 19.8% | 36.60% |
| Arizona | 1.87 | 6.5 | 23.3 | 34.3 | * |
| Arkansas | 0.31 | 3.8 | 9.5 | 18.8 | 8.07 |
| California | 4.73 | 9.3 | 33.2 | 49.7 | 9.38 |
| Colorado | 1.19 | 8.0 | 20.4 | 29.4 | 57.07 |
| Connecticut | 1.55 | 3.3 | 10.6 | 19.3 | |
| Delaware | 0.76 | 2.5 | 5.4 | 18.7 | |
| Florida | 2.01 | 4.3 | 7.9 | 10.1 | 16.06 |
| Georgia | 0.39 | 4.1 | 7.6 | 17.2 | 19.17 |
| Idaho | 2.32 | 10.6 | 36.5 | 27.6 | 54.66 |
| Illinois | | 6.2 | 17.5 | 37.0 | 2.54 |
| Indiana | 0.58 | 4.0 | 5.6 | 27.2 | 4.00 |
| Iowa | 1.17 | 6.9 | 28.1 | 34.6 | 4.65 |
| Kansas | 0.58 | 8.6 | 14.9 | 35.5 | 48.44 |
| Kentucky | 0.19 | 2.7 | 5.0 | 23.3 | 6.92 |
| Louisiana | 0.73 | 1.3 | 3.3 | 12.6 | 5.30 |
| Maine | 0.71 | 3.7 | 5.9 | 38.4 | 2.04 |
| Maryland | 1.67 | 3.6 | 13.2 | 25.6 | |
| Massachusetts | 1.77 | 5.4 | 12.5 | 30.1 | 0.82 |
| Michigan | 2.20 | 6.2 | 10.5 | 41.4 | 4.32 |
| Minnesota | 2.30 | 11.0 | 41.3 | 42.4 | 11.35 |
| Mississippi | 0.12 | 2.2 | 3.1 | 5.7 | 19.42 |
| Missouri | 0.25 | 3.5 | 6.4 | 18.8 | 7.59 |

| State | Wallace Progressive Party, 1948 | All Minor Parties, 1864–1936 | La Follette Progressive Party, 1924 | Roosevelt Progressive Party, 1912 | Populist (People's) Party, 1892 |
|---|---|---|---|---|---|
| Montana | 3.27 | 10.0 | 37.8 | 32.6 | 16.55 |
| Nebraska | | 8.2 | 22.9 | 30.8 | 41.00 |
| Nevada | 2.37 | 8.7 | 36.2 | 33.4 | 66.76 |
| New Hampshire | 0.85 | 2.6 | 5.4 | 20.9 | |
| New Jersey | 2.19 | 4.2 | 10.0 | 35.3 | 0.28 |
| New Mexico | 0.56 | 3.4 | 8.5 | 18.0 | * |
| New York | 8.12 | 5.4 | 14.4 | 26.0 | 1.20 |
| North Carolina | 0.49 | 2.1 | 1.4 | 28.5 | 15.94 |
| North Dakota | 3.81 | 11.2 | 45.3 | 32.9 | 48.96 |
| Ohio | 1.28 | 5.2 | 17.6 | 23.6 | 1.74 |
| Oklahoma | | 4.3 | 7.8 | 0.1 | * |
| Oregon | 2.86 | 9.5 | 24.5 | 31.5 | 16.24 |
| Pennsylvania | 1.47 | 5.7 | 14.3 | 39.9 | |
| Rhode Island | 0.79 | 3.9 | 3.2 | 22.5 | 0.43 |
| South Carolina | 0.11 | 0.6 | 1.0 | 2.5 | 3.42 |
| South Dakota | 1.12 | 12.4 | 37.0 | 54.6 | 37.58 |
| Tennessee | 0.34 | 2.8 | 3.5 | 22.1 | 8.92 |
| Texas | 0.33 | 4.5 | 6.5 | 9.7 | 23.64 |
| Utah | 0.97 | 6.5 | 20.8 | 23.5 | * |
| Vermont | 1.04 | 3.2 | 5.9 | 36.4 | 4.17 |
| Virginia | 0.49 | 1.7 | 4.6 | 16.1 | |
| Washington | 3.51 | 14.7 | 35.8 | 42.0 | 21.79 |
| West Virginia | 0.44 | 3.6 | 6.2 | 31.8 | 2.49 |
| Wisconsin | 1.98 | 9.9 | 54.0 | 17.5 | 2.66 |
| Wyoming | 0.92 | 9.0 | 31.5 | 23.6 | 46.14 |
| | | | | | |
| *National Percentage* | 2.3 | 5.7 | 16.85 | 29.6 | 8.63 |

Sources:

    Percentages of states' votes cast for all minor parties, 1864–1936, from Cortez A. M. Ewing, *Presidential Elections*, p. 128.

    Figures for La Follette Progressive Party, 1924, from Kenneth C. MacKay, *The Progressive Movement of 1924*, pp. 274–75.

    Figures for Roosevelt Progressive Party, 1912, from *Political Almanac for 1948*, pp. 276–77.

    Figures for Populist (People's) Party, 1892, from John D. Hicks, *The Populist Revolt*, p. 263.

\* Not yet admitted to Union.

## TABLE 9

VOTES RECEIVED BY PROGRESSIVE PARTY CANDIDATES,
NOVEMBER 2, 1948

| State | Votes for Wallace-Taylor Electors | Votes for Progressive Senatorial Candidates | Votes for Progressive House Candidates | Number of House Candidates |
|---|---|---|---|---|
| Alabama | 1,52? | | | |
| Arizona | 3,31? | * | 1,478 | 1 |
| Arkansas | 7?1 | | | |
| California | 190,3?1 | * | 228,180 | 14 |
| Colorado | 6,1?5 | 2,981 | | |
| Connecticut | 13,713 | * | 9,186 | 5 |
| Delaware | 1,050 | 681 | | |
| Florida | 11,020 | * | | |
| Georgia | 1,036 | | | |
| Idaho | 4,?72 | 3,154 | 3,130 | 2 |
| Illinois | | | 19,155 | 4 |
| Indiana | 9,?49 | * | 1,076 | 1 |
| Iowa | 12,?25 | 3,387 | 2,167 | 4 |
| Kansas | 4,?03 | | | |
| Kentucky | 1,?67 | 924 | 686 | 1 |
| Louisiana | 3,?35 | | | |
| Maine | 1,?84 | | | |
| Maryland | 9,?83 | * | 12,172 | 3 |
| Massachusetts | 38,?57 | | | |
| Michigan | 46,5?5 | | 1,608 | 4 |
| Minnesota | 27,8?6 | | | |
| Mississippi | 22? | | | |
| Missouri | 3,998 | * | 3,039 | 4 |
| Montana | 7,313 | | | |
| Nebraska | | | | |
| Nevada | 1,469 | * | | |
| New Hampshire | 1,970 | ?538 | 1,512 | 2 |
| New Jersey | 42,683 | 22,6?8 | 16,035 | 7 |
| New Mexico | 1,037 | 705 | 805 | 1 |
| New York | 509,559 | * | 512,148 | 44 |

| State | Votes for Wallace-Taylor Electors | Votes for Progressive Senatorial Candidates | Votes for Progressive House Candidates | Number of House Candidates |
|---|---|---|---|---|
| North Carolina | 3,915 | 3,490 | 3,345 | 6 |
| North Dakota | 8,391 | * | 1,758 | 1 |
| Ohio | 37,596 | * | | |
| Oklahoma | | | | |
| Oregon | 14,978 | | 18,741 | 2 |
| Pennsylvania | 55,161 | * | 6,969 | 2 |
| Rhode Island | 2,587 | | | |
| South Carolina | 154 | | | |
| South Dakota | 2,801 | | | |
| Tennessee | 1,864 | | 3,670 | 1 |
| Texas | 3,764 | | 1,449 | 4 |
| Utah | 2,679 | * | | |
| Vermont | 1,279 | * | | |
| Virginia | 2,047 | 5,347 | 3,037 | 2 |
| Washington | 31,692 | * | 13,739 | 3 |
| West Virginia | 3,311 | | | |
| Wisconsin | 25,282 | * | 10,382 | 5 |
| Wyoming | 931 | | | |
| *Total* | 1,157,140 | 44,865 | 875,467 | 123 |

Sources:

Statistics of the Presidential and Congressional Elections of November 2, 1948, compiled from official sources by William Graf under the direction of Ralph R. Roberts, Clerk of the House of Representatives—for all states except New Mexico.

State of New Mexico, *Official Returns of the 1948 Elections*, compiled under the supervision of Alicia Romero, Secretary of State.

* No senatorial seat was at stake.

# Bibliography

## INTERVIEWS

WHILE THE following does not purport to be a comprehensive listing of all personal interviews, it does serve to indicate some of those men and women who gave most generously of their time and recollections. To them the author is indebted for much material on the organization of the Progressive Party and on other groups related to the 1948 campaign of Henry A. Wallace.

Mr. John Abt, Chief Counsel, Progressive Party.

Mr. C. B. Baldwin, Campaign Manager for Henry A. Wallace and Secretary, Progressive Party.

Miss Charlotte Carr, former Assistant to Mr. Sidney Hillman in CIO Political Action Committee.

Mr. Barney Conal, Chief Field Organizer, Progressive Party.

Miss Hannah Dorner, Director, Independent Citizens' Committee of the Arts, Sciences and Professions.

Professor Thomas I. Emerson, Yale Law School, Chairman, Connecticut Wallace-for-President Committee and gubernatorial candidate of the People's Party in Connecticut.

Albert J. Fitzgerald, President, United Electrical Workers, Co-chairman, Progressive Party, and Chairman, National Labor Committee for Wallace and Taylor.

336

Miss Helen Fuller, member of the Editorial Staff, *New Republic.*

Mrs. Elinor S. Gimbel, Vice-Chairman, Progressive Party and Chairman, Women-for-Wallace.

Mr. Morris Goldin, member of the Executive Board, American Labor Party.

Mr. J. Albert Keefer, Administrative Assistant to Senator Glen H. Taylor and member of the Platform Committee, Progressive Party.

Miss Geraldine Shandross, Executive Secretary, New York County Committee, American Labor Party.

Mr. Ralph Shikes, Director of Publicity, Progressive Party.

Mr. Gael Sullivan, Executive Director, Democratic National Committee.

Hon. Glen H. Taylor, U.S. Senator from Idaho, 1945–50, and vice-presidential candidate of the Progressive Party, 1948.

Hon. Henry A. Wallace, Vice President of the United States, 1941–45, and presidential candidate of the Progressive Party, 1948.

## NEWSPAPERS

| | |
|---|---|
| *Baltimore Sun* | *Oklahoma Daily* (Norman) |
| *Baltimore Evening Sun* | *People's World* |
| *Chicago Sun-Times* | *Philadelphia Evening Bulletin* |
| *CIO News* | *Philadelphia Inquirer* |
| *Daily Worker* (New York) | *Pittsburgh Press* |
| *Gazette and Daily* (York, Pa.) | *PM* (New York) |
| *Manchester Guardian* | *Toledo Blade* (Ohio) |
| *National Guardian* (New York) | *Washington Daily News* |
| *New York Herald Tribune* | *Washington Post* |
| *New York Post* | *Washington Star* |
| *New York Times* | *Worker* (New York) |

## PERIODICALS

| | |
|---|---|
| *American Mercury* | *Collier's* |
| *American Political Science Review* | *Congressional Quarterly* |

| | |
|---|---|
| *Harper's Magazine* | *New York Times Magazine* |
| *Masses and Mainstream* | *Opinion News* |
| *Nation* | *Politics* |
| *New Leader* | *Public Opinion Quarterly* |
| *New Masses* | *Saturday Evening Post* |
| *New Republic* | *Time* |
| *Newsweek* | *U.S. News and World Report* |
| | *Worker Magazine* |

## CAMPAIGN LITERATURE
## AND UNPUBLISHED MATERIAL

Americans for Democratic Action. "Henry A. Wallace—the First Three Months." Washington, 1948. (Mimeographed.)

———. "Henry A. Wallace—the Last Seven Months of His Presidential Campaign." Washington, 1948. (Mimeographed.)

Brown, John Cotton. "The 1948 Progressive Campaign: A Scientific Approach." Unpublished Ph.D. dissertation, University of Chicago, 1949.

*New Leader.* Unpublished material from the files—made available by Mr. Louis Jay Herman.

*New Republic.* Unpublished material from the files—made available by Miss Helen Fuller.

Nixon, Russell. "Report on Organization." Chicago: National Labor Committee for Wallace and Taylor, 1948. (Mimeographed.)

Progressive Party. Brief of Plaintiffs, *Cooper* v. *Cartwright,* in the Supreme Court of the State of Oklahoma.

———. Consolidated Surplus Statement. January 1, 1948—October 31, 1948.

———. *Knock on Any Door* (a handbook for political workers). New York, 1948.

———. Official press releases, letters to local groups, and other campaign material.

———. "Report of the Rules Committee." Philadelphia, 1948. (Mimeographed.)

Henry A. Wallace. "A Century of Blood or Milk." Speech, November 12, 1950, Community Forum, New York, N.Y. (Mimeographed.)

———. "March of the Common Man: Constructive or De-structive?" Speech, January 21, 1951, Community Church of Boston, Mass. (Mimeographed.)

———. "Open Letter to Mao Tse-tung." September 30, 1950.

———. "Where I Stand." Speech, January 2, 1951, Brooklyn Jewish Center, Brooklyn, N.Y. (Mimeographed.)

GOVERNMENT DOCUMENTS,
PUBLICATIONS, AND REPORTS

*Budget of the United States Government,* for the fiscal year end-ing June 30, 1947.

Clerk of the House of Representatives, Financial Reports, 1948.
  Camper for Congress Citizens' Committee, Report 1808.

Communist Party, 1948 National Election Campaign Com-mittee Reports 1689, 1759, 1915.

Communist Party, 3rd District Election Campaign Committee of Virginia, Reports 1724, 1815.

D.C. Veterans for Wallace, Report 1619.

Fur and Leather Workers' Committee for Wallace, Taylor, and Progressive Candidates, Reports 1851, 1945.

National Council of the Arts, Sciences and Professions, Re-ports 1841, 1858, 1948.

National Wallace-for-President Committee, Reports 1568, 1614, 1657, 1694, 1832, 1971.

Progressive Citizens of America (PCA), California, Report 1617.

Progressive Citizens of America, Champaign, Ill., Reports 1616, 1672.

Progressive Citizens of America, Northfield, Ill., Report 1615.

Progressive Citizens of America, Montana, Report 1847.

Progressive Citizens of America, New York, Reports 1594, 1611.

Progressive Party (national), New York, Reports 1655, 1700, 1831, 1929.

Progressive Party, District of Columbia, Reports 1610, 1627, 1634, 1682, 1814, 1881, 1987.

Progressive Party, Maryland, Report 1907.

Progressive Party, Montana, Report 1845.

Progressive Party, North Carolina, Reports 1846, 1887.

United Farm Equipment and Metal Workers of America, CIO, Local 184, Auburn, N.Y., Report 1910.

Wallace-for-President Club of Atlantic City, N.J., Reports 1743, 1859.

Young Progressives of America, Reports 1693, 1796, 1960.

U.S. *Congressional Record.*

Court Cases Cited:

> *Cooper* v. *Cartwright,* 195 P. 2d 290.
>
> *Democratic Farmer-Labor State Central Committee* v. *Holm,* 33 N.W. 2d 831.
>
> *Feiner* v. *New York,* 340 U.S. 315.
>
> *MacDougall* v. *Green,* 80 F. Supp. 725, 335 U.S. 281.
>
> *Marcantonio* v. *Heffernan,* 82 N.E. 2d, 298 N.Y. 661.
>
> *Progressive Party* v. *Flynn,* 79 N.E. 2d 516.
>
> *State* v. *Hummel,* 80 N.E. 2d 899.

H.R. 4482, 80th Cong., 1st sess.

H.R. 4908, 79th Cong., 2d sess.

H.R. 5403, 80th Cong., 2d sess.

H.R. 5615, 80th Cong., 2d sess.

Senate Rept. 801, 81st Cong., 1st sess., to accompany S. Res. 141.

State of New Mexico. *Official Returns of the 1948 Elections.* Compiled under the supervision of Alicia Romero, Secretary of State. Santa Fe, New Mexico, 1949.

*Statistics of the Presidential and Congressional Elections of November 2, 1948.* Compiled from official sources by William Graf under the direction of Ralph R. Roberts, Clerk of the U.S. House of Representatives. Washington, D.C., 1949.

## BOOKS

Acheson, Dean. *A Democrat Looks at His Party.* New York: Harper & Brothers, 1955.

American Civil Liberties Union. *Violence in Peekskill.* New York: American Civil Liberties Union, 1949.

American Institute of Public Opinion. *Political Almanac for 1948*. New York: American Institute of Public Opinion, 1948.

*American Year Book, Record of the Year 1940*. New York: D. Appleton & Co., 1941.

Binkley, Wilfred E. *American Political Parties: Their Natural History*. New York: Alfred A. Knopf, Inc., 1944.

Binkley, Wilfred E., and Moos, Malcolm C. *A Grammar of American Politics*. 3rd edition. New York: Alfred A. Knopf, Inc., 1958.

Bruce, Harold R. *American Parties and Politics*. New York: Henry Holt & Co., Inc., 1927.

Byrnes, James F. *Speaking Frankly*. 1st edition. New York: Harper & Brothers, 1947.

Dennis, Eugene. *What America Faces*. New York: New Century Publishers, 1946.

DeWitt, Benjamin P. *The Progressive Movement*. New York: Macmillan Co., 1915.

Dimitrov, Georgi. *The United Front*. New York: International Publishers Co., Inc., 1947.

Douglas, Paul H. *The Coming of a New Party*. New York: McGraw-Hill Book Co., 1932.

Ewing, Cortez A. M. *Presidential Elections from Abraham Lincoln to Franklin D. Roosevelt*. Norman: University of Oklahoma Press, 1940.

Flynn, Edward J. *You're the Boss*. New York: Viking Press, Inc., 1947.

Haynes, Fred E. *Third Party Movements Since the Civil War*. Iowa City, Iowa: State Historical Society of Iowa, 1916.

Herring, E. Pendleton. *The Politics of Democracy*. New York: W. W. Norton & Company, Inc., 1940.

Hesseltine, William B. *The Rise and Fall of Third Parties*. Washington, D.C.: Public Affairs Press, 1948.

Hicks, John D. *The Populist Revolt*. Minneapolis: University of Minnesota Press, 1931.

Hinderaker, Ivan H. *Party Politics*. New York: Henry Holt & Co., Inc., 1956.

Hofstadter, Richard. *The Age of Reform*. New York: Harper & Brothers, 1955.

Key, V. O., Jr. *Politics, Parties and Pressure Groups.* 4th edition. New York: Thomas Y. Crowell Company, 1958.

Lord, Russell. *The Wallaces of Iowa.* Boston: Houghton Mifflin Co., 1947.

Lubell, Samuel. *The Future of American Politics.* New York: Harper & Brothers, 1952.

———. *Revolt of the Moderates.* New York: Harper & Brothers, 1956.

MacDonald, Dwight. *Henry Wallace, the Man and the Myth.* New York: Vanguard Press, 1948.

MacKay, Kenneth C. *The Progressive Movement of 1924.* New York: Columbia University Press, 1947.

McKean, Dayton D. *Party and Pressure Politics.* Boston: Houghton Mifflin Co., 1949.

Maxwell, Robert S. *La Follette and the Rise of the Progressives in Wisconsin.* Madison: State Historical Society of Wisconsin, 1956.

Merriam, Charles E., and Gosnell, Harold F. *The American Party System.* 4th edition. New York: Macmillan Co., 1949.

Mill, John Stuart. *On Liberty.* New York: Liberal Arts Press, Inc., 1956.

Mills, C. Wright. *The New Men of Power.* New York: Harcourt, Brace & Co., 1948.

Moley, Raymond. *27 Masters of Politics.* New York: Funk & Wagnalls Co., 1949.

Nash, Howard P. *Third Parties in American Politics.* Washington: Public Affairs Press, 1959.

Ostrogorski, Moisei. *Democracy and the Party System.* New York: Macmillan Co., 1926.

Richberg, Donald. *Tents of the Mighty.* New York: Willett, Clark & Colby, 1930.

Sait, Edward M. *American Parties and Elections.* 3rd edition. New York: D. Appleton-Century Company, Inc., 1942.

Scammon, Richard M. *America Votes.* New York: Macmillan Co., 1956.

Shannon, David A. *The Socialist Party of America: A History.* New York: Macmillan Co., 1955.

———. *The Decline of American Communism.* New York: Harcourt, Brace & Co., 1959.

Stedman, Susan W. and Murray S. *Discontent at the Polls*. New York: Columbia University Press, 1950.

Truman, Harry S. *Memoirs*. Garden City: Doubleday & Company, Inc., 1955.

Wallace, Henry A. *The Fight for Peace*. New York: Reynal & Hitchcock, 1946.

————. *New Frontiers*. New York: Reynal & Hitchcock, 1934.

————. *60 Million Jobs*. New York: Simon and Schuster, Inc., 1945.

————. *Statesmanship and Religion*. Milwaukee, Wis.: Morehouse Publishing Co., 1934.

————. *Toward World Peace*. New York: Reynal & Hitchcock, 1948.

————. *Whose Constitution: An Inquiry into the General Welfare*. New York: Reynal & Hitchcock, 1948.


## MAGAZINE AND NEWSPAPER ARTICLES
## OF SPECIAL INTEREST

Angoff, Charles. "Wallace's Communist-Front Party," *American Mercury*, 67 (October, 1948), 413–21.

Aptheker, Herbert. "The Face of the Lesser Evil," *Masses and Mainstream*, March, 1948.

Budenz, Louis F. "How the Reds Snatched Henry Wallace," *Collier's*, 122 (September 18, 1948), 14–15.

Cantril, Hadley C. "Polls and the 1948 U.S. Presidential Election," *International Journal of Opinion and Attitude Research*, 2 (1948).

Carroll, Luke P. "On the Road with Henry Wallace," *New York Herald Tribune*, October 20, 1948.

Fischer, John. "Unwritten Rules of American Politics," *Harper's Magazine*, 197 (November, 1948), 27–36.

Franklin, Julian H. "Why I Broke with the Communists," *Harper's Magazine*, May, 1947.

Fuller, Helen. "For a Better World Right Now," *New Republic*, August 2, 1948.

————. "New Party Meets," *ibid.*, 118 (April 19, 1948), 10.

————. "PAC and the Future," *ibid.*, 111 (November 27, 1944), 689–90.

————. "Report on the PCA Convention," *ibid.*, 118 (January 26, 1948), 9.

————. "Third Party Prospects," *ibid.*, 118 (March 22, 1948), 10–11.

————. "Throwing Wallace to the Wolves," *ibid.*, 111 (July 31, 1944), 121–22.

Gilbert, Rodney. "Thin Line of Heroes Backs Wallace's Party," *Saturday Evening Post*, 220 (March 6, 1948), 148.

Hale, William Harlan, "What Makes Wallace Run?" *Harper's Magazine*, 196 (March, 1948), 241–48.

Hesseltine, William B. "Is There a Bryan in Your Barn?" *Progressive*, May, 1948.

————. "Perversion of Progressives," *ibid.*, September, 1948.

Humphrey, Hubert. "A Reply to Rex Tugwell," *Progressive*, March, 1949.

Jackson, Gardner. "Henry Wallace, a Divided Mind," *Atlantic Monthly*, 182 (August, 1948), 27–33.

Johnson, Gerald W. "What a Sad Story," *New Republic*, 138 (January 6, 1958), 14.

Jones, Ken. "The FBI Wants You," *This Week Magazine*, November 12, 1950.

Kempton, Murray. "The Progressives' Long Winter," *Nation*, March 11, 1950.

Kenny, Robert W. "A Californian Looks Ahead," *Nation*, 167 (October 23, 1948), 460–61.

Kinkead, Robin. "Liberal Democrats in Fresno," *New Republic*, 117 (July 28, 1947), 9.

Kirchwey, Freda. "The Battle of Chicago," *Nation*, 159 (July 29, 1944), 118–20.

————. "Wallace: Prophet or Politician?" *ibid.*, 166 (January 10, 1948), 29–31.

————. "What Wallace Can Do," *ibid.*, 167 (July 24, 1948), 87–88.

————. "Word to Mr. Wallace," *ibid.*, 166 (March 13, 1948), 294.

Krock, Arthur. "Vote Tactic in Illinois," *New York Times*, October 20, 1948.

Lapin, Adam. "The Challenge of the New Party," *Masses and Mainstream,* October, 1948.

Laski, Harold J. "American Political Scene," *Nation,* 163 (November 16, 23, 30, 1946), 548–51, 582–84, 609–12.

Lasky, Victor. "Who Runs Wallace?" *Plain Talk,* June, 1948.

Lerner, Max. "Third Party Talk," *PM,* June 4, 1946.

Lord, Russell. "MacDonald's Wallace and the One I Know," *New Republic,* 118 (March 1, 1948).

McWilliams, Carey. "California's Third-Party Donnybrook," *Nation,* 116 (April 24, 1948), 434–36.

———. "Wallace in the West," *ibid.,* 116 (July 5, 1947).

Magil, A. B. "Antidote to Hooverism," *New Masses,* December 3, 1946.

———. "Cornerstone for Coalition," *ibid.,* October 15, 1946.

———. "November and After," *ibid.,* October 8, 1946.

———. "Reveille for Progressives," *ibid.,* January 14, 1947.

———. "Third Party in '48?" *ibid.,* June 3, 1947.

Minor, Robert. "Lessons of Past Third Parties," *Daily Worker,* August 2, 1948.

Moos, Malcolm C., and Kenworthy, E. W. "Dr. Shipstead Come to Judgment," *Harper's Magazine,* 193 (July, 1946), 21–27.

Neuberger, Richard. "Glen Taylor: Leftwing Minstrel," *Progressive,* April, 1948.

Padover, Saul K. "Party of Hope," *Saturday Review of Literature,* April 17, 1948.

Phillips, Cabell. "That Baffling Personality, Mr. Wallace," *New York Times Magazine,* February 8, 1948.

———. "Why They Join the Wallace Crusade," *ibid.,* May 23, 1948.

Rogge, C. John. "My New Plan for Peace," *New Leader,* January 29, 1951.

Shannon, William. "The Strange Case of Louis Budenz," *New Republic,* 125 (October 1, 1951), 9–10.

Sheean, Vincent. "Wallace Youth," *New Republic,* 119 (October 25, 1948), 7.

Sillen, Samuel. "One Fight," *Masses and Mainstream,* April 1, 1948.

Sroog, Arnold. "How the New Party Was Born," *Worker Magazine,* July 25, 1948.

Starr, Joseph R. "The Legal Status of American Political Parties," *American Political Science Review,* 34 (June, August, 1940), 439–55, 685–99.

Stewart, Kenneth. "Wallace the Symbol," *PM Sunday Magazine Section,* October 26, November 2, 1947.

Stone, I. F. "Plot Against Wallace," *Nation,* 159 (July 1, 1944), 7–8.

——. "PAC at Work," *ibid.,* 159 (October 14, 1944), 425–27.

Thompson, Craig. "America's Millionaire Communist," *Saturday Evening Post,* September 9, 1950.

Tugwell, Rexford Guy. "Progressives and the Presidency," *Progressive,* March, 1949.

Tyler, Gus. "Progressives and Communists," *New Republic,* (September 12, 1949).

Wallace, Henry A. "California and the New Party," *New Republic,* 118 (June 7, 1948), 12.

——. "Farewell and Hail," *ibid.,* 119 (July 19, 1948), 14–18.

——. "I Shall Run in 1948" (Address, December 29, 1948), *Vital Speeches,* 14 (January 1, 1948), 172–74.

——. "My Alternative for the Marshall Plan," *New Republic,* 118 (January 12, 1948), 13–14.

——. "My Commitments" (Acceptance Speech—Philadelphia), *Vital Speeches,* 14 (August 1, 1948), 620–23.

——. "One Course to Save the Democratic Party," *New Republic,* 117 (June 7, 1947), 14–15.

——. "Report on the New Party," *ibid.,* 118 (May 3, 1948), 11–13.

——. "Stand Up and Be Counted," *ibid.,* 118 (January 5, 1948), 4–10.

——. "Terrorism at Evansville," *ibid.,* 118 (April 19, 1948), 11.

——. "Third Parties and the American Tradition," *ibid.,* 118 (January 19, 1948), 12–14.

——. "The U.S., the U.N. and Far Eastern Agriculture," *Bulletin of the Atomic Scientists,* 6 (December, 1950).

————. "Way to Peace" (Madison Square Garden Speech), *Vital Speeches,* 12 (October 1, 1946), 738–41.

————. "Where I Stand," *New Leader,* August 26, 1950.

————. "Why a Third Party in 1948," *Annals of the American Academy of Political and Social Sciences,* 259 (September, 1948), 10–16.

Wechsler, James A. "My Ten Months with Wallace," *Progressive,* November, 1948.

————. "What Makes Wallace Run?" *ibid.,* February, 1948.

————. "The Philadelphia Pay-Off," *ibid.,* September, 1948.

Wheildon, L. B. "Third Party Movements," *Editorial Research Reports* 2 (July 16, 1947).

Williams, S. W. "People's Progressive Party of Georgia," *Phylon,* 10, No. 3, pp. 226–30.

Wright, Todd. "Whose Voice in Our Congress?" *Collier's,* 125 (April 1, 1950), 18–19.

*Yale Law Journal,* "Legal Obstacles to Minority Party Success," July, 1948.

Young, Jack. "California Started Something," *New Masses,* October 14, 1947.

# Index

349

# *Colophon*

HENRY A. WALLACE: *Quixotic Crusade 1948*
has been set in 10 point Linotype Times Roman,
leaded 2 points, printed on 60 pound P. H. Glat-
felter antique standard white text paper, R grade,
and bound in Columbia Bayside Linen over 70
point binder's board by the Vail-Ballou Press, Inc.

SIU
PRESS